art / shop / eat
NEW YORK

Carol von Pressentin Wright

The Metropolitan Museum and Museum Mile

The Silk Stocking District

Chelsea and the Meatpacking District

SoHo

The Museum of Modern Art in Queens

introduction

New Yorkers like to think that their city is the world's art capital and they are probably right. With more than 150 museums, hundreds of commercial galleries, and dozens of alternative art spaces, there is enough art in New York to satisfy the most avid artoholic.

This book is intended to help you make choices about what to see and then where to go when you have seen enough. It is organized into five art neighborhoods, which taken together will give you a good idea of what New York has to offer. The book focuses each neighborhood around an anchor - a major museum - to which are added a sampling of other sights, commercial galleries, and creature comforts - restaurants, bars, and shops.

Most of the art museums with great permanent collections are located on the affluent Upper East Side. The Metropolitan Museum moved to its location at the edge of Central Park while the neighborhood was still a suburb, but the wealthy followed soon afterward. The Frick Collection, the Cooper-Hewitt Design Museum, and the Neue Galerie occupy former mansions.

For a long time, the museum neighborhoods attracted the important galleries, but that changed in the 1970s when SoHo (SOuth of HOuston Street) became the center of contemporary art. Today the most important gallery area is Chelsea (with Williamsburg in Brooklyn beginning to come on strong). But the galleries moved to Chelsea (as they did to SoHo years earlier) because rents were cheap. And rents were cheap because there was nothing to attract people except space. Therefore some of these routes are heavy on galleries and others are heavy on permanent collections or sights en route. A couple of museums that shouldn't be overlooked but which fall beyond the geographic boundaries of the book are: The Cloisters at the upper tip of Manhattan, which houses part of the Metropolitan's medieval collection, and the Brooklyn Museum of Art, near Prospect Park in Brooklyn.

THE METROPOLITAN MUSEUM & MUSEUM MILE

The Metropolitan Museum of Art

OPEN	Sun, Tues-Thurs 9:30-5:30; Fri, Sat 9:30-9
CLOSED	Mon, Jan 1, Thanksgiving, Dec 25
CHARGES	$12.00 suggested for adults, $7.00 suggested for students and senior citizens, includes Main Building and The Cloisters on the same day; free to members and children under 12 with an adult. To help cover the cost of special exhibitions, for which there is no additional charge or special ticketing, the museum asks that you pay the suggested amount
TELEPHONE	(212) 879-5500 to reach a live person
RECORDED INFO	(212) 535-7710
WWW.	metmuseum.org
MAIN ENTRANCE	1000 Fifth Ave at 82nd St. Second entrance at 81st St/Fifth Ave
SUBWAY	4, 5, or 6 to 86th St
DISABLED ACCESS	Facilities for the disabled: ask at information desk or **T (212) 570-3764, TTY (212) 570-3828**
SHOPS	Several shops profusely stocked with books, postcards, posters, boutique and household items, toys
EATING	Cafeteria. Petrie Court Café with waiter service; reservations **T (212) 570-3964**. American Wing Café opening winter 2004

Changing exhibitions, gallery tours, lectures, concerts, special events, educational programs.

The Metropolitan Museum of Art is one of New York's most cherished institutions, a monumental presence on Fifth Avenue and in the city's cultural life, and a destination for some 5.2 million visitors yearly. Within its collections are more than two million works of art created over 5000 years and gathered from around the globe, the earliest culled from the mists of prehistory, the most recent produced in the 21st century.

THE BUILDING

The core of the Met's present home opened in 1880, a modest Victorian Gothic building faced with red-orange brick and white limestone, designed by Calvert Vaux and Jacob Wrey Mould, better known for their work on the bridges of Central Park. Most of this building has disappeared under later

The Metropolitan Museum of Art

architectural accretions, but you can see parts of the original façade from the Robert Lehman Wing and the European Sculpture Court. The architectural chunk that most people identify as the Met - the central pavilion on Fifth Ave including the main entrance - was begun in 1894 by Richard Morris Hunt, architect to the late-19c rich and famous, and completed in 1902 by his son Richard Howland Hunt. Wings to the north (1911) and south (1913) were added by the reigning architects of the next generation, McKim, Mead & White.

In 1971 the Metropolitan approved a schedule of major improvements, undertaken by Roche, Dinkeloo & Assocs, and completed over a 20-year span. The master plan included the redesign of the Fifth Ave stairs and the addition of glass-walled wings on the three other façades: on the west, the Lehman Wing (1975) with Robert Lehman's collection of paintings and decorative arts; on the north, the Sackler Wing (1979) with the Temple of Dendur; and on the south, the Rockefeller Wing (1982) for Arts of Africa, Oceania, and the Americas. Other new exhibition spaces within the expanded footprint of the museum have included the American Wing (1980) for American painting and decorative arts, the Lila Acheson Wallace Wing (1987) for modern art, and Henry R. Kravis Wing (1989), which houses part of the European Sculpture and Decorative Arts Collection. At present the museum is finishing a major reorganization of existing gallery space, including a complete renovation and reinstallation of the Greek and Roman Galleries.

HIGHLIGHTS

Impressionist and Post-Impressionist paintings: Manet, Monet, and Cézanne (19c European Paintings and Sculpture, second floor)

Old Master paintings including five Vermeers (Rooms 12 and 14), **as well as major works by Italian, Flemish, Dutch and French painters from the 12c-19c** (European Paintings, second floor, top of Grand Staircase)

The Egyptian collection and Temple of Dendur. Don't miss the Middle Kingdom wooden tomb models (Room 4) **and the painted coffins and funerary objects** (Room 21) (First floor, north of Great Hall)

The French period rooms (European Sculpture and Decorative Arts, galleries between Lehman Collection and café)

The Japanese armor (galleries right of entrance) **and full suits of European armor** (Arms and Armor, first floor, near the American Wing)

GREEK AND ROMAN ART
FIRST FLOOR

The Museum is working on the last stage of a three-part program to renovate the magnificent Beaux-Arts galleries designed (1917-8) by McKim, Mead & White, the dominant architectural firm of their era. Eventually the sky-lit atrium where the restaurant was located will be transformed into a Roman Court with sculpture, wall paintings, and decorative arts from the first to the third centuries AD.

Just beyond the Great Hall is the Roman cubiculum, a bedroom with beautifully frescoed walls; the villa was buried by the eruption of Vesuvius in AD 79.

The first three rooms (right to left) contain prehistoric and early Greek art, including, in the room on the right, an expressive marble statuette of a ***Seated Harp Player*** (c 2800-2700 BC), one of the earliest known representations of a musician.

CENTRAL GALLERY The long sky-lit barrel-vaulted central gallery contains Greek art of the 6c-4c BC, including beautifully painted prize amphorae, which were filled with olive oil and awarded to victorious athletes in the Panathenaic Games. Large-scale sculpture in this gallery includes Roman marble copies of Greek bronzes which had been made during the 5c-4c BC. The Romans, living 500 years later, replicated Greek statuary as decoration for public buildings and private villas and these copies are often the only records of lost masterpieces. Among the important pieces in this corridor are the *Wounded Amazon* and a *Statue of a Greek hero*, perhaps Protesilaos, the first Greek to set food on the sands of Troy during the Trojan War.

TO THE RIGHT OF THE CENTRAL GALLERY as you face the restaurant are three galleries with a fine collection of painted terracotta vases, arranged more or less chronologically. In the first are vases from about 600-525 BC, many painted in the black-figure technique. The acknowledged master of this technique is **Exekias** (c 550-530 BC), represented in the collection by a storage jar (its accession number is 17.230.14) depicting figures in a procession. The most important vase in the next room and perhaps the most important in the collection is a calyx-krater (a deep bowl for mixing wine and water), painted by **Euphronios**. It shows a scene from Homer's *Iliad*, *Sleep and Death Lifting the Body of the Fallen Sarpedon*. The red-figure technique, in which the background is black and the figures take the color of the unglazed clay, allows the composition to stand out with great clarity. Another vase painted with great skill by the so-called **Berlin Painter** shows a *Young Musician Playing the Kithara*. The subject of *Ganymede with a Hoop and Gamecock* on a nearby vase is the handsome Trojan prince pursued by Zeus; the hoop and rooster would have identified Ganymede to ancient viewers.

The last gallery on this side of the central corridor contains art from the 5c-early 4c BC, when the construction of the Parthenon (448-432 BC) influenced artists working in other media. Included here are vases depicting the life of women, warfare, and scenes from mythology. The great master of this period was the **Achilles**

METROPOLITAN MUSEUM OF ART
First Floor with Mezzanine Floor

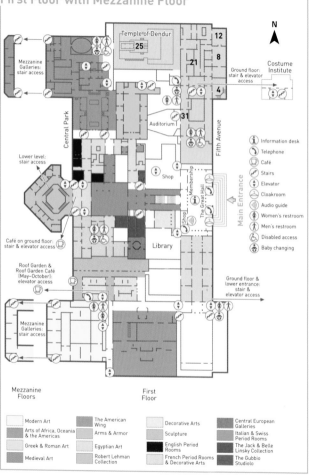

N

Temple of Dendur

25

12

8

21

4

Costume Institute

Ground floor: stair & elevator access

31

Auditorium

Central Park

Mezzanine Galleries: stair access

Lower level: stair access

Fifth Avenue

Shop

Membership

The Great Hall

Main Entrance

Café on ground floor: stair & elevator access

Shop

Library

Roof Garden & Roof Garden Café (May–October): elevator access

Ground floor & lower entrance: stair & elevator access

Mezzanine Galleries: stair access

ⓘ Information desk
☎ Telephone
☕ Café
⬆ Stairs
⬍ Elevator
Cloakroom
Audio guide
Women's restroom
Men's restroom
Disabled access
Baby changing

Mezzanine Floors

First Floor

Modern Art	The American Wing
Arts of Africa, Oceania & the Americas	Arms & Armor
Greek & Roman Art	Egyptian Art
Medieval Art	Robert Lehman Collection

Decorative Arts	Central European Galleries
Sculpture	Italian & Swiss Period Rooms
English Period Rooms	The Jack & Belle Linsky Collection
French Period Rooms & Decorative Arts	The Gubbio Studiolo

METROPOLITAN MUSEUM OF ART
Second Floor

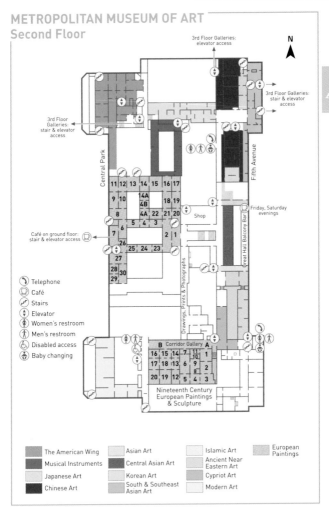

3rd Floor Galleries: elevator access

N

3rd Floor Galleries: stair & elevator access

3rd Floor Galleries: stair & elevator access

Central Park

Fifth Avenue

Friday, Saturday evenings

Shop

Great Hall Balcony Bar

Café on ground floor: stair & elevator access

11 12 13 14 15 16 17
9 10
14A
4B
8
4A 22 21 20
5 4 3
7
6
2 1
26
25 24 23
27
28 30
29

18 19

Drawings, Prints & Photographs

Telephone
Café
Stairs
Elevator
Women's restroom
Men's restroom
Disabled access
Baby changing

B Corridor Gallery A

16 15 14 7 11 10
17 18 13 6 9 2
8
20 19 12 5 4 1 3

Nineteenth Century European Paintings & Sculpture

The American Wing
Musical Instruments
Japanese Art
Chinese Art

Asian Art
Central Asian Art
Korean Art
South & Southeast Asian Art

Islamic Art
Ancient Near Eastern Art
Cypriot Art
Modern Art

European Paintings

Painter, represented by a lekythos (oil flask) in the white-ground technique showing a mourner and the deceased person at the tomb.

ON THE LEFT OF THE CENTRAL CORRIDOR are three galleries with original marble sculpture from the archaic and classical periods, much of it grave sculpture put up by landed families. In the first gallery stands an early **kouros** (c 590-580 BC), a marble statue of a nude youth, which once marked the grave of a young man from a wealthy family. The stiff pose with one foot forward is derived from Egyptian art. Among the sculpture in the next room (5c BC) is the famous *Grave Stele of a Girl with Doves*; the dead child is portrayed with great tenderness. The final room includes Greek Art of the 4c BC, when the power of Athens had diminished after the Peloponnesian War. The funeral monuments here are increasingly elaborate, and include those in the form of vessels to hold oil or water during funeral rites.

EGYPTIAN ART

The Egyptian Galleries contain the finest collection in the Western Hemisphere. The earliest objects date from 300,000 BC and the latest from the Roman period, 4c AD. The galleries are organized in a U-shape beginning on the Fifth Ave side of the building.

Statuette of a hippopotamus

Just inside the entrance is the **Tomb of Perneb** (c 2450 BC), which included an underground burial chamber; it still has a limestone offering chapel with a false door through which Perneb's spirit could emerge to enjoy the offerings arranged for it.

ROOM 4 Here is the finest **collection of tomb models** (c 1985 BC) ever found; it includes models of boats as well as scenes from daily life in the stable, garden, bakery, and brewery.

ROOM 8 Royal portrait statues here include a fragmentary brown quartzite face of Senwosret III, depicting the king as a solemn, careworn ruler. Among the royal jewelry is an exquisite pectoral with falcons and a scarab.

ROOM 12 One of the portrait statues of Hatshepsut is a life-size seated figure (c 1473-1458 BC) showing her definitely feminine body clad in the ceremonial clothing of the pharaoh, traditionally a male role; on her head is the headdress reserved for the ruler.

ROOM 21 The windowless Archaeological Room (c 1320-525 BC) contains **tomb groups and funerary objects** that illustrate the development of burial customs in Thebes during this period. Among them are painted and decorated coffins, canopic chests for the preservation of inner organs, and servant figurines to perform menial tasks for the dead.

ROOM 25 The **Temple of Dendur** (c 15 BC) once stood on the banks of the Nile, upstream from the Aswan Dam. Its decoration implies a stylized version of the natural world as the Egyptians

Temple of Dendur (Sackler Wing)

understood it, with depictions of river plants at the bottom and symbols of the sky (the disk of Horus, the sky god) at the top.

ROOM 31 Roman Art from the time of Augustus Caesar includes **Fayum portraits,** named for the Fayum oasis south of modern Cairo; in the Greco-Roman cemeteries there the customs of Egyptian, Roman, and Greek civilizations merged. The panel paintings may have been used as ordinary portraits until the owner died, and then were wrapped into the coverings of the mummy as a mask following Egyptian traditions.

MEDIEVAL ART

The Collection of Medieval Art contains Byzantine silver, glass, jewelry, metalwork, stained glass, sculpture, enamels, ivories, and Gothic tapestries. The works were created from the 4c-16c, roughly from the time of the fall of Rome to the beginning of the Renaissance. Financier J.P. Morgan, whose collections focused on books and decorative arts from every period of Western civilization, died in 1913 and left the museum a trove of objects which forms the nucleus of the more than 4000 works presently in the medieval collection. (If you want to see what Morgan donated, look for accession numbers in the format: 17.190. xxx.)

Unicorn Tapestry

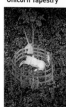

NOTE Medieval art is also on display at **The Cloisters,** the Metropolitan's only branch museum, in Fort Tryon Park at the upper tip of Manhattan. On view there are architectural elements from five medieval cloisters, the famous Unicorn tapestries, illuminated manuscripts, stained glass, Romanesque and Gothic architectural sculpture, ivories, paintings, and enamels. *S* A to 190th St, then M4 bus to museum.

In 2000, the Museum reopened the installation of **Byzantine Art,** adding a new exhibition space beneath the Grand Staircase. These three galleries showcase works from 330 (when the capital of the

Roman Empire moved to Constantinople) to 1453 (when the Byzantine Empire fell to the Ottoman Turks).

ROOM 1 On the left of the Grand Staircase are examples of Byzantine liturgical and secular art. The Syrian Attarouthi Treasure (6c-7c) includes silver and silver gilt chalices, censers, a wine strainer, and a silver dove representing the Holy Spirit. The Antioch treasure, in a case opposite, includes a "chalice" once touted as the legendary Holy Grail. Among the secular pieces are brooches, fibulas (ornamental pins for fastening clothing), and enamel bowls.

ROOM 2 Under the stairs is a gallery with jewelry, textiles, and architectural sculpture. From this cavelike space, you can see the unfinished underside of the Great Staircase and the supporting brickwork.

ROOM 3 The gallery on the north side of the staircase contains secular art from the Byzantine and early medieval world (4c-8c), including a delicate ivory diptych announcing Justinian's appointment as consul; Justinian, who became emperor six years later, had it made as a presentation gift to celebrate this major career step. Further along are six silver plates whose designs illustrate scenes from the life of the Old Testament king, David. The largest depicts David's upset victory over Goliath.

ROOM 4 The next gallery, to the west of the staircase, is arranged to suggest a Romanesque chapel. Near its entrance is a mutilated limestone *Head of King David* (c 1150), a rare survivor of many that once decorated portals of Notre-Dame in Paris. The statue it crowned was decapitated during the French Revolution, but the head has been identified from engravings made of the doorway before the Revolution. Near the staircase is a formal and symmetrical seated wooden *Virgin and Child in Majesty* (c 1150-1200) from the Auvergne. Among the tapestries are a rare *Annunciation Tapestry* and the elegant *Figures in a Rose Garden* depicting courtiers against a background of stripes and stylized rosebushes.

ROOM 5 An impressive 17c *choir screen* from Valladolid, Spain, dominates the room. Among the many small and beautiful objects usually on display is a *Reliquary Crib of the Infant Jesus*, a popular devotional object during the early 16c; these little cribs were venerated during the Christmas season; there would have been a figure of the infant Jesus beneath the silk coverlet. The beautifully carved *Alabaster Mourners* from the Tomb of the Duc de Berry represent relatives and allies of the duke, whose full-size effigy lay on top the sarcophagus. Another beautiful small object represents the *Visitation*, the visit of the Virgin Mary to St Elizabeth, who was also expecting a child; the crystal ovals probably covered tiny images of the Christ Child and the infant John the Baptist.

ROOMS 6-7 On the north side of the gallery, doors open into the Medieval Treasury with beautiful and precious objects of gold, silver, ivory, and enamel, many of them used for devotional purposes. The gallery of Medieval Secular Art offers everyday objects and ceramics including early Spanish lusterware.

ARMS AND ARMOR

The galleries of arms and armor are organized around a central Equestrian Court, with dramatic models of mounted knights in full suits of armor. On the right (as you enter from European Sculpture and Decorative Arts) are galleries with Japanese, Asian, and Islamic armor. An exceptional Japanese piece is an intricate 14c yoroi, made of iron, leather, and silk, which protected the torso and upper legs, usually of a mounted warrior. On the breastplate is the image of a powerful Buddhist deity Fudo Myo-o; there is a fierce larger-than-life statue of him in the second gallery of Japanese art.

American arms, displayed at the far end of the room, include Colt revolvers (the first mass-produced multi-shot weapons), "Kentucky" flintlock rifles, swords, other edged weapons, and a powder horn engraved with a map of the Hudson River Valley.

The galleries on the west side of the room (toward the American Wing) focus on European armor. Highlights here include a Germanic strap helmet dating back to the 6c, the type of helmet characteristic of the barbarians who brought down Rome. The beautiful hammered steel parade helmet (1543) made by the Milanese master armorer, Filippo Negroli, is decorated with a mermaid reclining over the crest; she holds the head of Medusa, whose eyes gaze toward the oncoming enemy. Ornately decorated suits of armor from the English royal workshops in Greenwich, which produced parade andtournament armor for Tudor courtiers; European firearms, and edged weapons complete the display.

EUROPEAN SCULPTURE AND DECORATIVE ARTS

The galleries themselves are not numbered and can seem mazelike in their arrangement, but the plan suggests the general layout by country and area of interest. This description begins north of the Grand Staircase (behind the gift shop) with the rooms of Northern European and Italian Decorative Arts. The galleries wrap around a large square, and are organized more or less by country.

NORTHERN EUROPEAN AND ITALIAN DECORATIVE ARTS are found in the first galleries and include period rooms from England, Switzerland, and Italy. The study or *Studiolo from the Ducal Palace in Gubbio* (c 1479-82), Italy, is intricately inlaid with walnut, beech, rosewood, oak, and fruitwood. The Swiss room has a superb ceramic stove. In the center of the large gallery is the magnificent *Farnese Table*, made of marble and alabaster, and inlaid with semiprecious stones and bits of colored marble; it was made by Jacopo Barozzi da Vignola for the Palazzo Farnese in Rome. The coats of arms on the supporting piers belong to Cardinal Alessandro Farnese, the greatest art patron of his day. Also in this room is the monumental *Wall Fountain* by Simone Mosca (1527-34), framed by a triumphal arch.

Near the entrance to Arms and Armor the galleries continue to the left. Around the corner is a *Venetian Bedroom* from the Palazzo Sagredo; the ornate ceiling and fluttering stucco cupids were intended for the eyes of visitors, since in 18c Venice it was customary to receive formal visits in bed.

ENGLISH PERIOD ROOMS are beyond the galleries with English furniture, against the west wall of the museum, and include two Neoclassical rooms by Robert Adam, the *Dining Room from Lansdowne House* and *Tapestry Room from Croome Court*, decorated with Gobelins tapestries. Across the corridor from Croome Court are a room with an imposing state bed and, next to it, a room with Elizabethan paneling.

A large gallery runs past the entrance foyer for the Lehman Collection. In it are goldsmiths' work, clocks, and selections from the museum's large collection of maiolica and glass, one of the finest in the world. There are plates, bowls, ewers, and pharmaceutical jars from important centers of ceramic art and glass in Florence, Faenza, and Venice.

FRENCH 18C PERIOD ROOMS are beyond, with a superb collection of furniture, paintings, ceramics, and carpets, which recreate the luxurious ambience of the wealthy during the reigns of Louis XV and XVI. In the 18c *Paris Shopfront*, to the left, are examples of Parisian silver. A great deal of silver was melted down to finance royal wars and examples from this period are rare. Along with the silver are elegant, decorative snuff boxes, with gold work, enamel flowers, and jewels. The two small paneled rooms across from the shopfront are a mirrored *Boudoir from the Hôtel de Crillon*, with a bed that belonged to Marie-Antoinette. The *Bordeaux Room* is a circular salon with carved paneling; on the table are pieces of black Sèvres porcelain. To the right of the Bordeaux Room is the *Early Louis XV Room* with cases on one side containing Sèvres porcelains in various glazes. The *Sèvres Room*, on the right, has elegant 18c paneling and furniture, some of it set with Sèvres plaques; master furniture makers represented here include Martin Carlin, Bernard II van Risen Burgh, and George Jacob.

The *Louis XVI Gallery* is decorated with a series of paintings with misty and watery themes by Hubert Robert, a French landscape painter with a particular interest in ruins. These were intended for the bathroom of the king's youngest brother. Robert held office as a curator of the Louvre under Louis XVI and was imprisoned during the Revolution. He was more fortunate than Louis, since another Hubert Robert was guillotined in his place and he lived to die in obscurity years later.

The centerpiece of the *Varangeville Room* is a red japanned writing table designed by Gilles Joubert, which was delivered to Versailles for use in Louis' study. It has been described as the most important piece of 18c French furniture to have crossed the Atlantic. On the floor is a Savonnerie carpet, one of 92 woven for the Grande Galerie at the Louvre.

The *Reception Room from the Hôtel de Cabris* in Grasse, near Cannes, has exceptional paneling (1775-8); the double doors bear carved designs of flaming torches and smoking incense burners. In the *De Tessé Room* is a mechanical table by Jean-Henri Riesener; Marie-Antoinette used it as a dressing, reading, and writing table.

The last period room (across the corridor) is the *Louis XIV State Bedchamber*, with needlepoint wall hangings after designs by Charles Le Brun, who became painter to the king in 1662 and head of the Gobelins works a year later; the tapestries were commissioned by the Marquise de Montespan, while she was mistress of Louis XIV.

DECORATIVE ARTS FROM CENTRAL EUROPE are beyond the State Bedchamber, with glass (Bohemian, German, and Venetian), ceramics (Meissen, Fulda, Nuremberg, and Höchst), goldsmiths' work, and furniture.

JACK AND BELLE LINSKY GALLERIES Between the Central European Galleries and the Patio of Vélez Blanco, the Jack and Belle Linsky Galleries contain a private collection of European paintings, sculpture, and decorative arts. The Linskys made their fortune manufacturing Swingline staplers; their onetime factory building is the temporary home of the Museum of Modern Art. The collection contains works by Giovanni di Paolo, Vittore Crivelli, and François Boucher. In the Rotunda is the earliest known dated painting by **Peter Paul Rubens**, *Portrait of a Man* (1597).

To see the rest of the galleries, return past the Louis XIV bedchamber and turn left into the **European Sculpture Court**, whose café overlooks Central Park. The sculpture is arranged chronologically from east to west. At the east end are figures representing *Flora and Priapus* (c 1616), by Pietro Bernini. Down the corridor to the right is a work by his more famous son, **Gian Lorenzo Bernini**. The young Bernini's *Bacchanal: A Faun Teased by Children* (c 1616-7), is an early work by a teenager who would become the pre-eminent sculptor and architect of the Baroque period. French works in the main sculpture court include Jean-Louis Lemoyne, *Fear of Cupid's Darts* (1739-40), and, near the café, Jean-Baptiste Carpeaux, *Ugolino and His Sons* (1865-7), a romantic rendering of the fate of the Pisan traitor who was starved to death for his sins; the tale is told in Dante's *Inferno*. Carpeaux's work foreshadowed the sculpture of Auguste Rodin, whose *The Burghers of Calais* (1885-95), portrays six citizens who volunteered for martyrdom at the hands of England's Edward III, to spare Calais from destruction.

The first gallery beyond the sculpture court offers examples of smaller scale 18c French sculpture, including Jean-Antoine Houdon's lovely portrait bust of his daughter, *Sabine Houdon* (1788). The following galleries contain 19c works dating from the Restoration of the Bourbon dynasty in 1815 to the Art Nouveau period at the beginning of the 20c.

ARTS OF AFRICA, OCEANIA, AND THE AMERICAS

The objects on display here come from sub-Saharan Africa, the Pacific Islands, and North, Central, and South America. Some are archaeological finds dating back 4000 years; others are African and Pacific works from the present.

AFRICA At the time of writing a special exhibition was installed in the first of the two African Galleries. The first gallery usually contains wonderful pieces of wooden sculpture from West and Central Africa, including many examples from the Dogon and Bamana cultures of Mali and the Baule culture of the Ivory Coast.

The Buli Master *Stool with female figure* (19c, Zaire)

The second African gallery, to the left, has works from Central Africa. In its own case near the center of the room is one of the finest pieces in the collection, a 9-inch carved ivory *pendant mask* from the 16c court of Benin in Nigeria. It is believed that the King of Benin wore this mask at ceremonies honoring his deceased mother. Also from Benin are bronze and brass objects, including a bronze *horn player* and several dark brass heads, wearing the royal regalia of coral beads, a cap and choker; they were kept on the royal altars as memorials to ancestors.

A 19c *helmet mask*, from the Kingdom of Bamum in Cameroon, is made of wood but decorated with cowrie shells, glass beads, and copper, all of them valuable materials. The arrangement depicts a stylized spider, symbolic of wisdom. An elongated 19c-20c

reliquary head of the Fang people from Gabon was once owned by the sculptor, Jacob Epstein. The head was originally mounted on a container that held ancestral skulls, to protect its contents from the forbidden gaze of women and uninitiated boys. Fang sculpture influenced Western artists, who began collecting it in the early 20c.

The Kongo "power" figure (19c-20c) is made of wood, copper, brass, iron, fiber, snakeskin, leather, fur, feathers, earth, and resin. It derives its special efficacy from symbolic substances inserted in its head, abdomen, and shoulders by a priestly figure. It would have been owned communally by a village, and consulted at public ceremonies.

THE AMERICAS These galleries lie behind and to the left of the African galleries. The first gallery, devoted to ***Mesoamerica***, includes Aztec stone sculpture of animals and female figures (possibly goddesses of agriculture or fertility). One such goddess was Chalchihuitlicue, goddess of water and springs. A 15c-16c statue carved from basalt shows her as a lady wearing a shawl and tasseled headdress. Unlike many Aztec figures, who wear ferocious expressions, she looks serene. A stone sculpture of ***Cihuateotl*** (late 15c-early 16c) represents a mythical woman who died in childbirth, became a deity, and brought misfortune to mankind. She is depicted as a grimacing skeleton.

On the right is an ***Olmec "baby" figure*** (12c-9c BC), a soft-bellied infantile figure who appears to be sucking his thumb. The figure may have represented a god or been an emblem of royal lineage. A ***wooden seated figure*** from the Maya peoples of Mexico or Guatemala dates back to the 6c and is one of only a few Pre-Columbian wooden objects to have survived the depredations of humidity and insects.

THE TREASURY (gallery to the left) has a remarkable display of Pre-Columbian gold. Among the fine pieces are figure pendants, possibly representing warriors, from the Tairona people of Colombia; pendants shaped like eagles, frogs, sharks, and other creatures; ear spools (primitive earrings), some inlaid with stone and shell; and impressive three-dimensional gold figures of hammered sheet gold from the Tolita-Tumaco culture (present Ecuador-Colombia border near the Pacific Ocean).

OCEANIA The rest of the wing to the south focuses on cultures of the *Pacific Islands*: the archipelagos of Melanesia, Micronesia, and Polynesia, Australia, and the island cultures of Southeast Asia. The most impressive gallery in this area with its glass wall facing south is devoted to the arts of Micronesia, including New Guinea, New Ireland, and the New Hebrides. Nelson A. Rockefeller (governor of New York state from 1959 until 1973) donated the wing in memory of his son, Michael C. Rockefeller, who died in a boating accident while collecting artifacts in Papua, New Guinea. The elder Rockefeller also donated his own collection of artifacts, which had previously been installed in The Museum of Primitive Art, which he had founded in 1954.

In the section devoted to the *Pacific Islands* (east wall of the gallery, turn left from the entrance) is an elaborately *inlaid shield*, woven of wicker, coated with nut paste, and inlaid with pearl shells. Fewer than two dozen of these 19c objects survive.

In the high-ceilinged main gallery, also on the east wall, are *funerary carvings* from northern New Ireland, complex figures embodying images from clan mythology, used in ceremonies honoring the dead (and the donors of the carvings). After the ceremonies, they were either destroyed or abandoned.

The most dramatic works in the wing are nine *bis poles* made by the Asmat people of Irian Jaya (western New Guinea) and collected by Michael Rockefeller in 1961. The poles, about 15 feet tall, are openwork structures with winglike projections and are carved with ancestor figures. They were used in the ceremonies that led up to headhunts and after a successful pursuit the heads of the victims were placed in hollows in the lower ends.

MODERN ART

The Metropolitan awakened to the 20c rather late, establishing a department of Twentieth Century Art only in 1967, although earlier gifts, for example Georgia O'Keeffe's bequest from the estate of Alfred Stieglitz, had nudged the museum in the direction of contemporary art. The collection includes paintings and sculpture by major European figures, but its strength lies in American art, particularly The Eight, the Alfred Stieglitz circle, and Abstract Expressionists.

NOTE Begin on the first floor beyond the elevators. The first-floor galleries are arranged in a square, with a special exhibitions gallery and a design gallery. The exhibit continues upstairs to the mezzanine, the second floor, and finally the roof, which is used for exhibits of large-scale sculpture during warm weather.

FIRST FLOOR

ROOMS 1-4 Works by European painters at the turn of the 20c, including Bonnard, Utrillo, Kandinsky, and Vuillard. The second room has one of the most famous paintings in the modern collection: **Pablo Picasso**, *Portrait of Gertrude Stein* (1906), painted when the artist was 24 and Stein was 32. When someone told Picasso that Stein did not look like the portrait, he replied, "She will." Among the works of influential Cubists is **Georges Braque**'s *Le Gueridon* (1921-2), a small round table, painted in the dulled colors favored by the early Cubists, but in Braque's later more figurative style. **Henri Matisse**'s, *Nasturtiums with the Painting "Dance"* (1912); a version of the painting *Dance* belongs to the Museum of Modern Art and is currently hung in MoMA QNS; here it is depicted leaning against the wall in Matisse's studio.

Sculpture in the gallery before the staircase includes work by Umberto Boccioni and Constantin Brancusi's *Bird in Space* (1923), a marble abstraction intended, according to the sculptor, "to catch the essence of flight."

ROOMS 5-8 In 1998 the museum inherited the collection of Jacques and Natasha Gelman (he produced and distributed the immensely successful films starring Cantinflas), which is shown in the galleries bearing their names. In the first gallery (Room 5) are **Fauve** artists, including André Derain and Maurice de Vlaminck. In the second, paintings are arranged chronologically to illustrate developments in **Cubism** between 1911 and 1924. The next section (Room 7) is devoted to Modigliani, Braque, and Bonnard, including a **Modigliani** portrait of a blue-eyed *Boy in a Striped Sweater* against a blue background, Braque's *Still Life with a Guitar* (1924), and two paintings by Bonnard featuring Marthe Boursin (later his wife): *After the Morning Bath* (1910) and *The Dining Room at Vernonnet* (1916).

Salvador Dalí's *Accommodations of Desire* (1929) introduces the section devoted to Surrealism. Several works by **Joan Miró** follow, including *Vine and Olive Trees, Tarragona* (1919), a view of Miró's family's Catalan farm, and *The Potato* (1928) in which a gigantic white female figure casts her arms across a blue sky. Here also are landscapes by Yves Tanguy and by Balthus, *Thérèse Dreaming* (1938).

ROOMS 9-12 The rooms beyond the Gelman Collection continue the survey of American 20c painting, with a rotating selection of favorites from the Metropolitan's holdings. **Thomas Hart Benton**, *July Hay* (1943) and Grant Wood, *The Midnight Ride of Paul Revere* (1931) are outstanding examples of American regionalism. **Edward Hopper**, *Tables for Ladies* (1930), with a waitress and cashier depicted in solitude in a restaurant setting, illustrates one of Hopper's frequent themes. Also on view are works by Georgia O'Keeffe, Milton Avery, Florine Stettheimer, and Lyonel Feininger. Members of **The Eight** exhibited include George Bellows, John Sloan, and William Glackens.

At the conclusion of the survey, a gallery contains changing exhibitions from the design collection, including furniture from Wiener Werkstätte and Bauhaus designers.

MEZZANINE The central high-ceilinged Mezzanine is used for large-scale paintings and pieces of sculpture. Flanking the sculpture gallery are two small rooms with low light, used for exhibits of the work of **Paul Klee** and for changing exhibitions of drawings, photography, and other fragile works.

SECOND FLOOR

The second floor galleries, not divided into separate rooms but articulated by dividers, contain primarily American (and a few European) painters working after World War II.

Works by **Roy Lichtenstein**, *Stepping Out* (1978) and James Rosenquist, *House of Fire* (1981) are followed by Ellsworth Kelly's large hard-edged color paintings and Morris Louis' soft-edged stripes. **Jasper Johns** is represented by *White Flag* (1955), the largest of his flag paintings and first one painted monochromatically.

Dominating one section is *Autumn Rhythm (Number 30)* (1950) by **Jackson Pollock**; dribbled, splashed, and poured, it is considered a masterpiece from his most important period, admired for its balance of control and spontaneity. His early work *Pasiphaë* (1943) was inspired by the story of Pasiphaë, daughter of Minos. Cursed by Poseidon to fall in love with a white bull, she became the mother of the Minotaur. **Willem de Kooning**'s early work is represented by *Attic* (1949), a monochromatic gestural painting, and the garishly colored *Woman* (1944).

ROOF GALLERY

In recent years the museum has mounted single-artist sculptural exhibitions in this beautiful space, including works from outside the museum's collection. Recent exhibitors have been Roy Lichtenstein, Claes Oldenburg-Coosje van Bruggen, and Joel Shapiro. There is a café, open from 10am until closing, including Friday and Saturday evenings. Along with the sandwiches come wonderful views of the skyline and Central Park.

The Metropolitan Museum of Art The Great Hall

THE AMERICAN WING

Organized on three levels, the American Wing offers an artistic survey of American life from the colonial period through the mid to late 20c. In addition to a fine collection of American painting and sculpture, you can browse your way through galleries of furniture and decorative arts ranging in style from Shaker simplicity to fin de siècle fussiness. The core of the wing is a three-story stack of period rooms, arranged chronologically from the top down.

Some of the galleries are numbered on the walls. Floor plans are posted strategically on each floor to help you find your way.

FIRST FLOOR

ROOMS 101-104 The entrance to the wing is via the tranquil Garden Court, overlooking Central Park. On display are examples of **19c and early 20c American sculpture and architectural elements**. The marble façade at the north end once adorned the United States Branch Bank (1924, architect Martin E. Thompson) on Wall St. At the south end is a stained-glass window, *View of Oyster Bay* (c 1905), the work of **Louis Comfort Tiffany** at his most dazzling. The gilded figure of *Diana* by **Augustus Saint-Gaudens** is a reduced replica of a statue that once topped the original Madison Square Garden (in Madison Square).

ROOMS 105-112 Behind the bank façade exhibits from the Early Federal Period (1790-1820), show the influence of French and English designers. There are period rooms from Boston, Baltimore, and Virginia, and galleries of furniture from such important makers as **Duncan Phyfe** and **Charles-Honoré Lannuier**. The *Shaker Retiring Room* (118) from New Lebanon, N.Y., is furnished in the austere manner of that austere religious sect.

ROOM 119 John Vanderlyn's huge *Panorama of the Palace and Gardens of Versailles* (1818-9) fills this large oval gallery. Vanderlyn hoped to make his fortune with this work and exhibited it in a custom-built rotunda in City Hall Park. Unfortunately the showing was not as successful as Vanderlyn had hoped, and he exhibited the panorama off and on for the rest of his life. Vanderlyn painted himself as the top-hatted figure at the right of the Latone Basin, pointing at the uniformed figures of Czar Alexander I and King Frederick William II of Prussia.

ROOMS 120-124 These rooms display mid- and late-19c furniture in a variety of Revival Styles - Greek, Gothic, Rococo, Renaissance, and Egyptian - as well as work by the firm of McKim, Mead, and White. Here you can see elaborate rosewood pieces by John Henry Belter, and ebonized and marquetried pieces by Herter Brothers, New York's most influential decorators in the late 19c.

Between the McKim, Mead, and White stair and the Frank Lloyd Wright Room are galleries containing examples of the work of **Louis Comfort Tiffany**, versatile designer of windows, lamps, furniture, mosaics, blown Favrile glass vases, pottery, enamelwork, and jewelry.

ROOM 129 The **Frank Lloyd Wright Room** reconstructs a living room (1914) from one of the architect's "prairie houses." Wright (1867-1959) designed every detail of this room, planning the furniture and finishes (red-brown bricks surrounding the fireplace, electroplated copper on the leaded windows) and even stipulating the arrangement of the furniture.

SECOND FLOOR

ROOMS 201-203 The balcony surrounding the Garden Court offers a survey of **American Decorative Arts**, from 17c-20c. On view are silver from the late Colonial and Federal periods, including work of that most famous of American silversmiths, **Paul Revere**. His father was a Huguenot silversmith who Americanized his name after arriving in Boston; other smiths represented are Myer Meyers (a Jewish silversmith of Dutch descent) and Cornelius Kierstede (also of Dutch descent). There are opulent late-19c examples from the Tiffany workshops, including the *"Magnolia" vase* (1893), worked in silver, gold, enamels, and opals and embossed all over with different American plant forms. Among the ceramics are humble salt-glazed stoneware from New York, red earthenware from Pennsylvania, and elaborate porcelains from the Union Porcelain Works in Greenpoint, Brooklyn. Glassware includes free-blown tableware and opalescent "Favrile" glass from **Louis Comfort Tiffany**.

ROOMS 209-215 Period rooms on this level date from the **Late Colonial Period** (1730-90) and include the *Pennsylvania German Room*, with colorful decorative motifs, and the *Alexandria Ballroom* from a Virginia tavern (c 1793).

Up a short staircase are the galleries of American Painting and Sculpture, arranged chronologically.

ROOMS 216-218, 223 are devoted to **18c paintings and sculpture**. Portraits include **John Smibert**, *Francis Brinley* (1729) and *Mrs Francis Brinley and her Son Francis* (1729); and **John Singleton Copley**, *Midshipman Augustus Brine* (1782) and *Daniel Crommelin Verplanck* (1771), the son of an influential Dutch family. Copley, recognized as the greatest 18c American painter, was almost entirely self-taught, but left for London (1775) when conflicts preceding the Revolutionary War threatened his Boston practice.

   Charles Willson Peale's portrait of *George Washington* (c 1780) is Peale's copy of his original now in Philadelphia; the artist copied the painting numerous times, updating Washington's uniform along the way and changing the background. **John Trumbull**'s heroic canvas, *The Sortie Made by the Garrison of Gibraltar* (1789) depicts a dramatic moment in the siege of the English fortress at Gibraltar. **Samuel F.B. Morse**, *The Muse: Susan Walker Morse* (1835-7), a portrait of his eldest daughter, painted shortly before Morse gave up painting and turned to telegraphy. Morse wanted to be a history painter, to devote himself to what he called "the intellectual branch of the art." When he failed to get major commissions for history painting, he abandoned art and turned to inventing, which eventually made him wealthy.

ROOMS 219-221 **19C painting**. Here are still lifes by members of the painterly Peale family, and **George Caleb Bingham**'s *Fur Traders Descending the Missouri* (c 1845), a masterful genre painting by an artist who had little formal training but a great deal of experience with the American West. Landscapes by members of the Hudson River School include works by **Thomas Cole** and **Asher B. Durand**. Later paintings include the large-scale *Heart of the Andes* (1859) by **Frederic Edwin Church**, displayed in an elaborate windowlike frame that reproduces the original. Somewhat larger is *The Rocky Mountains, Lander's Peak* (1864) by German-born **Albert Bierstadt**. Bierstadt's desire to paint the rugged landscapes of the American West was confirmed when he accompanied a surveying expedition headed by Frederick Lander.

ROOM 222 has paintings by **Winslow Homer** (1836-1910), now rated as one of the finest 19c American painters. Included here are genre paintings inspired by his early career as a magazine illustrator for *Harper's Weekly*: *Prisoners from the Front* (1866) was one of his first important works, an unsentimental portrayal of exhausted prisoners, a scene that Homer may have seen as a war correspondent. *Snap the Whip* (1872), is an equally realistic portrayal of Yankee schoolchildren at play. Also, *Eagle Head, Manchester, Massachusetts* (1870).

ROOM 223 Painted in Germany, **Emanuel Leutze**'s *Washington Crossing the Delaware* (1851) is a romantic reconstruction of history, inaccurate in many details, but deeply imprinted on the American consciousness. It was painted in Germany, using a single model for both Washington and the steersman. Sculpture in this room includes **Hiram Powers**' marble bust of an aged and toothless *Andrew Jackson* (1837).

BALCONY In room 225 are examples of trompe l'oeil painting and Western art, including bronzes by **Frederic Remington**, chronicler of cowboys, Indians, and army troopers. Also here are examples of the mysterious, visionary painting of **Albert Pinkham Ryder**, and others.

Emanuel Leutze *Washington Crossing the Delaware* (1851)

MEZZANINE

A staircase leads down to the mezzanine (rooms M1-M5), with **late 19c-early 20c American painting**, including paintings by **Thomas Eakins**: *The Champion Single Sculls (Max Schmitt in a Single Scull)* (1871), with Eakins himself rowing in the middle distance, a genre painting with one of Eakins' favorite subjects. Also, *The Thinker: Portrait of Louis Kenton* (1900), a brooding portrait of a man who was briefly Eakins' brother-in-law. Also here are domestic scenes of women and children by Mary Cassatt and portraits by James Abbott McNeill Whistler including *Arrangement in Flesh Colour and Black: Portrait of Theodore Duret* (1833). Paintings by John Twachtman, and Childe Hassam, and William Merritt Chase influenced by the French Impressionists. Among the most memorable paintings of **Winslow Homer** are *Northeaster* (1895), an austere New England seascape, and *The Gulf Stream* (1899), based on trips the artist had made to the Bahamas. The ship on the horizon may have been added some time after the picture was completed, to suggest the possibility of hope.

THE ROBERT LEHMAN COLLECTION

The Robert Lehman Wing, which juts off the west wall of the museum into Central Park, was the source of some consternation when it was built in 1976. The Lehman Collection, however, was one the museum could not turn down, remarkable for its range (early Renaissance to 20c) and its unsurpassed quality. Lehman, who died in 1969, insisted that his collection stay forever together, installed in rooms recreating those from his own town house, and so the museum added the present galleries. Drawings and other fragile works are shown downstairs in rooms with low light.

At the time of writing a special exhibition necessitated the rearrangement of some of the rooms.

THE GRAND GALLERY, facing the central courtyard, has 19c-20c French painting, with works by **Claude Monet**, **Vincent van Gogh**, **Paul Gauguin**, and **Edgar Degas**. Among the most-loved is **Pierre-Auguste Renoir**'s *Two Young Girls at the Piano* (1892), painted on commission for the Musée du Luxembourg; this is one of five versions Renoir painted as he developed the composition.

ROOMS 1-3 The period rooms from the Lehman apartment begin on the right (north side of wing). The collection is remarkable for its **Italian Renaissance paintings**, including works by Sienese and Florentine painters such as Ugolino da Nerio, Barna da Siena, Lippo Vanni, and other important painters.

THE SPECIAL GALLERY Beyond the third gallery, the Dining Room, the large Special Gallery is devoted to French painting and furniture. Usually on display here is **Jean-Auguste-Dominique Ingres**' *Portrait of the Princesse de Broglie* (1853), a portrait which captures the beauty and serenity of the princess as well as the luxury of her clothing and jewelry, and shows the painter's mastery of a genre he did not enjoy.

RED VELVET ROOM This room has paintings by **15c Masters** from Siena, Florence, and Venice, among them some of the most famous in the Lehman collection. Among the renowned works here are *The Temptation of St Anthony Abbot* (c 1444), by a painter known as the Osservanza Master, a student of Sassetta. One of eight panels illustrating the saint's life, it shows Saint Anthony tempted by a vision of a heap of gold to stray from the steep and stony path of righteousness; the gold, formerly in the lower left, has been scraped out and painted over. *The Creation of the World and the Expulsion from Paradise* (c 1445), by **Giovanni di Paolo**, was once part of an altarpiece. The concentric rings of the universe encircle the Earth, the outermost representing the constellations of the zodiac. **Alessandro Botticelli**'s *Annunciation* (c 1490), a small painting intended for private devotion, shows the Virgin in a complex architectural setting rendered with perspective.

THE SITTING ROOM on the second floor of the Lehman townhouse held some of the most imposing paintings in the collection - masterpieces by **Spanish painters of the 16c-18c** and **Dutch painters of the 17c**. El Greco's *St Jerome as a Cardinal* (c 1600-10) is one of five known versions of this painting: the Frick Collection has another. **Rembrandt**'s *Portrait of Gérard de Lairesse* (c 1665) sympathetically portrays a young man, also a painter, whose face was ravaged by syphilis. **Francisco de Goya**, *Condesa de Altamira and Her Daughter, Maria Agustina* (1787-8), a portrait remarkable for its technique (the fabrics of the countess's gown and the baby's dress) and its psychological insights. Don Manuel Osorio Manrique de Zuñiga, whose portrait is displayed in the galleries of European Paintings, was also a member of this powerful family whose patronage furthered Goya's career.

THE FLEMISH ROOM Here are **15c Northern European paintings and decorative arts**. **Hans Memling**, *Portrait of a Young Man* (1470-5) and *The Annunciation* (1480-89). **Petrus Christus**, *A Goldsmith in His Shop*, possibly St Eligius (1449), patron saint of goldsmiths, an early example of genre painting. The *Portrait of Margaret of Austria* (1490), by Jean Hey, shows the ten-year-old princess, who had been betrothed, aged three, to the future Charles VIII of France; a year later her future husband repudiated her.

EUROPEAN PAINTING

The galleries at the top of the Grand Staircase hold the Metropolitan's collection of **Old Master paintings**, one of the high points of the museum. Fortunately these rooms are numbered on the doorways so that you can find your way through this maze of rooms.

ROOM 1 **Giovanni Battista Tiepolo** was the greatest Venetian, Italian, and possibly European painter of the 18c; his work represents the summit of the Italian decorative tradition. *The Triumph of Marius*, *The Capture of Carthage*, and *The Battle of Vercellae* all belonged to a series of heroic canvases painted (1725-9) to decorate the main room of the Ca' Dolfin in Venice, a palace owned by the patriarch of Aquileia. The paintings depict incidents that established Rome's ascendance, and presumably had reference to recent Venetian campaigns. In *The Triumph of Marius*, Tiepolo painted himself on the left in front of the torch bearer.

ROOM 2 **French Neoclassical painting**. Dominating Room 2 is **Jacques-Louis David**, *The Death of Socrates* (1787), an iconic painting of the Neoclassical movement in France, expressing the virtues of self-sacrifice and austerity. David's *Antoine-Laurent Lavoisier and His Wife* (1788) is a masterful portrait of the scientist best known for his studies of water, oxygen, and gunpowder. His wife was thought to have studied with David, and a portfolio of her work sits on the armchair at the left edge of the painting. Also in this room are portraits by Jean-Baptiste Greuze, Adélaïde Labille-Guiard, and Élisabeth Louise Vigée Le Brun.

The galleries opening from the right of Room 2 are devoted to Italian Renaissance painting. Those opening from the left contain Netherlandish and northern European paintings.

ROOMS 3, 4A-B, AND 14A contain **13c-15c Italian painting**. In Room 3 are works by **Giovanni di Paolo**: *Madonna and Child with Saints* (1445?) and *Paradise* (perhaps part of an altarpiece to which the *Expulsion from Paradise* in the Lehman Collection belongs). Also in this room are **Sassetta**, *Journey of the Magi* (c 1435), and Simone Martini, *St Andrew*. In Room 4, **Giotto**'s *Epiphany* (c 1320) is innovative both in the carefully organized space within the frame and in the naturalism of several of the figures. Lorenzo Monaco's depictions of *Noah, David, Moses*, and *Abraham*, were probably parts of an altarpiece; although the meaning of the figures is debated, often Old Testament prophets were considered to prefigure events of the New Testament (the ark prefiguring the Church, the sacrifice of Isaac was interpreted as an emblem for the sacrifice of Christ). Room 4A contains a rare double portrait by **Filippo Lippi**, *Man and Woman at a Casement* (c 1440).

When department store magnate Benjamin Altman died in 1913, he left his magnificent collection to the Metropolitan with the stipulation that his paintings be kept together in adjoining rooms, which accounts for the arrangement of Rooms 4A-14, which hold his Italian and Dutch paintings. Renaissance painting in Room 4B includes **Andrea Mantegna**, *The Holy Family with St Mary Magdalene* (1490-1506) and **Alessandro Botticelli**, *The Last Communion of St Jerome* (early 1490s), an unusual portrayal of a saint characteristically shown as a scholar.

ROOM 5, beyond the Italian secular painting gallery, contains works from northern Italian painters: **Giovanni Bellini**, *Madonna Adoring the Sleeping Child* (early1460s), an early work showing Mantegna's influence; **Carlo Crivelli**, *Pietà* (1476; and **Andrea Mantegna**, *The Adoration of the Shepherds* (after 1450).

ROOMS 6-7 **15c-16c Italian painting**: Lippi, Ghirlandaio, Botticelli, Signorelli, and Perugino. Here are **Luca Signorelli**'s beautiful *Madonna and Child* (1505) with grotesque figures and golden coins in the background, and the eccentric *Hunting Scene*, by **Piero di Cosimo**, a whimsical gathering of humans, satyrs, and wonderfully painted animals. **Agnolo Bronzino**'s *Portrait of a Young Man* (c 1540), a self-consciously aristocratic nobleman, is one of his finest. Also in this room is an early altarpiece by **Raphael**, *Madonna and Child Enthroned with Saints* (1504).

The Italian paintings continue in Room 8, which opens from Room 6 (the entrance near the staircase is presently closed).

ROOMS 8-9 16c Venetian and Italian painting. In the first room are **Titian**'s *Venus and the Lute Player* (1565–70), a late painting completed by his studio, and *Venus and Adonis* (1560s), a scene from Ovid's *Metamorphoses*, with the goddess of love embracing her mortal lover as he departs on the fatal boar hunt. Also on view are Tintoretto, *The Miracle of the Loaves and Fishes* (1545-50) and Paolo Veronese, *Mars and Venus United by Love* (1570s).

ROOM 10 17c French painting includes **Nicolas Poussin**, *The Abduction of the Sabine Women* (c 1637), and the mysterious *The Blind Orion Searching for the Rising Sun* (1658), painted late in Poussin's careeer. **Claude Lorrain**'s idealized Italian landscapes include *View of La Crescenza* (c 1649) and *The Trojan Women Setting Fire to Their Fleet* (1643).

ROOMS 11-14 contain **17c Dutch portraits and landscapes**, with works by Hobbema, Ruisdael, and Cuyp. Fewer than 40 universally accepted works by **Johannes Vermeer** are known to exist; the Metropolitan has five: *A Maid Asleep* (1656-7), in the Altman Collection (Room 14); *Young Woman with a Lute* (early 1660s); *Young Woman with a Water Pitcher* (c 1660-7); *Study of a Young Woman* (c 1665-7); and the less compelling *Allegory of the Faith* (c 1670), commissioned by a Catholic patron and filled with Christian symbols.

Among the 17c Dutch portraits are several by **Rembrandt**: *Man in Oriental Costume* ("The Noble Slav"; 1632), *Flora* (1650s), *Woman with a Pink* (1662-5), and a fine *Self-Portrait* (1660), painted when the artist was 54. *Aristotle with a Bust of Homer* (1653), perhaps the most famous of the Metropolitan's Rembrandts, is often interpreted as a study of contrasting material and spiritual values.

ROOM 15 18c English portraits of assorted aristocrats include Thomas Gainsborough, *Mrs Grace Dalrymple Elliott* (1778), a portrait apparently commissioned by Mrs Elliott's lover, and **Sir Joshua Reynolds**, *Captain George K.H. Coussmaker* (1782).

Diego Velázquez
Juan de Parjea (c 1650)

ROOMS 16-19 At the time of writing these galleries were closed for reinstallation. However, Room 16 usually contains works by Murillo, Zurbarán and **Diego Velázquez**, including *Juan de Parjea* (c 1650), a celebrated portrait of the painter's assistant. The next rooms offer French painting from the 17c-18c, with works by Georges de la Tour, Jean-Baptiste Greuze, and Jean-Baptiste Chardin.

ROOMS 20-22 **Francisco de Goya** is well-represented in the collection by a number of portraits of the Spanish aristocracy, including two well-known and touching portraits of children, *Manuel Osorio Manrique de Zuñiga* (1784–92) and *José Costa y Bonells, Called Pepito*. The next two rooms offer French and Venetian painting from the 18c, with Rococo paintings by Boucher and Fragonard, and views of Venice by Guardi and Canaletto.

RENAISSANCE PAINTING FROM NORTHERN EUROPE AND 18C ITALIAN PAINTING (Rooms 23-30) open from the left of Room 2 near the top of the Grand Staircase.

ROOMS 23-26 Here, arranged chronologically, are **Netherlandish painting from the 15c-16c** and **German painting from the 16c**. Highlights include **Jan van Eyck**, *The Crucifixion* and *The Last Judgment* (1425-30), the former acutely detailed, the latter schematic and iconographic. **Rogier van der Weyden**'s cool aristocratic portrait of *Francesco d'Este* (c 1460), the illegitimate son of the duke of Ferrara, has an unusual white background. *The Harvesters*, by **Pieter Breugel the Elder**, part of a cycle representing the months, is remarkable for the distant panoramic landscape and the immediacy with which the peasants are painted. **Hans Holbein**, *Member of the Wedigh Family* (1532), is outstanding in its fine characterization. Also on view here is **Lucas Cranach**'s *The Judgment of Paris* (c 1528).

ROOMS 27-28 Dominating Room 27 are works by **Peter Paul Rubens**, *Venus and Adonis*, influenced by Titian, and *Rubens, His Wife Helena Fourment and Their Son, Peter Paul* (c 1639), a portrait of domestic happiness; Rubens married Helena when he was 53 and she was 16. **Anthony van Dyck**, *James Stuart, Duke of Richmond and Lennox*, is a flattering portrait of the cousin of Charles I by a painter who excelled in flattering portraits.

ROOMS 29-30 **El Greco**. Here are his *Portrait of a Cardinal* (c 1600), perhaps Don Fernando Niño de Guevara, the Grand Inquisitor and archbishop of Seville, and *View of Toledo* (1597), his only landscape. In the final room are examples of **17c Italian painting**, notably **Caravaggio**'s *The Musicians* (c 1595) and work by Annibale Carraci, Mattia Preti, and Guido Reni.

19C EUROPEAN PAINTINGS AND SCULPTURE

The museum's collection of 19c European paintings and sculpture, with its outstanding work by the French Impressionists and Post-Impressionists, is one of New York's prime cultural attractions.

The corridor gallery contains **Salon paintings**, including Rosa Bonheur's monumental *The Horse Fair* (1853-5), bronze animal sculptures by Antoine-Louis Barye, and, further along, sculptures by **Auguste Rodin**, including bronzes from *The Gates of Hell* and a terracotta portrait bust, a study for the monument to Balzac, and a bronze figure of the novelist wrapped in a monk's robe.

The first two galleries (northeast corner, near Cypriot Art) are devoted to **Romanticism and Neoclassicism**, precursors of Impressionism.

ROOMS 1-2 **Eugène Delacroix**, *Basket of Flowers* (1848), *The Abduction of Rebecca* (1846), and *The Natchez* (c 1835). Also works by John Constable, Joseph Mallord William Turner, Théodore Gericault, and Théodore Rousseau. Aristocratic portraits by two of the great Neoclassical painters, **Jacques-Louis David** and his student, **Jean-Auguste-Dominique Ingres**, including *Joseph-Antoine Moltedo* (c 1810), a sympathetic portrait of a high-ranking bureaucrat.

ROOMS 3-4 The corner gallery features the work of the prolific **Jean-Baptiste-Camille Corot**, including figure paintings as well as the more familiar landscapes. Among the painters in the next room are Charles-François Daubigny and Jean-François Millet of the **Barbizon School** and Honoré Daumier, whose *The Third-Class Carriage* (c 1863-5) offers a poignant portrait of working-class travelers.

ROOM 5 The Museum has one of the world's largest holdings of the work of **Gustave Courbet**, a leader of French 19c Realists, whose work is displayed in two galleries at opposite ends of the Manet gallery: critics attacked *Woman with a Parrot* (1865-6) for its sensuality and general bad taste, though Manet and other contemporaries liked it.

ROOM 6 This large central gallery exhibits paintings by **Édouard Manet**. Among them are *Woman with a Parrot* (1866), sometimes considered Manet's response to Courbet's painting with the same title; *Mlle. V...in the Costume of an Espada* (1862), like the previous painting using Victorine Muerent as the model; *The Spanish Singer* (1861), one of the two pictures with which Manet made his name in the Salon of that year; *Young Man in the Costume of a Maja* (1863); *Boy with a Sword* (1861); *A Matador* (1865–70); *Boating* (1874). *The Dead Christ and the Angels* (1864) is one of Manet's few paintings with a religious subject.

ROOMS 8-11 These galleries with **Degas sculpture, paintings, and pastels** contain many works collected by Mrs. H.O. Havemeyer, one of the museum's major benefactors. Through her friendship with Mary Cassatt, she knew the Impressionist painters and was especially captivated by the work of Degas. On exhibit is his most famous sculpture, *Little Fourteen-Year-Old Dancer*, the only piece of the artist's sculpture exhibited during his lifetime. Degas

Édouard Manet *Boating* (1874)

paintings include *The Dancing Class* (1871), *Woman Seated Beside a Vase of Flowers* (1858), and *The Collector of Prints* (1866).

ROOM 12 Next to the room with the Barbizon painters is a gallery featuring **Pierre-Auguste Renoir**: *Mme Charpentier and Her Children*, a society portrait of a publisher's wife, which is more detailed than most of Renoir's portraits. *By the Seashore* (1883) is an example of Renoir's "dry" style, influenced by a trip to Italy where he came to admire Renaissance painters; *Tilla Durieux* (1914), a portrait of a famous German actress, was painted at the end of Renoir's life when he worked with his brush strapped to his arthritic hand. Also other Renoir landscapes and portraits and work by Berthe Morisot and Alfred Sisley.

ROOMS 14-15 Works by **Claude Monet** span his long career from

Impressionist paintings done while the artist was in his 20s to his studies of changing light during the day, to some of his late abstract paintings of water lilies. *Regatta at Sainte-Adresse* (1867); *Garden at Sainte-Adresse* (1867); *La Grenouillière* (1869); *Rouen Cathedral: The Portal (in Sun)* (1894); *The Houses of Parliament (Effect of Fog)* (1903); *Rouen Cathedral: The Portal*; *Bridge over a Pool of Water Lilies*; *Haystacks (Effect of Snow and Sun)* (1891); *Poplars* (1891), and others.

ROOM 16 This gallery is largely devoted to work by **Camille Pissarro**, a central figure of the Impressionist group, who was influenced by the great English landscape painters, especially Constable and Turner. On display are: *Barges at Pontoise* (1876); *The Garden of the Tuileries on a Spring Morning* (1899); and *The Boulevard Montmartre on a Winter Morning* (1897).

ROOM 19 In this room is a wonderful group of paintings by **Paul Cézanne**. *The Gulf of Marseilles Seen from L'Estaque* (1884-6) depicts a landscape Cézanne often painted, studying the forms of the houses and mountains from different viewpoints. Among the portraits are *Dominique Aubert* (1865-6), an early work closer to the style of the Impressionists than, for example, *Mme Cézanne in a Red Dress* (c 1890). *The Card Players* (1892) is a genre painting, unusual for Cézanne. Also on view are several landscapes and fine still lifes, for example, *Still Life with Apples and a Pot of Primroses* (early 1890s).

ROOMS 17-20 **Vincent van Gogh** and **Paul Gauguin**. The Metropolitan has the nation's largest collection of paintings by van Gogh. In this room are *Wheat Fields with Cypresses* (1889), the first appearance of this theme to which the painter often returned. Also *Cypresses* (1889); *Mme Ginoux (L'Arlésienne)* (1888); *Shoes* (1888); *The Potato Peeler*, with *Self-Portrait with a Straw Hat* (1886-8), painted on the reverse; and *Irises* (1890).

Paul Gauguin: *Ia Orana Maria* (1892), an Annunciation scene; *Two Tahitian Women* (1899). **Georges Seurat**: *Circus Sideshow* (1887-8) and *Study for a Sunday Afternoon on the Island of La Grande Jatte*

(1884). This was Seurat's final study for his masterpiece, now in the Chicago Art Institute; Seurat began the painting itself in the summer of 1884. The following year he met Camille Pissarro who suggested he repaint the canvas using different pigments; unfortunately by 1892 these new paints began to lose their brilliance. So the study gives an idea of the way Seurat intended the finished painting to look.

The southeast corner of the second floor of the museum has galleries largely devoted to the art of the eastern Mediterranean and the Near East.

CYPRIOT ART

The Metropolitan has the best collection of ancient Cypriot art outside of Cyprus, much of it gathered by Luigi Palma di Cesnola (1832-1904), first director of the museum. An immigrant from Italy with a military background, Cesnola fought valiantly in the American Civil War and was rewarded by being made consul on Cyprus. There he was overcome by a mania for archaeology and devoted his considerable energy and money to unearthing thousands of works and having them shipped to New York.

   The collection is installed in four rooms, organized chronologically. In the first room are prehistoric pieces including bronze tripods. Among the highlights from Geometric and Archaic Cyprus (second room) is a silver gilt bowl (c 725-675 BC) whose decoration shows a mix of Mesopotamian and Egyptian motifs, an Assyrian winged god wrestling with a lion in the center and Egyptianized animals in the borders. The most outstanding piece (third room) from the Classical period is the limestone *Amathus sarcophagus*, whose decoration shows the influence of Greek, Cypriot, and Near Eastern influences. The basic shape and architectural ornaments (for example the sphinxes on the lid) are Greek while the figures on the short sides are Oriental. The sarcophagus is unusual because of its monumental size and the preservation of traces of color.

ANCIENT NEAR EASTERN ART

These galleries contain pre-Islamic works dating from the 6th millennium BC up to the Arab conquest of the Near East (mid-7c). The galleries begin with a room of monumental **Assyrian Art** featuring large stone reliefs and carvings taken from the palace of King Assurnasirpal II in Nimrud (now northern Iraq) on the upper Tigris River. Two huge winged creatures, a bull and a lion with human heads, flank the door. Originally they functioned to support an arch.

In the adjacent galleries are objects from Mesopotamia (5th-1st millennium BC), Pre-Islamic Antiquities from Iran, and Achaemenid, Parthian, and Sasanian Art.

ISLAMIC ART

The galleries of Islamic Art, installed 30 years ago, closed in the spring of 2003 for enlargement and re-installation. During the four years the galleries are under restoration, highlights will be on view on the south balcony overlooking the Great Hall. The display has been chosen from the Metropolitan's collection of 12,000 examples of Islamic art, whose works date from the 7c-18c and were created in the area that extends from Spain in the west to Central Asia and India in the east. The collection includes miniatures frm the royal courts of Persia and Mughal India, glass and metalwork from Egypt, Mesopotamia, and Syria, beautiful ceramics, and luxurious carpets (some of which will be hung in rotation in the Great Hall, the grand entrance to the museum from Fifth Avenue).

ASIAN ART

The Asian Art Galleries begin with the Great Hall Balcony and continue to the northern wall of the museum. Fragile works - for example, Chinese, Korean, Japanese, Indian, and Tibetan paintings - rotate every six months; some textiles, lacquers, and woodblock prints change approximately every four months.

Equestrian portrait of Shah Jahan (17c Indian miniature)

Two displays on **Chinese ceramics** on the **Great Hall Balcony** explore the impact of Chinese and Japanese ceramics on European traditions, and the relationship between Chinese blue-and-white wares and those made in Japan, Korea, and Vietnam. Examples date from the 6c BC to the 18c. Benjamin Altman collected Qing dynasty (1644-1912) porcelain as well as European Old Master paintings, and the cases contain many examples of elaborately painted, sumptuously glazed vessels that he donated to the museum upon his death.

CHINESE ART

The exhibit begins with **Neolithic and Bronze Age** works and continues chronologically. The earliest objects, from about 1500-2000 BC include a famous *Tuan Fang altar set* with ritual vessels. Further along, in the Han Dynasty section are ceramic tomb figurines appealing to modern sensibilities for their depiction of everyday activities: people playing games or dancing.

Art from the **Six Dynasties Period** focuses on early Buddhist sculpture from northern China, notably a *Maitreya altarpiece* (c 524) with figures from the Buddhist pantheon. The **Tang Dynasty** section contains gold and silver vessels and ornaments, jade belt plaques, and other rich objects illustrating the wealth and cosmopolitan spirit of the age. Further along are ceramic Tang *tomb figures* representing soldiers, servants, camels, and horses, which were buried to serve the dead.

Return to the large gallery of **later Chinese Buddhist sculpture**, which opens off the center of the long chronological gallery. The large dry-lacquer *seated Buddha* (7c), one of the few remaining in the world, was made by laboriously molding layers of lacquer-soaked cloth over a clay core, a costly labor-intensive process. Traces remain of former gilding and painting.

The long gallery close to Fifth Ave contains Chinese paintings, shown on a rotating basis. Beyond is the **Chinese Garden Court**, modeled on a 12c scholar's garden, a group of domestic buildings around an open courtyard in which there was an artistic representation of nature, with carefully arranged rocks, plants, and flowing water. The garden, built in large part by Chinese craftsmen who came to the museum and used materials brought from China, was the first permanent cultural exchange between the United States and the People's Republic of China.

The galleries on the east side of the Garden Court contain selections from the museum's extraordinary collection of Chinese paintings and calligraphy, including works from the 8c-18c, which are rotated for conservation. There are also 19c-20c paintings and decorative arts: jades, lacquers, metalwork, textiles, and other objects from the 12c-19c.

JAPANESE ART

Here are nine roughly chronological galleries containing painting, sculpture, ceramics, and lacquer, textiles, and woodblock prints, spanning more than 4000 years. The first galleries contain Pre-Buddhist and Shinto art, including cylindrical clay sculptures (for example a bust of a warrior) from the Kofun culture (5c-6c). Images in the gallery of Buddhist art reflect different schools of Japanese Buddhism, imported from China in the 6c. Among them is a scowling image of the Buddhist deity, Fudo Myo-o, who fought the enemies of Buddha with his sword and ensnared evil forces with his noose.

The next galleries feature **Kamakura narrative painting** (1185-1333) and **art of the Muromachi period** (1392-1568), including monochromatic landscapes, and ceramics.

Beyond is the **Shoin Room**, from the Momoyama period (1568-1615), modeled on a guest room at a temple outside Kyoto. Painted on the door panels is *The Old Plum* (c 1645), a wonderfully gnarled and abstracted plum tree, which was a symbol of rejuvenation and fortitude because it put up new shoots each spring. The panel was probably one of four that encircled the room.

The next gallery displays paintings and ceramics from the Edo period (1615-1868). Among the best-known paintings by Ogata Korin is *Yatsuhashi or Eight Plank Bridge* (also called *The Irises*) painted in the 18c, which renders abstractly a motif from a 10c literary work. *The Great Wave at Kanagawa* (c 1831-3) by Katsushika Hokusai is one of 36 prints depicting views of Mount Fuji. In this one the mountain is seen as a small triangle over which towers a wild and turbulent sea. The print is said to have inspired Debussy's *La Mer* and Rilke's *Der Berg*. The remaining galleries offer ceramics, decorative arts including textiles, and woodblock prints.

ARTS OF SOUTH AND SOUTHEAST ASIA

The galleries of Indian art open from the northeast corner of Early Chinese Sculpture (off the Great Hall Balcony).

ROOMS 1-3 **Early India**: Kushan, Ishvaku, and Gupta periods. On view in the first gallery, among statues of nature gods and female fertility figures, is a pair of *gold earrings* (1981.398.3,4), the most elaborate early Indian jewelry known to exist. In the Kushan gallery is an exceptional *Torso of a standing Bodhisattva*, a being who has attained enlightenment, thus escaping the cycle of death and rebirth, but decides to remain on earth to help others do the same. A red sandstone *Standing Buddha* (5c) from the Gupta period, considered the Golden Age of Indian art, is one of the most important pieces in the collection. The buddha is portrayed in a typical pose with the right hand (missing) raised in a protective gesture and the left holding the edge of the garment; the figure is remarkable for its serenity.

ROOM 7 **South India**. Here are several fine bronze images from the Chola period (880-1279): *Standing Parvati* depicts the Hindu goddess, consort of Shiva, in the graceful traditional "thrice bent" pose. The iconography of *Shiva as Lord of the Dance* (11c) depicts the god as creator, preserver, and destroyer.

ROOM 8 In the Medieval Sculpture Gallery are arts that flourished from the 8c-13c, derived from the styles of the Gupta period. *Loving Couple*, a stone temple sculpture from the 13c, shows a bejeweled couple embracing, symbolic not only of physical pleasure but of the soul's longing for union with the divine.

ROOM 11 Shown here are changing exhibitions of Indian painting from the 17c-18c.

ROOMS 12-13 Arts of **Nepal** and **Tibet** include Buddhist and Hindu sculpture, showing the influence of northern Indian styles. The *Paramasukha-Chakrasamvara mandala* (c 1100) is the earliest known Nepalese painting done on cloth. Another highlight is a *Standing Bodhisattva Maitreya*, the Buddha of the Future, from 9c-10c Nepal, one of the largest early Nepalese bronzes in the Western Hemisphere.

A staircase leads down to the Southeast Asian Art Galleries.

ROOM 14 **Southeast Asia, Thailand, Vietnam, and Indonesia** from the Bronze Age and Iron Age (3rd millennium BC-4c AD). Among these ancient objects is a large (41 inches), mysterious bronze ceremonial object shaped like an ax standing on its blade, only one of two known to exist. Its precise function is not known.

ROOM 17 **Khmer Courtyard**, Angkor Period (9c-13c). *Avalokiteshvara, the Boddhisattva of Infinite Compassion, Seated in Royal Ease* (late 10c-early 11c), is one of the finest surviving Khmer bronzes, with a smooth, reflective surface.

MUSICAL INSTRUMENTS

The Metropolitan's collection of instruments spans six continents, with the oldest pieces dating from about 300 BC.

EUROPEAN INSTRUMENTS are in the galleries to the left. Highlights include European and American keyboard instruments, among which is a richly painted Double Virginal (1581) by Hans Ruckers the Elder, a Flemish harpsichord builder, discovered in Peru in 1915. **Bartolomeo Cristofori**'s Grand Piano (1720) is the oldest known piano; Cristofori developed the first successful hammer-action keyboard instrument and therefore gets credit as the inventor of the modern piano. Probably one of the most elaborate pianos ever built is a gilded Erard piano with engraved ivory, mother-of-pearl, and abalone decoration, made for the wife of an English baron; Liszt and Chopin used Erard instruments but the keys of this one were barely touched, no surprise given the excessive decoration. Stringed instruments include one of the few violins by **Antonio Stradivari** that has been restored to its Baroque condition; most instruments by this famous maker were modified to produce a bigger, more brilliant sound.

AMERICAN AND NON-WESTERN INSTRUMENTS occupy the end and right hand galleries. Here you will find pottery whistles, whistling jars, and rattles, including the kind used by *shamans*. From Africa come thumb pianos and a marimba with gourd resonators. The Chinese, Japanese, and Korean instruments are especially beautiful, including a sonorous stone and a mouth organ of bamboo pipes in a lacquered bowl.

The pipe organ (1830) was built by a famous Boston craftsman, Thomas Appleton, whose reputation and instruments reached as far as California by the time he retired in 1869. This one was probably built for a church in Hartford, Connecticut, but was discovered almost 150 years later, unused and neglected, in Plains, Pennsylvania.

The Guggenheim Museum

OPEN	Sat-Wed 10-5:45; Fri 10-8
CLOSED	Thurs, Dec 25; open other holidays, but check holiday hours
CHARGES	Adults, $15.00; students and seniors with valid ID, $10; Children under 12, free
TELEPHONE	(212) 423-3600
RECORDED INFO	(212) 423-3500
WWW.	guggenheim.org
MAIN ENTRANCE	1071 Fifth Ave, between 88th/ 89th Sts. The café entrance is also on Fifth Ave, close to 88th St
SUBWAY	4, 5, 6 to 86th St
DISABLED ACCESS	Manual wheelchair users may need a companion to assist with the ramp. Museum accessible to wheelchairs, except one gallery. Wheelchairs available without charge
SHOPS	Two shops with art books, catalogues, posters and postcards, apparel, jewelry, accessories, toys and books for children, and household objects, including a teapot shaped like the museum
EATING	Café

Changing exhibitions, tours and gallery talks, lectures, events.

The Guggenheim Museum is an unmistakable presence both on uptown Fifth Avenue and in the city's cultural life. Its home, Frank Lloyd Wright's unforgettable concrete spiral, confronts its staid rectilinear neighbors with considerable edginess. The building itself is wonderful to look at, but artists have complained that the narrow ramp and low ceilings of the dome are hostile to art and to visitors trying to look at the art. The collection, an amalgam of six different private collections each with a different thrust, nonetheless is recognized as one of the great holdings of 20c Masters from the years before World War II.

THE BUILDING

Frank Lloyd Wright's landmark building is probably the most famous thing about the Guggenheim Museum. In form it is a spiral with a ramp cantilevered out from its interior walls, sitting above a horizontal slab. Wright explained that the building was "organic art," imitating the forms of nature. Artists, including Willem de Kooning and Robert Motherwell, declared it unsuitable for the sympathetic display of art. Critics have called it the wrong building in the wrong place. Its yellowish concrete facing has been likened to jaundiced skin. But it has one of the great interior spaces in the city.

Wright got the commission for the building in 1943. A letter from the museum's director, Baroness Hilla Rebay von Ehrenwiesen, explained (or exclaimed): "I want a temple of spirit, a monument!" That is precisely what she got, though sixteen years later.

Those years were spent in redesigning the museum, either because Wright's ideas continued to evolve, or because zoning and construction regulations as expressed by the Department of Buildings differed monumentally from Wright's creative notions. At different stages early plans showed the spiral either getting smaller toward the top or larger, the solution Wright eventually chose. At one point in order to create the largest interior space allowed by zoning laws, Wright planned the spiral to swell to a size that would overhang the footprint by 24 feet. He also wanted a great deal of glass to illuminate the interior with natural light. The city vetoed both the overhang and the glass. After years of arguing and compromising, ground was broken in 1956 and the building completed three years later. In 1992 Gwathmey Siegel & Assocs added the rectangular building on 89th St to provide much-needed exhibition and administrative space.

HIGHLIGHTS

The view from the ramp up to the skylight and down to the main floor	The Rotunda
Post-Impressionist and Modern Masters	Thannhauser Galleries

The Solomon R. Guggenheim Museum

The collection brings together the tastes of several individual collectors. The most important was Solomon R. Guggenheim, who had risen from itinerant peddler to mining and smelting magnate. In 1927 Guggenheim sat for a portrait by a young German artist, Baroness Hilla Rebay von Ehrenwiesen. Rebay believed passionately in the spiritual qualities of abstract art, or as she called it "non-objective" art, and under her influence Guggenheim stopped collecting Old Master paintings and switched to early-20c European abstraction. Rebay recommended artists who shared her views: Robert Delaunay, Vasily Kandinsky, Fernand Léger, and especially Rudolf Bauer, her former lover and longtime confidant. The Guggenheim Museum today owns more Kandinskys than any other museum in the United States and more Bauers than any in the world.

A second major influence in the collection was Peggy Guggenheim, Solomon's niece, who collected Surrealist art (she was married for a year to Max Ernst) and abstract painting and sculpture, including works by Cubists, and Futurists, Metaphysical painters, European Abstractionists, and American Abstract Expressionists. She installed her collection in her home, the Palazzo Venier dei Leoni in Venice. Ownership of these works was transferred to the museum upon her death in 1979, though Peggy stipulated that her paintings and sculptures should stay in her palazzo unless Venice sank.

There are several other important players in the permanent collection. Justin K. Thannhauser, a successful German art dealer who fled to New York before World War II, ceded important Impressionist, Post-Impressionist, and early Modern masterpieces to the museum in 1978. They are displayed in the galleries bearing his name. The museum bought works by German Expressionists and Paul Klee from the estate of Karl Nierendorf, a German art dealer who came to the United States in 1936, and also from Katherine S. Dreier, an artist and collector, who was friendly with early 20c American and European avant-garde artists and collected their work. Finally, the museum acquired many works by European and American Minimalist, Post-Minimalist, and Conceptual artists from Giuseppe Panza di Biumo, an Italian industrialist and real estate investor.

Highlights from the permanent collection are rotated through the Thannhauser Galleries, the Tower Galleries, and sometimes the Rotunda. You can always see some of the permanent collection, but the number of works on view depends on what else the museum is showing at the time. The description below will give you a good idea of the size and scope of the permanent collection. It is organized more or less chronologically, as the galleries usually are.

THANNHAUSER GALLERIES The exhibition of highlights begins on Level 2 with **Impressionist and Post-Impressionist paintings and sculpture**. This oval gallery is organized chronologically; begin to the left of the entrance. The earliest painting in the collection is **Camille Pissarro**, *The Hermitage at Pontoise* (c 1867), an early naturalistic but idyllic painting of the village where the artist lived off and on for 17 years. **Pierre-Auguste Renoir**, *Woman with Parrot*

(1871), a subject also explored by Manet and Courbet (paintings in the Metropolitan Museum); the formal composition and somber use of color precede his later Impressionist style. Also by Renoir, *Still Life with Flowers* (1885). **Édouard Manet**, *Before the Mirror* (1876) is thought to be a painting of a courtesan; Manet and the other Impressionists frequently painted these women, seeking to represent on canvas the conditions of "modern" life. *Woman in Evening Dress* (1877-80) perhaps represents a fashionable middle-class Parisian woman, holding a stylish Japanese fan. Also by Manet, *Portrait of Countess Albazzi* (1880). **Edgar Degas**, *Dancers in Green and Yellow* (c 1903). **Claude Monet**, *Le Palais Ducal Vu de Saint-Georges Majeur* (1908).

Édouard Vuillard, *Place Vintimille* (1908-10); the painter lived in a fourth floor apartment looking down on the square and clearly painted these panels from upstairs. **Paul Gauguin**, *Haere Mai* and *In the Vanilla Grove, Man and Horse* were both painted in 1891, the year Gauguin made his first trip to Tahiti. The words "Haere Mai" mean "Come here" in Tahitian, but don't seem to bear much relation to the contents of the painting. Although the painter claimed he was going to the South Pacific to render reality "the way a child would" using only the primitive means of painting, the pose of man and horse in *The Vanilla Grove* are derived from the famous frieze on the Parthenon.

Paul Cézanne is well-represented in the collection. Currently on view are *Bend in the Road through the Forest* (1873-5), *Still Life: Flask, Glass, and Jug* (c 1877), *Still Life, Plate of Peaches* (1879-80), *Mme Cézanne* (1885-87), and *The Neighborhood of Jas de Bouffan* (1885-7). Jas de Bouffan was Cézanne's family estate, which the painter inherited upon the death of his father in 1886. Also in the collection are *Bibémus* (c 1894-5), a view of abandoned quarries near Aix-en-Provence, and *Man with Crossed Arms* (1899), sometimes considered an especially important precursor of Cubism in its distortions and multiple points of view: the left and right eyes are seen from different angles.

From the earlier part of **Pablo Picasso**'s career come *Le Moulin de la Galette* (1900), painted when the artist was only 19 years old, on his first visit to Paris, influenced by Toulouse-Lautrec. *Woman*

Ironing (1904) is an image of poverty and fatigue from his Blue Period. *Fernande with a Black Mantilla* (1905-6) depicts his mistress at the time, Fernande Olivier; although naturalistic and romantic, this picture is sometimes considered a precursor to his later abstract work in its stylization of her face.

In addition to these paintings presently on view, the collection contains works by Seurat, Van Gogh, notably *Mountains at Saint-Rémy* (1889), Henri de Toulouse-Lautrec, and Pierre Bonnard. There are two paintings by **Amedeo Modigliani**, a *Nude* (1917) and *Jeanne Hébuterne with a Yellow Sweater* (1918-9), both of whose faces suggest his interest in African masks at the time.

20C PIONEERS Here are examples of Cubism as originated by **Braque** and **Picasso**. Picasso's *Carafe, Jug and Fruit Bowl* (1909) shows an early form of this influential style, in which the surfaces of the objects in the still life are broken into planes but still seem to have volume, and the colors, while grayed, are still appropriate to the objects. Georges Braque's *Violin and Palette and Piano and Mandorla* (both 1909-10) are composed of fragmented, monochromatically shaded planes. In Picasso's *Accordionist* (1911), the instrument and its player can be perceived only with difficulty. Juan Gris' *Newspaper and Fruit Dish* (1916) exemplifies the later development of Synthetic Cubism, which introduced brighter colors, ornamental patterns, and the overlapping of forms that were (or seemed to be) cut out and glued to the canvas.

The last section of highlights on this floor contains Picasso's *Woman with Yellow Hair* (1931), a portrait of Marie-Thérèse Walter, then his mistress, drawn in a sweeping curvilinear style. Next to it is *Head of a Woman (Dora Maar)*, painted in 1939.

MAPPLETHORPE GALLERY, LEVEL 4 Currently on view in these galleries are examples of **Geometric Abstraction**, another strong area in the collection. To right of the entrance are several examples by **Piet Mondrian**. The museum has many examples of this Dutch artist's work, including early representational pictures of flowers, and still lifes from the years before he went to Paris.

Amedeo Modigliani *Jeanne Hébuterne with a Yellow Sweater* (1918-9)

Composition VII (1913) reflects his regard for Cubism, with which he became acquainted in Paris. The painting was inspired by a tree, which has been broken down into black lines and areas of color. *Composition 8*, painted a year later, is based on the façades of buildings in Paris. *Composition 16*, dating from 1916, is one of the last works known to be based on an actual object. Mondrian's later works in this gallery, for example *Composition 2* (1922), are restricted to black horizontal and vertical lines on a white ground with small blocks of yellow, black and red.

Lázlo Moholy-Nagy, a Hungarian painter, sculptor, and theorist who taught at the Bauhaus in the 1920s, moved to London in 1935, where he joined the Constructivist group. His *Space Modulators* (1939-45) of molded plexiglass date from this period. The work of Naum Gabo, who was in London during the same time period, also makes use of new synthetic materials and has clear architectural qualities. Gabo had been trained as an engineer and was interested in modern concepts of the nature of space. On view here are a reconstruction of the early *Column* (1923), *Construction on a Plane* (1937-9), *Construction in Space: Arch* (1937), and his later *Linear Construction in Space No. 1* (1942-3) which makes use of nylon monofilament to create mathematical curves.

Josef Albers was one of the first Bauhaus teachers to immigrate to the United States, where he held positions at the experimental Black Mountain College in North Carolina, and later at Harvard and Yale. His *Homage to the Square* series began in 1950 and continued for 25 years. All these paintings consist of squares within squares, their sizes and subtly graded colors carefully calculated.

The Red Balloon (1922) by **Paul Klee**, is an abstract arrangement of squares, circles, and triangles, which simultaneously suggests the façades of buildings along a city street. *New Harmony* (1936), a composition of colored rectangles, is said to express the artist's interest in musical notation, which Klee (a fine amateur violinist) related to color theory. The painting is symmetrical (the top right matches the bottom left) and makes use of 12 hues (not counting the gray and black), which may signify the 12-tone row used as a basis for music composition by Arnold Schönberg and others.

THE ROTUNDA has been the site of several installations including Jenny Holzer's *Truisms*, quizzical epigrams installed on LED signboards that circled the Rotunda during a retrospective of her work in 1989. In 2003 the blockbuster installation of Matthew Barney's *Cremaster Cycle* filled most of the museum with Barney's mysterious but compelling videos and the sculptural pieces that accompanied the films.

PHOTOGRAPHY In 1992 the Robert Mapplethorpe Foundation gave the Guggenheim more than 200 photographs by Mapplethorpe, who died of AIDS in 1989, and a major grant to support photography. The gallery named after him presents at least one major photography show every two years and the grant has enabled the museum to establish photography as an area within the permanent collection. In addition to Mapplethorpe's self- and celebrity portraits, flowers, and erotic images, the collection contains work by artists as disparate as Josef Albers, Cindy Sherman, Thomas Struth, Bernd and Hill Becher, and Barbara Kruger.

on route

Because this route runs straight up Fifth Ave, the points of interest are arranged geographically from south to north.

Neue Galerie, 1048 Fifth Ave (86th St), Sat, Sun, Mon 11-6, Fri 11-9. Closed Tues, Wed, Thurs, Jan 1, July 4, Labor Day, Thanksgiving, Dec 25. *T* (212) 628-6200, www.neugalerie.org. The Neue Galerie (New Gallery), like its 1923 predecessor in Vienna, features Austrian and German fine and decorative arts from the early 20c. If your taste runs either to Beckmann and Bauhaus or strudel and schnitzel, this museum and its café should be on your short list. The mansion was built by a railroad entrepreneur whose daughter married an English baron; later a

Vanderbilt lived here. Gustav Klimt, Egon Schiele, changing exhibitions. **S** B, C to 86th St; 4,5, 6 to 86th St

The National Academy of Design, 1083 Fifth Ave (89th/90th Sts), Wed, Thurs 12-5, Fri-Sun 11-6. Closed Mon, Tues, major holidays. **T** (212) 369-4880, www.nationalacademy.org. Housed in a mansion that once belonged to Archer Milton Huntington, son of railroad baron, Collis P. Huntington, the Academy dates back to 1825. Elected members must donate a sample of their work, so the Academy over the past 179 years has acquired an impressive collection of American art, shown in changing exhibitions. **S** 4, 5, 6 to 86th St

The Cooper-Hewitt National Design Museum: Smithsonian Institution, 2 East 91st St (Fifth Ave), Tues 10-9, Wed-Fri 10-5, Sat 10-6, Sun 12-6. Free admission Tues 5-9. Closed Mon, federal holidays. **T** (212) 860-6868, www.ndm.si.edu. Before it became the home of the national design collection, this ornate mansion belonged to steel baron Andrew Carnegie. Selections from the permanent collection (product design and decorative arts, drawings, prints and graphic design, textiles, and wall coverings) rotate through the galleries, and there are intelligent changing exhibitions. **S** 4, 5, 6 to 86th or 96th St

The Jewish Museum, 1109 Fifth Avenue (92nd St), Sun, 11-5:45, Mon, Tues, Wed, 11-5:45, Thurs 11-8 (pay what you wish after 5), Fri, 11-3. Closed Sat, major Jewish holidays, Jan 1, Martin Luther King Jr. Day, Thanksgiving. **T** (212) 423-3200, www.thejewishmuseum.org. The two-floor permanent exhibition illuminates Jewish experience from ancient times to the present using painting, sculpture, archaeological and ceremonial objects. The collection of Hanukkah lamps is famous. Fine special exhibitions. Part of the building was built as financier Felix Warburg's mansion. **S** 4, 5, 6 to 86th St

Museum of the City of New York, 1220 Fifth Ave (103rd/104th Sts), Wed-Sat 10-5, Sun 12-5. Closed Mon, legal holidays. **T** (212) 534-1672, www.mcny.org. The Museum of the City of New York is the city's history museum; its artifacts document the city's past from Native American days onward. If the great collection of toys, dolls, and dollhouses doesn't qualify as Art, the paintings, prints, photographs, sculptures, and decorative arts surely do. Top-notch collection of Currier and Ives hand-colored lithographs, examples of New York silver that span four centuries. **S** 6 to 103rd St; 2, 3 to 110th St/Lenox Ave

Central Park, Conservatory Gardens, Fifth Ave (104th/106th Sts). The gates that once guarded the mansion of Cornelius Vanderbilt II now fence these six acres, divided into English, French, and Italian gardens. Thousands of tulips and daffodils in the spring; thousands of Korean chrysanthemums in the autumn; fountains, and a pergola heavy with wisteria, but no glass conservatory (it was torn down in 1934). **S** 6 to 103rd St

Central Park

El Museo del Barrio, 1230 Fifth Ave (104th/105th Sts), Wed-Sun 11-5. Closed Mon, Tues, legal holidays. **T** (212) 831-7272, www.elmuseo.org. New York's only Latino Museum, El Museo focuses on Puerto Rican, Caribbean, and Latin American culture. Check out the changing exhibitions and the long-running show, "Taíno: Pre-Columbian Art and Culture from the Caribbean," which explores the achievements of a people who dominated the Caribbean when Columbus waded ashore on Hispaniola in 1492. **S** 6 to 103rd St

commercial galleries

Most galleries are open Tuesday-Saturday from about 10 or 11 until 5 or 6. Many are closed part of the summer.

Aquavella, 18 East 79th St (Fifth/Madison Aves), **T** (212) 734-6300, www.acquavellagalleries.com. Established family-owned gallery since 1925, big-name 19c-21c artists, Lucian Freud. **S** 6 to 77th St

Adam Baumgold, 74 East 79th St (Madison Ave), **T** (212) 861-7338, www.adambaumgoldgallery.com. Post-war 20c and contemporary art. Exhibitions of individual artists, thematic group shows, works by Saul Steinberg and David Wojnarowicz. **S** 6 to 77th St

CDS, 76 East 79th St (Madison/Park Aves), **T** (212) 772-9555. 20c art from the Americas, Europe, Australia. Historical and contemporary shows. **S** 6 to 77th St

Mitchell-Inness & Nash, 1018 Madison Ave (78th/79th Sts), **T** (212) 744-7400, www.miandn.com. Impressionist, modern and contemporary masters; estates of Willem De Kooning, Roy Lichtenstein, Tony Smith, and Jack Tworkov. **S** 6 to 77th St

Salander-O'Reilly, 20 East 79th St (Madison/Fifth Aves), **T** (212) 879-6606, www.salander.com. Fine art from the Renaissance to the present, focus on American Modernism, 19c European and contemporary art. **S** 6 to 77th St

Allan Stone, 113 East 90th St (Park/Lexington Aves), **T** (212) 987-4997, www.allanstonegallery.com. Contemporary art; mid-20c art; Abstract Expressionism; tribal art. Venerable and respected gallery, opened 1960.

Artists include Joseph Cornell, Dennis Clive, John Anderson, Wayne Thiebaud. *S* 4, 5, 6 to 96th St

Michael Werner, 4 East 77th St (Madison/ Fifth Aves), *T* (212) 988-1623, www.artnet.com/mwerner.html. The New York branch of a Cologne gallery, focuses on American and European artists, especially Germans. Artists include Georg Baselitz, Sigmar Polke, Marcel Broodthaers, and Per Kirkeby. *S* 6 to 77th St

eating and drinking

AT THE MUSEUMS

THE METROPOLITAN MUSEUM

The **Cafeteria** on the ground floor (access from the first floor behind the Medieval Hall or from the second floor at the rear of the European Paintings) offers hot entrées, grilled and cold sandwiches, salads, pizza, snacks, and desserts. Lunch, snacking, and dinner. Child-friendly. Open Fri and Sat 11-7; Sun-Thurs 11-4:30.

The **Petrie Court Café** on the first floor in the European Sculpture Garden overlooks Central Park. Self-service continental breakfast; waiter service at lunch and dinner. Open Fri and Sat 9:30am-10:30pm; Sun, Tues-Thurs 9:30-4:30. Reservations recommended. *T* (212) 570-3964.

On Fri and Sat, you can have a drink and a snack on the **Great Hall Balcony**, with live music from 4-8:30.

From May-Oct, weather permitting, the **Roof Garden Café** serves up light food along with excellent skyline views. Fri, Sat 10-8:30 and Sun, Tues-Thurs 10-4:30.

THE GUGGENHEIM MUSEUM

Attractive café, opens a half hour before the museum so you can fortify yourself for the trip up (or down) the ramp. *T* (212) 423-3670. Sat-Wed 9:30-5:45, Thurs 9:30-3 and Fri 9:30-8.

THE NEUE GALERIE

Café Sabarsky, *T* (212) 288-0665. A full restaurant with Viennese and Eastern European fare. The Viennese pastries and the coffee are worth a detour. Closed Tues.

THE JEWISH MUSEUM

Café Weissman, *T* (212) 423-3307. Open during museum hours, serves updated kosher food, including sandwiches, soups, and hot entrées.

SURROUNDING AREA

Fifth Ave and Park Aves are mostly residential, so you'll have to look for restaurants on the side streets, Madison Ave, and east of Park Ave. Most of the following restaurants and bars lie between Fifth and Third Aves, 77th-90th Sts, with some of the less expensive ones a little further east. If you're willing to venture further south, check the dining suggestions on the Silk Stocking route.

$ **Barking Dog Luncheonette**, 1678 Third Ave (94th St), *T* (212) 831-1800. Old-fashioned American food for kids and adults. Not too far from the Cooper-Hewitt and the Jewish Museum. Cash only. *S* 6 to 96th St

Beyoglu, 1431 Third Ave (81st St), *T* (212) 650-0850. Dinner. Mezes (Middle-Eastern tapas) and other good Turkish fare in second floor restaurant. *S* 4, 5, 6 to 86th St

Blockheads Burritos, 1563 Second Ave (81st/82nd Sts), *T* (212) 879-1999. Heavy-duty Tex-Mex, with beer and margaritas. Also Biscuit Barn Barbecue menu with Southern style dishes. *S* 4, 5, 6 to 86th St

Comfort Diner, 142 East 86th St (Lexington Ave), *T* (212) 426-8600. The name says it all: standard diner food and other familiar favorites. Open for breakfast and until 2 am on Sat and Sun. *S* 4, 5, 6 to 86th St

Good Health Café, 324 East 86th St (First/Second Aves), *T* (212) 439-9680. Pleasant, inexpensive vegetarian-vegan-health food place. Also organic grocery and juice bar. *S* 4, 5, 6 to 86th St

Jackson Hole, 1270 Madison Ave (91st St), *T* (212) 427-2820. Big burgers in unremarkable surroundings, but a handy location. Breakfast. *S* 6 to 86th or 96th St

Miss Saigon, 1425 Third Ave (80th/81st Sts), *T* (212) 988-8828. Inexpensive Vietnamese in an okay dining room. *S* 6 to 77th St

Pintaile's, 26 East 91st St (Fifth Ave), *T* (212) 722-1967. Thin-crust pizza with a wealth of toppings. *S* 6 to 96th St

Wu Liang Ye, 86 Restaurant 215 East 86th St (Second/Third Aves), *T* (212) 534-8899. Uptown link in a small Chinese restaurant chain; spicy Sichuan food, modest atmosphere. *S* 6 to 86th St

$$ **Bandol**, 181 East 78th St (Third/Lexington Aves), *T* (212) 744-1800. Intimate surroundings, French-Provençal food. Dinner only; also wine bar. *S* 6 to 77th St

Blue Grotto, 1576 Third Ave (88th/89th Sts), *T* (212) 426-3200. Uptown Italian with downtown chic. Pizza and mainstream Mediterranean. Lounge scene. Relative newcomer. *S* 4, 5, 6 to 86th St

Caffe Grazie, 26 East 84th St (Fifth/Madison Aves), *T* (212) 717-4407. Italian café on two levels (quieter upstairs). Handy location for the Metropolitan Museum. *S* 4, 5, 6 to 86th St

Heidelberg, 1648 Second Ave (85th/86th Sts), *T* (212) 628-2332. One of the few leftovers from the days when Yorkville was German-American. Family-owned restaurant. *S* 4, 5, 6, to 86th St

Luke's Bar and Grill, 1394 Third Ave (79th/80th Sts), *T* (212) 249-7070. Pub atmosphere in neighborhood restaurant serving burgers and brew. Open late. *S* 6 to 77th St

92, 45 East 92nd St (Madison Ave), *T* (212) 828-5300. An upscale diner with daily specials. *S* 6 to 96th St

Osso Buco, 1662 Third Ave (93rd St), *T* (212) 426-5422. Neighborhood, family-style Italian. *S* 6 to 96th St

Pasaclou, 1308 Madison Ave (93rd St), *T* (212) 534-7522. Small neighborhood French-eclectic bistro. *S* 6 to 96th St

Sarabeth's, 1295 Madison Ave (92nd/93rd Sts), *T* (212) 410-7335. Long lines for this very popular American restaurant, especially for weekend brunch. Desserts, breakfast. Afternoon tea. *S* 6 to 96th St

Serafina Fabulous Pizza, 1022 Madison Ave (79th St), *T* (212) 734-2676. Designer pizzas baked in wood-burning oven, home-made pasta; served with attitude. *S* 6 to 77th St

Zócalo, 174 East 82nd St (Lexington/Third Aves), *T* (212) 717-7772. Cheerful, noisy Mexican, good food, exotic drinks and margaritas. *S* 4, 5, 6 to 86th St

$$$ Butterfield 81, 170 East 81st St (Third/Lexington Aves), *T* (212) 288-2700. Small, intimate, New-American Upper East Sider, good food, good service, high tabs. Dinner only. Before telephone exchanges became numbers-only, this part of town was designated by Butterfield 8. *S* 6 to 77th St

Café Boulud, 20 East 76th St (Madison Ave), *T* (212) 772-2600. One of the city's finest French restaurants. Understandably, très très cher. Most people probably don't come here by subway, but if you break with tradition, the nearest stop is the 6 at 77th St

Centolire, 1167 Madison Ave (85th/86th Sts), *T* (212) 734-7711. Commodious upstairs-downstairs trattoria with appealing food that will set you back a lot more than "cento lire." Lunch weekdays; dinner every day; brunch weekends. *S* 4, 5, 6 to 86th St

Clove, 24 East 80th (Fifth/Madison Aves), *T* (212) 249-6500. Inventive American food in townhouse setting. *S* 6 to 77th St

Demarchelier, 50 East 86th St (Madison/Park Aves), *T* (212) 249-6300. Small French bistro, friendly, attractive. Classic food. *S* 4, 5, 6 to 86th St

Orsay, 1057 Lexington Ave (75th St), *T* (212) 517-6400. Hickory-smoked and bistro food with international touches; trendy clientele, noisy. *S* 6 to 77th St

Parma, 1404 Third Ave (79th/80th Sts), *T* (212) 535-3520. Northern Italian veteran, comfortable, classic dishes. *S* 6 to 77th St

BARS

Auction House, 300 East 89th St (First/Second Aves), *T* (212) 427-4458. Wood-paneled lounge, sofas, curtains, candles, and dress code (no baseball hats). *S* 4, 5, 6 to 86th St

Back Page, 1472 Third Ave (83rd St), *T* (212) 570-5800. Popular sports bar with fervent fans. *S* 4, 5, 6 to 86th St

Bar @ États-Unis, 242 East 81st St (Second/Third Aves), *T* (212) 396-9928. Small Yorkville bar in restaurant, nice bar food. *S* 6 to 77th St

Bar at the Stanhope Hotel, 995 Fifth Ave (81st/82nd Sts), *T* (212) 650-4773. After you've seen the inside of the Met, you can sit down here and see the outside; outdoor terrace in warm weather. Polite and elegant. *S* 6 to 77th St.

Bemelmans Bar, in the Carlyle Hotel, 35 East 76th St (Madison Ave), **T** (212) 570-7189. Classic upscale bar with Ludwig Bemelmans' (think *Madeline*) murals on the walls, piano music, white-jacketed waiters all around. **S** 6 to 77th St

Big City Bar and Grill, 1600 Third Ave (90th St), **T** (212) 369-0808. Big-screen TV for sports fans and tables on the street for people-watchers. **S** 4, 5, 6, to 86th St

Dorrian's Red Hand, 1616 Second Ave (84th St), **T** (212) 772-6660. White baseball cap set quaffs brew and chomps burgers in this infamous bar. **S** 4, 5, 6, to 86th St

Mustang Grill, 1633 Second Ave (85th St), **T** (212) 744-9194. Hundreds of tequillas, good margaritas, distressed leather couches and overstuffed chairs, nachos and other Tex-Mex appetizers in New-York-Meets-Santa Fe grill. **S** 4, 5, 6, to 86th St

Trinity Pub, 229 East 84th St (Second/Third Aves), **T** (212) 327-4450. Small Irish pub, owned by the people who run Banshee at First Ave/74th St. **S** 4, 5, 6 to 86th St

shopping

Manhattan between 79th and 96th Streets from Fifth to Third Ave is mainly residential and well-to-do. The shopping here provides a mix of boutiques carrying upscale children's wear, unusual book and specialty shops, designer consignment shops, and housewares.

ACCESSORIES

Artbag, 1130 Madison Ave (84th/85th Sts), **T** (212) 744-2720, www.artbag.com. In business 65 years, two-level shop with classy leather handbags, small leather goods; repair service. **S** 4, 5, 6 to 86th St

Gruen Optika, 1225 Lexington Ave (82nd/83rd Sts), **T** (212) 628-2493. Designer frames by Vera Wang, Gucci, Oliver Peoples, others. **S** 4, 5, 6 to 86th St

Le Sportsac, 1065 Madison Ave (80th/81st Sts), *T* (212) 988-6200, www.lesportsac.com. Sun 12-5. Flagship store offers signature nylon bags in modern prints, eye-catching colors. *S* 6 to 77th St

ANTIQUES

Bernard & S. Dean Levy, Inc., 24 East 84th St (Fifth/Madison Aves), *T* (212) 628-7088; www.levygalleries.com. Closed Sun, Mon. Since 1901, this five-floor townhouse gallery has offered an impressive selection of American art and antiques. *S* 4, 5, 6 to 86th St

BABIES, KIDS, & TEENS

Bonpoint, 1269 Madison Ave (90th/91st Sts), *T* (212) 722-7720, www.bonpoint.com. Closed Sun. Exquisitely displayed, high-end clothing for babies and children. *S* 4, 5, 6 to 86th St

Greenstones, Too, 1184 Madison Ave (86th/87th Sts), *T* (212) 427-1665. Closed Sun. Bright, cheerful, everyday clothing for babies and kids. *S* 4, 5, 6 to 86th St

Infinity, 1116 Madison Ave (83rd/84th Sts), *T* (212) 517-4232. Closed Sun. Moderately-priced clothes for pre-teens, teens. *S* 4, 5, 6 to 86th St

Magic Windows, 1186 Madison Ave (86th/87th Sts), *T* (212) 289-0028, www.magicwindowsny.com. Sun 11-5. Well priced babies' and children's clothes. Custom-made party dresses. *S* 4, 5, 6 to 86th St

Marsha D.D., 1574 Third Ave (88th/89th Sts), *T* (212) 831-2422. Sun 12-5:30. If you're visiting New York with a teenager who shops, this Third Ave megastore is a must. *S* 4, 5, 6 to 86th St

Peter Elliot Jr., 1067 Madison Ave (80th/81st Sts), *T* (212) 570-5747. Sun 1-5 (Mar-June and Sept-Dec only). Elegant clothes for kids. *S* 6 to 77th St

Tartine et Chocolat, 1047 Madison Ave (79th/80th Sts), *T* (212) 717-2112, www.tartine-et-chocolat.com. Sun 12-4. Beautifully made babies' and children's clothes from Catherine Painvin Paris. *S* 6 to 77th St

BOOKS

Archivia, 1063 Madison Ave (80th/81st Sts), 2nd floor, *T* (212) 439-9194, www.archivia.com. Sun 12-5. Specializes in architecture, design, fashion, landscaping. New and used books from here and abroad. *S* 6 to 77th St

Kitchen Arts & Letters, 1435 Lexington Ave (93rd/94th Sts), *T* (212) 876-5550. Closed Mon morning and Sun. A unique selection of books about cooking and food around the world. The friendly staff can help you locate hard-to-find out-of-print volumes. *S* 6 to 96th St

CLOTHES FOR MEN & WOMEN

agnès b., 1063 Madison Ave (80th/81st Sts), *T* (212) 570-9333, www.agnesb.com. Sun 12-6. Stylish, understated clothes for women from Parisian designer, accessories, cosmetics. *S* 6 to 77th St

Anik, 1122 Madison Ave (83rd/84th Sts), *T* (212) 249-2417, www.aniknyc.com. Sun 11-7. The "in" spot to find urban basics for young women. Labels include Easel and Alice & Olivia. *S* 4, 5, 6 to 86th St

Betsey Johnson, 1060 Madison Ave (80th/81st), *T* (212) 734-1257, www.betseyjohnson.com. Sun 12-6. Always-hip designer offers fun, flirty dresses in mesh and floral fabrics. *S* 6 to 77th St

Montmartre, 1157 Madison Ave (85th/86th Sts), *T* (212) 988-8962. Sun 11-6. Boutique with hard-to-resist feminine clothes, designers Nanette Lepore, Rebecca Taylor. *S* 4, 5, 6 to 86th St

Olive & Bette's, 1070 Madison Ave (80th/81st Sts), *T* (212) 717-9655, www.oliveandbettes.com. Sun 11-6. Small shop, trendy tops and bottoms for teens and young women. *S* 6 to 77th St

Peter Elliot, 1070 Madison Ave (80th/81st Sts), *T* (212) 570-2300. Sun (Mar-June, Sept-Dec only) 1-5. Classic Upper East Side menswear with flair. *S* 6 to 77th St

Peter Elliot Women, 1071 Madison Ave (80th/81st Sts), *T* (212) 570-1551. Sun (Mar-June, Sept-Dec only) 1-5. Across the street from Peter Elliot, traditional women's loungewear, outerwear, and everything in between. *S* 6 to 77th St

Super Runners Shop, 1337 Lexington Ave (88th/89th Sts), *T* (212) 369-6010, www.superrunnersshop.com. Sun 12-5. Buy your running shoes here, knowledgeable staff, top brands. *S* 4, 5, 6 to 86th St

Vilebrequin, 1070 Madison Ave (80th/81st), *T* (212) 650-0353,

Vilebrequin, 1070 Madison Ave (80th/81st), *T* (212) 650-0353, www.vilebrequin.com. Sun 11-5. Check out these boxer-style swimsuits from St. Tropez for men and boys in matching patterns. *S* 6 to 77th St

CONSIGNMENT SHOPS

La Boutique Resale, 1045 Madison Ave (79th/80th Sts), 2nd floor, *T* (212) 517-8099, www.laboutiqueresale.com. Sun. 12-6. Scarves, shoes; fun-to-browse vintage section. *S* 6 to 77th St

Encore Designer Consignment, 1132 Madison Ave (84th/85th Sts), 2nd-3rd floors, *T* (212) 879-2850, www.encoreresale.com. Sun 12-6 (except July to mid-August). Fairly-priced designer consignment shop. *S* 4, 5, 6 to 86th St

Michael's, 1041 Madison Ave (79th/80th Sts), 2nd-3rd floors, *T* (212) 737-7273, www.michaelsconsignment.com. Closed Sun, and Sat in July, Aug. The designer section (loads of Chanel), accessories, and the eveningwear and bridal salon make this a standout. *S* 6 to 77th St

HEALTH & BEAUTY

Fresh, 1061 Madison Ave (80th/81st Sts), *T* (212) 396-0344, www.fresh.com. Sun 12-6. Health and beauty products, made from natural ingredients (milk, honey, soy, and Umbrian clay). *S* 6 to 77th St

L'Occitane, 1046 Madison Ave (79th/80th Sts), *T* (212) 396-9097, www.loccitane.com. Sun 12-6. Products made in the South of France: soaps, candles, and room sprays in scents such as cinnamon orange, verbena, and green tea. *S* 6 to 77th St

HOUSEWARES

Keesal & Mathews, 1244 Madison Ave (89th/90th Sts), *T* (212) 410-1800, www.keesalandmathews.com. Sun 12-5. Reasonably-priced housewares, perfect spot to find a hostess gift. *S* 4, 5, 6 to 86th St

S. Feldman Housewares, 1304 Madison Ave (92nd/93rd Sts), *T* (212) 289-3961, www.wares2u.com. Sun 11-5. Founded as a 5-and-10-cent store; everything from toasters to gift wrap to power strips. *S* 6 to 96th St

Schweitzer Linens, 1132 Madison Ave (84th/85th Sts), *T* (212) 249-8361, www.schweitzerlinen.com. Closd Sun. Neighborhood favorite for high-quality sheets, towels, slippers, robes. *S* 4, 5, 6 to 86th St

Straight From The Crate, 1251 Lexington Ave (84th/85th Sts), *T* (212) 717-4227, www.straightfromthecrate.com. Sun 12-6. Compact, funky furnishings for the apartment dweller. Desks, tables, unique wine and CD racks. *S* 4, 5, 6 to 86th St

JEWELRY

Cécile & Jeanne, 1100 Madison Ave (82nd/83rd Sts), *T* (212) 535-5700, www.cecilejeanne.com. Sun 10-6. Modern, playful designs from Paris. The silver bracelets with semi-precious stones are a knock-out. *S* 4, 5, 6 to 86th St

Michael Eigen, 1200 Madison Ave (87th/88th Sts), *T* (212) 996-0281, www.michaeleigen.com. Closed Sun. Contemporary pieces from well-established (Me & Ro) and new (Julie Baker) designers. *S* 4, 5, 6 to 86th St

LINGERIE

Roberta's Lingerie, 1252 Madison Ave (89th/90th Sts), *T* (212) 860-8366. Mon-Sat 10-6. Closed Sun. Robes, nightgowns, underwear, lots of socks by Lauren, hosiery by DKNY, Spanx, and CK. *S* 6 to 96th St

PETS

Karen's for People & Pets, 1195 Lexington Ave (81st/82nd Sts), *T* (212) 472-9440, www.karensforpets.com. Closed Sun. Pet lovers will go ga-ga over the gourmet snacks and pet paraphernalia (coats, sweaters, pet carriers) at this one-of-a-kind store. *S* 6 to 77th St

Pets-on-Lex, 1271 Lexington Ave (85th/86th Sts). *T* (212) 426-0766. Sun 11-6. How much is that doggie in the window? Step inside to find out and explore aisles and aisles of pet gear. *S* 4, 5, 6 to 86th St

SHOES

Easy Spirit, 1518 Third Ave (85th/86th Sts), *T* (212) 828-9593, www.easyspirit.com. Sun 11-6. Your feet will thank you for buying a pair of these truly comfortable shoes. *S* 4, 5, 6 to 86th St

Eric Shoes, 1222 Madison Ave (88th/89th Sts), *T* (212) 289-5762. Sun 12-6. High-quality dressy and casual shoes and boots for women. *S* 4, 5, 6 to 86th St

Steve Madden, 150 East 86th St (Lexington/Third Aves), *T* (212) 426-0538, www.stevemadden.com. Platforms with attitude for the young, brave female! Plus David Aaron's hip, comfortable shoes for everyone else. *S* 4, 5, 6 to 86th St

SPECIALTY

Big City Kites, 1210 Lexington Ave (82nd/83rd Sts), *T* (212) 472-2623, www.bigcitykites.com. Closed Sun. Kites of all sizes, shapes, and colors. *S* 4, 5, 6 to 86th St

E.A.T. Gifts, 1062 Madison Ave (80th/81st Sts), *T* (212) 861-2544. Sun 12-5. So much to look at! Unusual gifts for all ages, favors for kids' parties, books, candy, kitchenware, cards, and much more. *S* 6 to 77th St

Feller's Judaica & Gift Gallery, 1205 Lexington Ave (81st/82nd Sts), *T* (212) 472-2300. Open Sun 12-5; closed Fri after 1:30 and Sat. Wide selection of books, posters, yarmulkes, CDs, other gift items. *S* 6 to 77th St

Game Show, 1240 Lexington Ave (83rd/84th Sts), *T* (212) 472-8011. Sun 12-5. Games and puzzles to delight all ages. *S* 4, 5, 6 to 86th St

Tiny Doll House, 1179 Lexington Ave (80th/81st Sts), *T* (212) 744-3719. Closed Sun. One-of-a-kind doll house shop offers furnishings beyond your wildest dreams (even parquet flooring). *S* 6 to 77th St

TOYS

Penny Whistle Toys, 1283 Madison Ave (91st/92nd Sts), *T* (212) 369-3868. Closed Sun. Small neighborhood favorite. *S* 4, 5, 6 to 86th St

Zany Brainy, 112 East 86th St (Park/Lexington Aves), *T* (212) 427-6611, www.zanybrainy.com. Educational and fun toys. *S* 4, 5, 6 to 86th St

WINE

Best Cellars, 1291 Lexington Ave (86th/87th Sts), *T* (212) 426-4200, www.bestcellars.com. Weekdays until 9, Fri, Sat until 10. Closed Sun. Many reasonably-priced wines (most are under $15). Tastings Mon-Fri 5-8; visiting chefs pair food with wine, Sat 2-4. *S* 4, 5, 6 to 86th St

K&D Wines & Spirits, 1366 Madison Ave (95th/96th Sts), *T* (212) 289-1818, www.kdwine.com. Mon-Sat 10-8, closed Sun. If the wine you're looking for isn't already here, the staff will gladly help you find it. *S* 6 to 96th St

THE SILK
STOCKING
DISTRICT

The Frick Collection

OPEN	Tues, Wed, Thurs, Sat 10-6; Fri 10-9; Sun, Feb 12, and Election Day (first Tues in Nov) 1-6
CLOSED	Mon, Jan 1, July 4, Dec 25-26.
CHARGES	$12, adults; $8, senior citizens (62 and over); $5, students. Members, unlimited free admission. Children under 10 are not admitted to the museum; those under 16 must be accompanied by an adult. Admission price includes ArtPhone audio guide
TELEPHONE	**(212) 288-0700**
WWW.	**frick.org**
MAIN ENTRANCE	1 East 70th St (Fifth/Madison Aves)
LIBRARY	The Frick Art Reference Library is located at 10 East 71st St. Library hours are Mon-Fri 10-5 and Sat 9:30-1. The library is closed Sundays, holiday weekends, Saturdays in June and July, and during the month of August
SUBWAY	6 to 59th or 68th St
DISABLED ACCESS	Telephone the museum or ask at the information desk
SHOPS	The shop is stocked with art books and exhibition catalogues, postcards, posters, prints, and stationery items; online shopping available; for telephone shopping, call (212) 547-6848
EATING	No café, but on Fri evenings when the museum is open until 9, there is a cash wine bar after 6:30

Small-scale but much admired changing exhibitions, lectures, and concerts.

The Frick Collection occupies Fifth Avenue's most elegant and most faithfully preserved mansion, the onetime residence of Henry Clay Frick (1849-1919), a pioneer in the coke and steel industries. Frick is remembered as perhaps the most brilliant industrialist of the Age of Steel, the partner and later the rival of Andrew Carnegie. Frick's style of management, and particularly his brutal treatment of the strikers at the Homestead Steel Mills in 1892, made him the object of hatred and envy, leaving a bitter and enduring legacy in industrial relations. A taciturn workaholic whose mastery of detail and quick decision-making style gave him advantages over his competitors, Frick was also a heroic risk taker, an affectionate family man, and a dedicated learner.

The Frick Collection Fragonard Room

Johannes Vermeer *Officer and Laughing Girl* (1655–60)

Both the house and its contents are a monument to him and to the passion for collecting that energized many of the city's other newly minted millionaires at the turn of the 20c. Frick, however, was a collector in a class by himself. His fortune allowed him to afford the best. And he chose the best - sometimes selling earlier purchases in favor of later ones. He started out choosing paintings by Bouguereau, Daubigny, and the members of the Barbizon School (as did many of his contemporaries), but guided by his art dealer Joseph Duveen, his taste matured as he grew older. His last purchase, one of the jewels of the collection, was Vermeer's *Mistress and Maid*, acquired the year of his death.

The Frick Collection has superb European paintings from the

Renaissance to the end of the 19c, fine 18c French furniture, Italian Renaissance bronzes, and superb French and Chinese ceramics. Although the building was altered when it became a public museum, it still retains the aura of a domestic past, allowing a glance into the lives of the (very) rich at the beginning of the 20c. The house and its fine appointments, the paintings and sculptures, and the interior garden court with its splashing fountain and seasonal plantings convey an atmosphere of serenity and grace, set apart from the hustle of the city.

THE BUILDING

Henry Clay Frick left Pittsburgh for New York in 1905 and a year later bought this chunk of prime Fifth Avenue real estate for $2.47 million, a huge sum a century ago. At the time, the Lenox Library, the pet project of an earlier millionaire, stood on the lot. The library was considered one of the masterpieces of Richard Morris Hunt (whose work you can see today at the Metropolitan Museum and elsewhere) and its contents soon formed part of the foundation of the New York Public Library.

At the urging of art dealer Joseph Duveen, Frick commissioned the firm of Carrère & Hastings to build a house that would showcase his growing collection during his lifetime and become a museum after his death. In this desire Frick was influenced by London's Wallace Collection. Carrère & Hastings, who were then in the midst of building the New York Public Library, thirty blocks downtown on Fifth Ave, persuaded their client to save the Lenox Library, one of Hunt's masterpieces.

The Frick Collection Garden

Frick agreed, and offered to pay to have the Lenox Library disassembled and reconstructed where the Arsenal stands, at the edge of Central Park, if (and only if) the City would tear down the Arsenal at *its* expense. The City refused, and Frick in turn refused to consider any alternate plans.

Although Mr Lenox's books found a new home in the New York Public Library downtown, the Lenox Library itself was torn down.

After a couple of false starts, architect Thomas Hastings came up with this Neoclassical design, based on 18c European, especially French, domestic architecture of the most opulent kind. The building has a steel frame and is faced with limestone; it is built on an axial plan, with the "living" rooms along Fifth Avenue and Frick's art gallery along 71st St. Attilio Piccirilli, better known for the *Maine* monument at Columbus Circle, executed the sculpture on the pediments over the windows. The nude reclining above the entrance door is the work of Sherry Edmundson Fry, an Iowa-born sculptor who had studied in Rome at the American Academy, which Frick supported financially. Frick was aware that Andrew Carnegie, by now his rival, was embarked on planning his own mansion uptown; Frick opined that his own house would "make Carnegie's place look like a miner's shack."

After Mrs Frick's death, John Russell Pope, later architect of the National Gallery in Washington, D.C., remodeled the interiors to make them suitable for the general public and added extra gallery space.

HIGHLIGHTS

Works by Holbein, El Greco, Titian, & Bellini	Living Hall
Fragonard's Rococo masterpieces plus superb 18c French furniture	Fragonard Room
Frick's Vermeers	South Hall & Room 16
Works by Rembrandt, Velázquez & Goya	Room 16

ROOM 5 The **South Hall** is a smallish room with great paintings. **Johannes Vermeer**'s *Officer and Laughing Girl* (c 1655–60), the earliest of Frick's three paintings by this great Dutch master, is a beautifully illuminated interior scene. A second painting by Vermeer, *Girl Interrupted at Her Music* (c 1660), is probably a courtship scene, a notion reinforced by the picture of Cupid barely

THE FRICK COLLECTION

16 Enamel Room

15 West Gallery

17 Oval Room

18 East Gallery

Portico

Music Room

13 Library

14 North Hall

19 Garden Court

Lawn

12 Living Hall

11 Fragonard Room

5

4

Cabinet

Museum Shop

Terrace

10

3

1 Entrance Hall

2 Reception Hall

Garden

9 Dining Room

6

8 Boucher Room

7

Coat Room

⬆ Entrance

visible in the background. Between the Vermeers is **Francisco de Goya**'s *Don Pedro, Duque de Osuna* (probably 1790s); the sitter was a wealthy patron of the arts in general and of Goya in particular.

François Boucher's charming portrait of his wife, *Madame Boucher* (1743), suggests that she was an indifferent housekeeper and the picture has been nicknamed "Boucher's Untidy Venus," though critics have remarked that the composition is a witty parody of classical Renaissance depictions of Venus (e.g. Giorgione and Titian). Frick's taste did not extend in general to the Impressionists, though he did acquire **Pierre-Auguste Renoir**'s *Mother and Children* (c 1876-8) and works by Degas and Manet late in his collecting career. This is an early treatment of a theme Renoir returned to repeatedly. The subjects are thought to be the two daughters of a prosperous Parisian family with their nanny in a park near Renoir's studio.

ROOM 7 The **Anteroom** on the other side of the Vestibule contains some of the earlier paintings in the collection. Hans Memling's *Portrait of a Man* (c 1470) may be the first portrait this Flemish master painted with a landscape background. In the picture by Jan van Eyck and his workshop, *Virgin and Child with Saints and Donor* (1441-3), the saints depicted are St Barbara with her symbol and the tower where she was imprisoned, and St Elizabeth of Hungary, who gave up her crown to become a nun. **El Greco**, *Purification of the Temple* (c 1600); during the Counter-Reformation this New Testament incident served as an image for the purification of the Catholic Church from heresy. Pieter Breugel the Elder, *The Three Soldiers* (1568) is a small monochromatic panel showing mercenary foot soldiers; the painting belonged to both Charles I and Charles II of England.

ROOM 8 The **Boucher Room** is decorated with panels by **François Boucher** depicting *The Arts and Sciences* (probably 1750-2). The arts and sciences being practiced by rosy, cherubic children include Fowling and Horticulture, Fishing and Hunting, Architecture and Chemistry, Poetry and Music, Comedy and Tragedy, Painting and Sculpture, and Singing and Dancing. While the Fricks lived here, the panels were upstairs in Mrs Frick's sitting room, but they were originally installed in one of Madame de Pompadour's residences - the Château de Crécy near Chartres - while Mme de Pompadour was the official mistress of Louis XV. Details of the decoration seem to refer to Mme de Pompadour's own interests as a patron of the arts and sciences, the clavichord, for example, suggesting her own skill at the keyboard. Scholars have been hard pressed to figure out how fishing related to the lady in question, but have noted that her maiden name was Poisson ("fish" in French). The marble *Bust of a Young Girl* is a 19c copy of an original by François-Jacques-Joseph Saly; Boucher includes the bust in his depiction of Sculpture. Perhaps the girl was Mme de Pompadour's beloved

El Greco *Purification of the Temple* (c 1600)

daughter, Alexandrine D'Étiolles. Among the furnishings are pieces by master furniture makers: **Jean-Henri Riesener**, **André-Louis Gilbert**, and **Martin Carlin**.

ROOM 9 The **Dining Room** demonstrates Frick's fondness for 18c English painting and decorative arts. Because the Fricks used this room for their dinner parties, the furniture is modern, designed for this room by Sir Charles Allom, Britain's leading designer of the period, knighted for his work at Buckingham Palace. Many of the interiors, with their fine plasterwork and carved wood paneling, were constructed in Allom's London workshops and then shipped to New York, where they were reassambled in the house.

On the walls are aristocratic portraits by Sir Joshua Reynolds, George Romney, and John Hoppner, as well as **William Hogarth**'s *Miss Mary Edwards* (1742), a wealthy woman who chose poorly from among her many suitors: when her husband's gambling habits threatened her fortune, she repudiated the marriage, essentially making her son a bastard. Hogarth paints her in a fine red dress with expensive jewelry. **Sir Thomas Gainsborough**'s *Mall in St James' Park* (probably 1783) shows the artist's skill as a landscape painter; the Mall, near his London home, was a fashionable place to stroll. The subject of **Sir Joshua Reynolds**: *General John Burgoyne* (probably 1766) is best known in this country for his defeat at the Battle of Saratoga in the Revolutionary War; back in the 18c he was also known as a dandy, a gambler, and an amateur actor.

At the far end of the room is a silver *écuelle*, a serving dish for stew, by **Paul de Lamerie**, the most famous of the exiled Huguenot silversmiths working in London during the reign of the first two Georges.

ROOM 10 The **West Vestibule** offers another group of paintings by Boucher, *The Four Seasons*, also painted for Mme de Pompadour.

ROOM 11 Four of the large canvases by **Jean-Honoré Fragonard** in the **Fragonard Room** were commissioned by Mme du Barry, who succeeded Mme de Pompadour in Louis XV's affections. When the paintings - *The Pursuit*, *The Meeting*, *The Lover Crowned*, and *Love Letters*, known together as *The Progress of Love* - were completed, Mme du Barry rejected them in favor of a set by

Jean-Honoré Fragonard *The Meeting* (detail; 1771–3)

Joseph-Marie Vien. Vien is not a household name today but in 1773 when Fragonard finished the four canvases, he was a champion of the up-and-coming Neoclassical style. Fragonard then had the rejected paintings installed in his cousin's house, where he added two more large panels, the overdoors, and the narrow Hollyhock paintings. Frick bought the set for $750,000 from the estate of J. Pierpont Morgan, who had them in his London home. Today they are often considered Fragonard's masterpieces.

Also in the room are Clodion's delicate terracotta *Zephyrus and Flora* (1799) and **Jean-Antoine Houdon**'s *Comtesse du Cayla* (1777), a marble bust of a 22-year-old countess portrayed as a nymph, with grape leaves around her neck and in her hair.

On the table in the center of the room is a set of three Sèvres porcelain vases. The central one in the shape of a ship represents the acme of French 18c porcelain, since the elaborate form was technically difficult to make and the painting - of exotic birds in lush landscapes - is exceptional. There are only about a dozen examples of this form of porcelain in existence, including some at the Metropolitan. The ship was intended as a pot-pourri, to hold flower petals or fragrant leaves, whose odor wafted through the holes in the lid.

Also in this room is a mechanical table by **Martin Carlin** with Sèvres porcelain plaques; its top tilts up so that it could be used for reading or raised and used as a music stand. The three-legged table with porcelain plaques is probably also by Carlin, whose rich and powerful clients included Mme du Barry and the daughters of Louis XV.

ROOM 12 The oak-paneled **Living Hall** has six truly extraordinary paintings. **Giovanni Bellini**'s *St Francis in the Desert* (c 1480), a mysterious landscape, reveals Bellini's mastery of perspective, his attention to the details of the real world, and his simultaneous mastery of Christian iconography. This was one of Frick's three favorite paintings. Flanking it are portraits by **Titian**, Bellini's greatest student. His *Portrait of a Man in a Red Cap* (c 1516) is an early work. *Pietro Aretino* (1548-51), who wrote both satirical verses and the lives of saints, became wealthy through a shrewd combination of flattery and blackmail; he was both a talented and worldly man as the rich clothing and the gold chain in Titian's portrait suggest.

Across the room is **El Greco**'s *St Jerome* (c 1590-1600), another version of a portrait in the Metropolitan Museum; it depicts the ascetic saint who translated the Bible into Latin. **Hans Holbein the Younger**, *Sir Thomas More* (1527), the second of Frick's three favorites, depicts the author, scholar, and statesman, who served Henry VIII in several capacities, finally as Lord Chancellor. More resigned that office over the issue of Henry's divorce from Catherine of Aragon and later refused to subscribe to the Act of

Giovanni Bellini *St Francis in the Desert* (c 1480)

Supremacy, which made the King head of the Church of England. This refusal that led to his conviction for treason and his execution. The heavy gold chain around his neck is an emblem of service to the king. On the other side of St Jerome is *Thomas Cromwell* (c 1532), More's enemy, who worked to Protestantize the English Church under Henry VIII and was directly opposed to Thomas More's position. Cromwell was eventually accused of treason himself and was in turn executed. Frick enjoyed grouping paintings thematically, and having these portraits of two arch enemies face one another across the mantel must have pleased him.

Hans Holbein the Younger
Sir Thomas More (1527)

Complementing the paintings are examples of furniture by **André-Charles Boulle**, cabinetmaker to Louis XIV. Boulle's furniture, often of ebony or ebonized wood, is known for its veneers and inlays of tortoise shell and mother-of-pearl. The matching cabinets flanking the fireplace are by Bernard Vanrisamburgh II and his son Bernard III. These comparatively simple pieces are embellished with black and gold Japanese lacquer panels.

Here also are some of the Renaissance bronzes, which Frick began to collect at the end of his life. J. Pierpont Morgan had swept up large numbers of these small sculptures from European collections and after the banker's death in 1913, Frick purchased many from his estate. Also here are Chinese porcelains, and a Persian carpet from the later 16c.

Look out the west windows to the Fifth Avenue garden, with three beautiful magnolia trees, planted in 1939.

ROOM 13   In the **Library** are portraits by Thomas Gainsborough, Sir Joshua Reynolds, Sir Henry Raeburn, and Sir Thomas Lawrence. The only two American portraits in the room are Gilbert Stuart's *George Washington*, a copy of the famous original he painted for John Vaughan of Philadelpha, and John C. Johansen's portrait of *Henry Clay Frick*, painted in 1943. On the shelf between these two is **Antoine Coysevox**'s marble sculpture of *Louis XV as a Child of Six* (1716), a year after he became king. This portrait bust simultaneously shows the young king as a beautiful child and a regal figure, and it is easy to understand how Coysevox was both the most popular and most highly regarded portrait sculptor of his generation.

   On the north wall is John Constable's *Salisbury Cathedral from the Bishop's Garden* (1826), one of several he painted of this subject. The Bishop asked Constable for a sunny version; Constable's painting of 1823 with storm clouds gathering above the spire is in now the Victora and Albert Museum, in London.

Jean-Auguste-Dominique Ingres
The Comtesse d'Haussonville (1845)

ROOM 14   The main attraction of the **North Hall** is **Jean-Auguste-Dominique Ingres**' *The Comtesse d'Haussonville* (1845), a beautiful painting of a spirited and outspoken young aristocrat. The portrait reveals both the painter's ability as a draughtsman and his sensitivity to personality. Louise, Princesse de Broglie (1818-82), was a granddaughter of Madame de Staël and sister-in-law of the Princesse de Broglie, whose portrait, painted shortly after this one, hangs in the Metropolitan Museum. Both are among Ingres' finest. It was purchased by Frick's son.

Jean-Antoine Watteau, *The Portal of Valenciennes* (1709-10), the only Watteau in the collection, was not chosen by Frick himself, but was purchased in 1991. It was painted at the time Watteau was just gaining public recognition after years of poverty and obscurity. Watteau came from Valenciennes, in northern France, which had long been a battleground; during his early years he painted a series of genre paintings depicting the peripheral events of war.

Also on view in this hall are Degas, *The Rehearsal* (1878-9), purchased by Frick, and Monet's *Vétheuil in Winter* (1878-9), purchased after Frick's death. Sculpture includes Verrocchio's *Bust of a Young Woman* (date unknown), a marble portrait of a gentlewoman of wealth and style; and a small terracotta *Head of an Angel* (c 1655) by Gian Lorenzo Bernini.

ROOM 15 The **West Gallery** was Frick's own picture gallery, planned as a setting for his collection and intended to be reminiscent of the galleries in English country houses. Its grand scale, 96 x 33 feet with a two-story ceiling, surely impressed Frick's visitors and also allowed Frick to hang the paintings in thematic arrangements as he preferred.

Along the south wall landscapes alternate with portraits, most of them Dutch. Here are landscapes by **Jean-Baptiste-Camille Corot**, **Jacob van Ruisdael**, **Meyndert Hobbema**, and **John Constable**. To the left and right of the van Ruisdael landscape are two portraits by **Sir Anthony van Dyck**, *Frans Snyders*, a fellow artist and close friend of Van Dyck's, and *Margareta Snyders*, Frans' wife. Both were painted around 1620, but were separated from 1793 until Frick bought them in 1909.

In the middle of the long wall is **J.M.W. Turner**'s *The Harbor of Dieppe* (1826?) facing its companion piece across the room: *Cologne: The Arrival of a Picket-Boat: Evening*. Both are remarkable for the luminosity of the color.

There are four paintings by **Frans Hals** in the collection, most of whose portraits bear general names since their sitters are not known; most appear to be prosperous burghers: *Portrait of a Man*, *Portrait of a Painter*, *Portrait of a Woman*. The *Portrait of an Elderly Man* (probably 1626-30), shows a heavyset man wearing a black

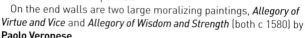

doublet, a starchy white ruff, and a cloak, which is painted with the forceful brushstrokes characteristic of Hals' style.

John Constable, *The White Horse* (1819), was admired by the painter himself; he bought it back from the original purchaser and kept it for the rest of his life. The last of the portraits on this side of the room is **Agnolo Bronzino**'s aristocratic *Lodovico Capponi* (c 1550-5), a page at the court of Cosimo dei Medici, where Bronzino was official painter.

On the end walls are two large moralizing paintings, *Allegory of Virtue and Vice* and *Allegory of Wisdom and Strength* (both c 1580) by **Paolo Veronese**.

ROOM 16 At the west end of the gallery, the **Enamel Room** contains several cabinets with enamels from the workshops of Limoges, most of them acquired from J. Pierpont Morgan's estate. **Piero della Francesca**'s relatively large *St John the Evangelist* (between 1454 and 1469) is one of four side panels of an altarpiece and one of the few major works by this painter outside Italy. Although no symbols identify the saint, St John was the patron of the donors' wife and father. Duccio di Buoninsegna, *The Temptation of Christ on the Mountain* (1308-11) was purchased by Frick's son and was at one time part of Duccio's *Maestà*, the famous altarpiece that stood for 200 years in the Duomo in Siena.

Just beyond the Enamel Room on the other side of the West Gallery is **Gerard David**, *The Deposition* (c 1510-5), painted with cool colors and a lowering sky; it is one of the earliest known northern European paintings done in oil (instead of water-based tempera) on canvas. **Rembrandt**'s *The Polish Rider* (c 1655) is an elusive and mysterious painting, which has inspired several theories as to its meaning: an allegory of life, an illustration of a literary or historical figure, a tribute to the soldiers who were at the time defending eastern Europe against Turkish invaders. Its attribution to Rembrandt has also been questioned, though today it is thought that Rembrandt himself painted the face of the rider, the head of the horse, and important parts of the background scenery, while a less skilled assistant did the weaker areas of the painting: in particular, the horse's legs and the rider's hands.

Nearby is *The Education of the Virgin* (c 1650) by either Georges de la Tour or his son Étienne. It shows St Anne teaching her daughter, the Virgin Mary, to read the Bible.

Beyond the large Turner painting are three of the greatest works in the collection. **Rembrandt**'s *Self Portrait* (1658) is

Rembrandt Harmensz van Rijn *Self Portrait* (1658)

considered one of the best of the more than 60 the artist painted throughout his professional life. The artist, then 52 years old and bankrupt, portrays himself in regal clothing, monumentally posed, but with his face scarred by time. *Mistress and Maid* (1665-70) by **Johannes Vermeer** was the last painting bought by Frick before his death. Although the painting was not finished, the effect of light on the sparkling jewelry, the silver and glass objects on the table are beautifully rendered, as is the sense of mystery. **Diego Velázquez**, *King Philip IV of Spain* (1644) was the third of Frick's favorites during his long collecting career. The king is seen wearing a silver and red colored outfit commemorating a campaign against the French in Catalonia; Philip was a great arts patron, but not a successful ruler. The painting was done in a makeshift studio during the campaign, while the army paused at the town of Fraga.

To the left of the doorway is El Greco's *Vincenzo Anastagi* (1571-6), a military leader who defended Malta during the Turkish siege in 1565. El Greco painted this portrait in his youth, before he had left Italy for Spain. To the right of the doorway is **Franciso de Goya**'s *The Forge* (c 1815-20), a dark and forceful painting of blacksmiths at work over a glowing fire. It is different in subject and tone from most of Frick's choices. According to his daughter, he preferred paintings that were "easy to live with," but perhaps the subject matter had special meaning for the coke and steel industrialist.

ROOM 17 The **Oval Room** was added to the building when it became a museum. On the left side is a large terracotta statue of *Diana the Huntress* (probably between 1776-95) by **Jean-Antoine Houdon**. It is only one of five known large terracottas by Houdon, was fired in at least 10 sections, and is supported by metal armatures inside. Also in the room are four full-length portraits; those on the left are by **Sir Anthony van Dyck**: *Sir John Suckling* (1632-41), a minor poet in the court of Charles I, and *The Countess of Clanbrassil* (1636). Opposite them are two by **Gainsborough**: *Mrs Peter William Baker* (1781) and *The Hon. Frances Duncombe* (c 1777), a painting that shows Gainsborough's admiration for Van Dyck not only in the idealized setting and grace of the pose but

Diego Velázquez *King Philip IV of Spain* (1644)

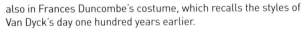

also in Frances Duncombe's costume, which recalls the styles of
Van Dyck's day one hundred years earlier.

James Abbott McNeill Whistler
*Symphony in Flesh Color and Pink:
Mrs Frances Leyland* (1872–3)

ROOM 18 The **East Gallery**, filled with portraits and a few genre paintings, has notable work by **James Abbott McNeill Whistler**. At one end of the room are *Symphony in Flesh Color and Pink: Mrs Frances Leyland* (1872-3), the wife of one of Whistler's patrons. Whistler designed the dress Mrs Leyland is wearing. At the other end of the room is Whistler's *Arrangement in Black and Gold: Robert, Comte de Montesquiou-Fezensac* (1891-2), a dandified aristocrat, one of the models for the Baron de Charlus in Proust's *A la recherche du temps perdu*. Also on view are his *Arrangement in Black and Brown: Miss Rosa Corder* (1875-8) and *Harmony in Pink and Grey: Lady Meux*. The abstract or musical titles Whistler bestowed on his work were intended to suggest that painting, even society portraiture, like music, doesn't convey moral or literary ideas, but exists for its own sake.

On the left wall is **Sir Anthony van Dyck**'s *James, Seventh Earl of Derby, His Lady and Child* (1632-41), one of a large group of portraits Van Dyck painted during his last English period, between 1632 and 1641. The earl, a Royalist during the Civil War, was captured and executed in 1651. Van Dyck went to Italy in 1621 and during this period painted portraits of the Genoese nobility, creating the type of proud, slender aristocratic figure that would appear in his portraits thereafter. Nearby and on the opposite wall are two works from this Italian period: *Portrait of a Genoese Noblewoman* (formerly thought to be Paola Adorno, Marchesa di Brignole Sale; 1622-7) and *Marchesa Giovanna Cattaneo* (1622-7).

On the end wall is **Claude Lorrain**'s, *The Sermon on the Mount* (1656), an exceptionally large painting for Claude, which shows Christ surrounded by the apostles preaching to an astonished multitude. On the right side of the room is Jean-Baptiste Chardin's *Lady with a Bird-Organ* (1753), a painting commissioned by Louis XV and the last of Chardin's genre paintings before he turned entirely to still lifes and portraiture.

ROOM 19 The **Garden Court**, with its trickling fountain, natural light, and seasonal plantings is one of the city's great indoor oases. Formerly the Frick's carriage entrance, it was converted to its present appearance by John Russell Pope when the house was remodeled as a museum. In the corners of the room are sculptures. Jacques Jonghelinck's bronze bust of the *Duke of Alba* (1571) portrays a Spaniard, fanatically loyal to the Catholic church and the Spanish throne; his arrogance and repression of civil and religious opposition when he served as governor-general to the Low Countries were unacceptable even to the Spanish government that hired him. *Robert de Cotte* was architect to Louis XIV and designed many official buildings in France and major palaces elsewhere in Europe. **Antoine Coysevox** depicts the forcefulness and worldly confidence of this talented man who was also the sculptor's friend and colleague. The earliest piece in the room, a bronze *Angel* (dated 1475), bears an inscription stating it was made by Jean Barbet. Barbet was probably not the designer but the artisan who cast the figure. Documents of the period identify him as "Cannonnier du Roi," and his job seems to have involved casting cannon and cannonballs for the city of Lyon.

On the walls are paintings by Daubigny, Constable, Whistler, and Édouard Manet, *The Bullfight* (1864), originally the upper part of a larger painting; the lower half, known as *The Dead Toreador* is in the National Gallery in Washington.

The Whitney Museum of American Art

OPEN	Wed-Thurs 11-6, Fri 1-9 (6-9pm pay-what-you-wish), Sat-Sun 11-6
CLOSED	Mon, Tues, Jan 1, Thanksgiving, Dec 25
CHARGES	Adults $12; seniors (62 and over) and students with valid ID $9.50. Members, New York City Public High School students with valid student ID and children under 12 free
TELEPHONE	**(212) 570-3676**. For tickets call (800) WHITNEY; there is a $2.25 service charge for each ticket ordered by phone or online. Advance tickets may be purchased or reserved without a service charge at the Museum Admissions Desk
WWW.	**whitney.org**
MAIN ENTRANCE	945 Madison Ave (75th St)
SUBWAY	6 to 77th St
DISABLED ACCESS	The museum is wheelchair accessible. Wheelchairs are available free of charge at the coat check in the museum lobby
SHOPS	The Whitney Museum Store has a fine selection of art books and exhibition catalogues on late-20c and 21c American art. Downstairs near the café a second shop offers household objects, arty T-shirts and neckties, stationery, posters, and toys. Online shopping available
EATING	Café

*Changing exhibitions, guided tours, lectures, seminars, symposia, and readings. On some Fri evenings there is live music; performances start at 7pm. The Whitney Museum has a satellite facility, **The Whitney Museum of American Art at Altria** (formerly Philip Morris) at 120 Park Ave (42nd St), near Grand Central Terminal, with a large sculpture court and a smaller exhibition gallery.*

The Whitney Museum was founded in 1931 by Gertrude Vanderbilt Whitney to exhibit living American artists. Mrs Whitney was an aspiring sculptor with gilt-edged social connections. A Vanderbilt by birth, the great-granddaughter of the founding father, Cornelius Vanderbilt - aka the Commodore - she was also the wife of Harry Payne Whitney, whose family fortune came from oil, railroads, and street cars. In 1907, she opened a studio in Greenwich Village to get away from the

The Whitney Museum of American Art

oppression of too much money and too confining a social position. Eventually she bought the building next to her studio, remodeled it as a gallery, and began showing and also buying the work of young American artists she admired; Stuart Davis, Robert Henri, George Luks, and John Sloan had their first exhibitions at her gallery. These artists still form the core of the early-20c collection.

Mrs Whitney preferred painting to sculpture and realism to abstraction. Only after her death did the museum give equal importance to collecting sculpture and abstract art. The museum today is rich in works by Louise Nevelson, Alexander Calder, Claes Oldenburg, Alex Katz, Ad Reinhardt, and others. The museum is also a major showcase for video artists and film makers.

Even so the Whitney is known best for its changing exhibitions, especially the **Whitney Biennial**, its signature show, a survey of contemporary American art that takes place every even-numbered year. In 2002, the Whitney Museum held maybe its most controversial Biennial. The exhibition - organized around the themes "Beings, Spaces, Tribes" - presented the work of 113 artists and moved away from traditional painting and sculpture to emphasize sound and video presentations, installation pieces, and Internet-based and computer-generated works. Critics faulted the show for being too inclusive and undiscriminating. Many of the installations (for example one that consisted of a séance to raise the ghost of Joseph Cornell) seemed more like activities than art. But Biennial bashing has been a sport since the first show in 1932, which caused one critic to remark that "no more telling evidence of the deplorable state of American art has ever been assembled."

THE BUILDING

The Whitney first opened its doors (1931) in three remodeled brownstones (townhouses faced with brown sandstone) on West 8th St in Greenwich Village. In 1954 it moved uptown West 54th St, near the Museum of Modern Art, almost quadrupling its

attendance. In 1966 the present building opened, designed by
Marcel Breuer, Hungarian-born, Bauhaus-trained and best-
known for his tubular stainless steel chairs.

Constructed of site-cast concrete, sheathed in dark gray
granite, cantilevered over a pseudo-moat used as a sculpture
court, and punctuated by seven apparently random trapezoidal
bay windows, the building was considered intrusive and ugly, even
brutal, when it arrived. Today it is generally considered a
masterpiece and is landmarked to protect it from wanton
alteration or destruction.

Within a couple of decades the museum outgrew Breuer's
building and the trustees hired architect Michael Graves to design
an expansion. Neighborhood and civic groups were enraged with
Graves' proposal and in 1985 the museum abandoned the plan.
Since then, the museum has expanded modestly from within,
moving offices and archives to nearby brownstones and opening
up more gallery space.

HIGHLIGHTS

Calder *Circus*	Ground Floor
Sculptures by Louise Nevelson **Abstract Expressionist and Pop Art collections**	Second Floor
Survey of American painting from the early 20c until 1945, especially the room devoted to Edward Hopper	Fifth Floor

GROUND FLOOR

Calder's *Circus* (1926-31), beloved by museum visitors since 1976
when it was first exhibited in the lobby, is sculptor **Alexander
Calder**'s most famous work. Made from wire, cork, wood, cloth
and other familiar and homey materials, the *Circus* has the
whimsy of a child's toy and the ingenuity of an extraordinary
imagination. Some of the animals and performers are made by

bending wire to form realistic figures, a method so easy and simple that Calder began to make wire portraits, which combined line drawing and sculpture, representing a new possibility in three dimensional art. Calder used to carry the animals and performers around in a suitcase and put on performances with narration in English or French, sound effects, and a phonograph for background music. A video of Calder "performing" accompanies the *Circus*.

LOWER LEVEL

In the stairwell down to the lower level is Alex Katz's *Red Coat* (1982). The windows of the lower level, including the restaurant, look out onto the Whitney's Sculpture Court.

To see the permanent collection in chronological order, take the elevator (or walk up the stairs) to the **Fifth Floor**. If you walk up the stairs, you will see on one of the **stairwell landings** a part of Charles Simonds' sculpture, *Dwelling* (1981), commissioned by the Whitney. The window nearby looks out on the other two parts of the work, one on the windowsill of the former bank across the street, the other on a rooftop chimney of the same building. Simonds' "dwellings" first appeared downtown in SoHo and on the Lower East Side during the 1970s. Made of unfired brick, tucked on window ledges or in other out-of-the-way places, they were fragile, subject to the weather and the whims of passersby. Consequently many got destroyed. Simonds often constructed them as if they were partially ruined, suggesting the life and death of a community.

FIFTH FLOOR

The **lobby** directly in front of the elevators is devoted to **Urban Realism** and offers works mainly from the 1920s. **Robert Henri**'s *Portrait of Gertrude Vanderbilt Whitney* (1916) shows her dressed in a silk lounging suit, leaning casually against a sofa. Her husband did not let her hang the painting in their Fifth Ave home, because

Robert Henri *Portrait of Gertrude Vanderbilt Whitney* (1916)

she was wearing pants, so the high-spirited Gertrude hung it in her studio in Greenwich Village.

Also here are Guy Pène de Bois' cool pictures of featureless wealthy women: *Opera Box* (1926) and *Woman with Cigarette* (1929). **George Bellows'** *Dempsey and Firpo* (1924) shows a moment in the fight between the unpopular champion Jack Dempsey and his Argentinian challenger, Luis Firpo. Though Dempsey won the fight by a knockout in the second round, Bellows recorded the moment in the first when Firpo knocked Dempsey through the ropes.

Other painters of the urban scene whose work appealed to Whitney were **John Sloan**, here represented by *The Picnic Grounds* (1906-7) and **William Glackens**, whose *Hammerstein's Roof Gardens* (c 1909) depicted a site of seedy entertainment. **Gaston Lachaise**'s *Standing Woman* (1912-27) is one of his most successful nudes and one of the few significant acquisitions of sculpture made by Mrs Whitney.

EARLY AMERICAN MODERNISM **Marsden Hartley** belonged to a group of painters promoted by Alfred Stieglitz, photographer and gallery owner. Like other members of the Stieglitz circle, Hartley was interested in abstraction. *Painting, Number 5* (1914-5) belonged to a series known as the War Motif paintings, its abstract symbols (the Iron Cross, the red cross) commemorating a young German officer, Hartley's lover, who had been killed in World War I.

Max Weber's *Chinese Restaurant* (1915) is a fragmented representation of the bustle and activity of such an eating place, then a novelty in America. Oscar Bluemner, *Space Motive*; and *Situation in Yellow* (1933), a painting of dark trees and yellow buildings in front of a red sky. For Bluemner, colors had specific symbolic meanings.

Georgia O'Keeffe, like Hartley a member of the Stieglitz circle, is well-represented in the Whitney collection. *Summer Days* (1936), a dreamlike evocation of the southwestern landscape, was painted during the heyday of Surrrealism. Also by O'Keeffe: *Flower Abstraction* (1924), with sexual overtones; *The White Calico Flower* (1931); and the almost completely abstract *Black and White* (1930).

In the other corner of the room are landscapes by Marsden Hartley, who after years of travel across the United States and in Europe settled in Maine, where he had been born. His later expressive landscapes depict the rugged scenery of his native state: *Robin Hood Cover, Georgetown, Maine* (1938) and *Granite by the Sea* (1937). Arthur G. Dove, another painter of the Stieglitz group, is represented by *Ferry Boat Wreck* (1931), an abstraction of an actual wreck he saw in Long Island Sound.

LANDSCAPE PAINTING In this small gallery are further landscapes and abstractions by Georgia O'Keeffe and Marsden Hartley. John Marin: *Boat, Sea, and Sky: Green and Red Sea, Grey Sky* (1944) and *Wave on a Rock* (1937), a choppy sea rendered by jagged brush strokes.

THE LONG GALLERY beyond the room devoted to Early American Modernism focuses on **The Machine Age and Geometric**

Abstraction. **Charles Demuth**'s *My Egypt* (1927), showing a grain elevator in Demuth's hometown, is an eloquent example of Precisionist painting, a movement that used modernist principles to represent and sometimes glorify the architecture of industrial America. The title suggests comparison between the wonders of American industry and the monuments of Egyptian civilization, particularly the pyramids. Also by Demuth, *Buildings, Lancaster* (1930). Elsie Driggs' depiction of the smokestacks of *Pittsburgh* (1927) simultaneously evokes the geometric beauty of the tubular pipes and smokestacks and suggests the darkness and menace implicit in them.

In 1927 when **Charles Sheeler** visited the *River Rouge Plant* (1932), a Ford motor car factory outside Detroit, to document it for an advertising campaign, he considered such industrial monuments to be the modern equivalent of cathedrals. By 1932, when Sheeler created the painting from his five-year-old photographs, the country had sunk into the Depression and bitter hostilities broke out at River Rouge between workers and management. Peter Blume's *New England Barn* (1926) was painted when Blume was only twenty; this geometric depiction of rural architecture hints at his later dreamlike Surrealist canvases. Ralston Crawford's *Steel Foundry, Coatesville, Pa.* (1936-7) is an example of his early optimistic Precisionist work.

At the far end of the gallery is **Joseph Stella**'s famous *Brooklyn Bridge, Variation on an Old Theme* (1939), an evocation that suggests the bridge's almost religious significance to Stella. Some viewers have seen a connection between this large canvas and the paneled altarpieces painted during the Renaissance. Also here is **Lyonel Feininger**'s *Gelmeroda VIII* (1921), an abstract, modernist rendering of a traditional church in Gelmeroda, a town near Weimar, Germany.

Stuart Davis, *Egg Beater No. 1* (1927); Davis nailed an eggbeater, a rubber glove, and an electric fan to a table, and looked at them to find their inherent geometric structure. Usually the artist chose overtly American subjects, for example the street fronts, buildings, and signs in *House and Street* (1931), and rendered them in the style of Picasso's Synthetic Cubism. Davis was also one of the first to use text in jazzy ways, along with intense color, as in *Owh! In San Paõ* (1951).

The next gallery shows the work of **Edward Hopper**, whose representational paintings of American scenes are often empty and tinged with loneliness. When Hopper's wife died, she left the museum 2500 works - paintings, drawings, preliminary sketches - from her husband's estate in recognition of the museum's long-term commitment to him.

The earliest picture in the gallery, *Italian Quarter, Gloucester* (1912), was painted when Hopper was 20. *Railroad Sunset* (1929) is an exploration of natural light in the evening, just as *Seven A.M.* (1948), painted almost 20 years later, beautifully renders the morning light (the hour is registered by the clock in the shop window). Hopper claimed that *Early Sunday Morning* (1930) is simply a visual record of New York's Seventh Avenue, though no people are present and the shop fronts have been reduced to geometric simplicity. *A Woman in the Sun* (1961) and *Second Story Sunlight* (1960) do include human beings, but the figures are

Edward Hopper *Early Sunday Morning* (1930)

mysterious, alone, or unconnected to one another. Also on view, *Railroad Crossing* (1922-3) and *New York Interior* (1921).

REALISM IN THE 1930s Just beyond the entrance is **Ben Shahn**'s large *The Passion of Sacco and Vanzetti* (1931-2), part of a series illustrating the story of two Italian immigrants, both self-acknowledged anarchists, who were executed for the murder of a shoe company employee. Many, Shahn included, believe that Sacco and Vanzetti were convicted because of their ethnic background and their political beliefs. John Steuart Curry was one of the foremost American Regionalists. His *Baptism in Kansas* (1928) records and honors the values of rural America that the movement sought to enshrine. Curry was himself a Kansan.

Reginald Marsh, who had worked as a newspaper illustrator during the 1920s, focused on urban life as lived by common people, especially in places like Coney Island and the Times Square arcades. *Negroes on Rockaway Beach* (1934), *Twenty Cent Movie* (1936), and *Ten Cents a Dance* (1933) depict life in New York during the Depression and are painted without clear social commentary. **Thomas Hart Benton**, like Curry, was a mid-Westerner, the most vocal of the American Regionalists. *The Lord Is My Shepherd* (1926), painted on Martha's Vineyard, depicts a deaf-mute couple who lived near Benton's summer studio.

Arshile Gorky, usually remembered as a transitional figure between the modernists of the 1930s and the Abstract Expressionists a decade later, worked intermittently on *The Artist and His Mother* for ten years (c 1926-36). The painting, a meditation on the memory of his mother who had died a year before Gorky and his sister came to the United States from Armenia, was recreated from a photograph that had been sent to his father years before.

The next gallery is devoted to **Alexander Calder**. The museum has more than 70 of his works, from all phases of his long career. In addition to the *Circus* on display downstairs, the museum owns *The Brass Family* (1927), a group of humorous and daringly balanced circus acrobats, the largest of Calder's works in wire.

Object with Red Discs (1931) is an early abstract work, as is *Half-circle, Quarter-circle* (1932).

The final gallery, **Surrealism in America**, offers **Joseph Cornell**'s *Grand Hôtel, Bon Port* and more traditional Surrealist paintings - Philip Evergood, *Lily and the Sparrows* (1939), Peter Blume, *Light of the World* (1932), and Jared French, *State Park* (1946).

SECOND FLOOR

The survey of American art continues downstairs with **De Kooning to Today**, a survey of works made after World War II. During this period the United States became an international leader in avant-garde art.

In the foyer facing the elevators are two large sculptures by **Louise Nevelson**, *Dawn's Wedding Chapel, II* (1959) and *Royal Tide, II* (1961-3), both large assemblages of painted wood. Nevelson is one of the artists the museum has acquired in depth, and the collection now includes about 90 works by this seminal modern sculptor. In the 1950s, Nevelson began making painted wood sculptures, often incorporating found objects - finials, scraps of wood, chair legs - and often painting them black. *Dawn's Wedding Chapel, II* was part of a much larger installation called *Dawn's Wedding Feast*, which had hundreds of boxes and filled a large gallery space.

If you walk around the galleries counterclockwise, beginning to the right of *Royal Tide*, you can view the works of art in roughly chronological order. (The rooms are not labeled or numbered.) Also to the right, when you exit the elevator, is the **Kaufman Astoria Studios Film and Video Gallery**, with changing exhibitions.

In the first gallery are examples of **Early Abstract Expressionism**. Arshile Gorky's *The Bethrothal II* (1947), an abstract vision of biomorphic forms, perhaps a man and a woman; the painting is often considered a precursor of Abstract Expressionism in that accidental drips and marks of the paint on the canvas are used create other forms. **Isamu Noguchi**, *Humpty Dumpty* (1946), a biomorphic composition of black slate, constructed to fit together without glue or screws. Also here: Adolph Gottlieb, *Vigil* (1948), Lee Krasner, *The Guardian* (1960), and Louise Bourgeois, *One and Others* (1955). **Jackson Pollock**, the reigning figure of Abstract Expressonism, is represented in the collection by early representational work and by canvases from his most famous pour-and-drip period, for example, *Number 27* (1950), not on display at the time of writing.

In the next room are other followers of **Abstract Expressionism**, whose work was sometimes lumped under the term **Post-Painterly Abstraction**. **Morris Louis**' first mature works were a series of *Veil* paintings, created by thinning the paint and pouring it onto unprimed canvas, which was angled up against the wall. As the paint dripped down, Louis manipulated the canvas to create patterns of diaphanous color. *Tet* (1958) refers to the ninth letter of the Hebrew alphabet. **David Smith**, *Running Daughter* (1956), an image of a girl in motion, based on a photo of his older daughter running across the grass. In the last years of his life Smith's work became larger in scale and less linear. **Willem de Kooning**, *Door to the River* (1960), painted in broad strokes with housepainters' brushes. The rectangle in the center with a strip of blue beneath may refer to the title. The museum also owns one of De Kooning's famous paintings of women, *Woman and Bicycle* (1952-3), a grinning female figure in a yellow low-cut dress.

In the next two rooms are **Pop Art paintings** from the late 1950s and early 1960s. Jim Dine's *Double Isometric Self Portrait* (Serape), painted in 1964, is part of the Bathrobe Series, for which Dine used a newspaper ad for a robe with the man airbrushed out. Alex Katz, *Ada Ada* (1959) and *Eli* (1963). In the 1950s Katz reacted against the dominant gestural style of Abstract Expressionism by working with collages of figures cut from paper. In his later work he retained the flat look of these cutouts, though he began working at a much larger scale. Also, Marisol, *Women and Dog* (1964). Not presently on view is Roy Lichtenstein's *Little Big Painting* (1965), a parody of Abstract Expressionism, rendering the slashing, confrontational brushstrokes of that movement in a careful, mechanical way. The painting has his typical Ben-Day dots, but they are used to render the paint dripping from the brush of the invisible painter.

Jasper Johns' *Three Flags* (1958), is a rendering of the American flag in triplicate, one his favorite motifs in the late 1950s. Also, *White Target* (1957), a de-colorized bull's eye, and *Studio with Beer Cans* (1964), which incorporates actual cans. The painter's admirers find that his representations of targets, flags, and other simple objects explore the boundary between art and reality.

Around the corner in the next large gallery is one of Lucas Samaras' *Chair Transformations*, a witty permutation of the idea and form of a chair. The chairs in the series include a Pointillist version, another that looks like a Constructivist version, all angles and hard surfaces, and the one currently on view made of melamine laminate and multi-colored yarn. Yayoi Kusama's *Accumulation* (1963) is another chair onto which the artist has sewn dozens of stuffed, organic-looking pouches. Kusama, who had herself committed to a mental institution in Japan, describes her work as "obsessional," the result of her mental illness. Richard Artschwager, *The Bush* (1971), gray oils on coarse Formica panels.

Susan Rothenberg's *For the Light* (1978-9) is an image of a horse galloping towards the viewer, with a strange bone-like projection from its forehead. Rothenberg was one of the artists responsible for the return of figure painting - human or animal - after the years of Conceptualism.

The remaining galleries contain **Contemporary Art** from the late 1980s until the present, including Chris Burden's *America's Darker Moments* (1994), a mirrored diorama with small tin figures representing the bomb in Hiroshima, the murder of Emmett Till, John F. Kennedy's assassination, the My Lai massacre, and the Kent State University shootings; Paul McCarthy's *Class Fool* (1976); Kiki Smith's *Untitled* (1990), two battered-looking nude wax mannequins; and Lisa Yuskavage's *Big Northview* (2001), two provocative, high-breasted sex kittens in lurid light.

on route

The Arsenal, 821 Fifth Ave (64th St), weekdays 9-5. Now home of the Department of Parks & Recreation, once upon a time it really was an arsenal. Upstairs gallery has exhibits, mostly about New York, its parks, and historic preservation. **S** N, R to Fifth Ave

Asia Society Museum, 725 Park Ave (70th St), Tues-Sun 11-6, Fri until 9; closed Mon, major holidays. **T** (212) 288-6400, www.asiasociety.org. The core collection of works from South, Southeast, and East Asia (paintings, ceramics, and sculpture) was gathered by Mr and Mrs John D. Rockefeller 3rd. Exhibitions of traditional and contemporary Asian art, performances. **S** 6 to 68th St

Central Park Wildlife Center and Children's Zoo, Fifth Ave between 63rd and 66th Sts, April-Oct, Mon-Fri 10-5, weekends until 5:30; closes earlier in winter. **T** (212) 439-6500. A great little urban zoo with a much-loved central seal pool. Check out the Delacorte Musical Clock, whose sculptural animals play nursery tunes on musical instruments every hour. **S** N, R to Fifth Ave

China Institute Gallery, 125 East 65th St (Park/Lexington Aves), Mon-Sat 10-5, Tues and Thurs until 8. Closed Sun, holidays, and between exhibitions. **T** (212) 744-8181, www.chinainstitute.org. If you're interested in traditional Chinese art, this is one of the two best places in New York to see it (the Met is the other). **S** 6 to 68th St

Seventh Regiment Armory, 643 Park Ave (66th/67th Sts). Once the home of New York's "Silk Stocking Regiment," this landmark building has magnificently decorated interiors, some by Louis Comfort Tiffany. The huge drill hall is used for antiques shows and other large-scale events. **S** 6 to 68th St

Spanish Institute, 684 Park Ave (68th/69th Sts), closed Sun. **T** (212) 628-0420, www.spanishinstitute.org. Spanish-American cultural organization has changing exhibits, from well-known masters to newly emerging artists from Spain, Latin America and Europe. The Institute occupies a neo-Federal townhouse (1927) designed by McKim, Mead & White for a wealthy banker. **S** 6 to 68th St

THE FIFTH AVENUE CORRIDOR:
57TH STREET TO 42ND STREET

Fifth Avenue cuts a swathe along Manhattan's midline from the Harlem River to Washington Square. Between the southern boundary of the Silk Stocking District and the northern edge of Chelsea, it passes by some of the borough's most famous cultural and architectural landmarks as well as some of its historic commercial establishments. Many of these sights lie close to MoMA's permanent home on West 53rd St.

These sights along Fifth Avenue and close to it are arranged from north to south. For the continuation of this section see Chelsea p 129.

Bergdorf Goodman, 754 Fifth Ave (57th St), open Mon-Sat 10-7, Thurs to 8, Sun 11-6. *T* (212) 753-7300. Elegant clothing, stunning window displays, in this old-line department store that sits on the site of a Vanderbilt mansion. *S* E, V to Fifth Ave-53rd St; N, R, W to Fifth Ave 60th St

Henri Bendel, 712 Fifth Ave (56th St), open Mon-Fri 10-7, Thurs until 8, Sat 10-7, Sun noon-6. *T* (212) 247-1100. Smaller but more genteel than some of the other big name luxury department stores. The building, former home of Coty perfumes, has several windows by René Lalique. *S* E, V to Fifth Ave-53rd St; N, R, W to Fifth Ave-60th St

Dahesh Museum of Art, 580 Madison Ave (56th/57th Sts), Tues-Sun 11–6; first Thurs of each month open until 9pm (pay what you wish 6-9). Closed Mon, federal holidays. *T* (212) 789-0606, www.daheshmuseum.org. Changing exhibitions of 19c-20c European (mainly French and British) academic art in sumptuous galleries. If Barye, Bonheur and Bouguereau are your cup of tea, put this jewel of a museum at the top of your list. *S* F to 57th St; N, R, W to 5th Ave; 4, 5, 6 to 59th St; 1, 9 to Columbus Circle

American Folk Art Museum, 45 West 53rd St (Fifth/Sixth Aves), open Tues-Sun 10:30-5:30, Fri until 7:30; free Fri 5:30-7:30. Closed Mon, holidays. *T* (212) 265-1040; www.folkartmuseum.org. Eight floors of folk art - everything from trade signs and quilts to baseball-themed artifacts to the visionary paintings of Henry Darger and other outsider artists. Changing exhibitions and selections from the permanent collections are displayed in a beautifully designed sliver of a building. *S* E, V, to Fifth Ave-53rd St

Fifth Avenue, 53rd Street

H&M, 640 Fifth Ave (51st St), open Mon-Sat 10-8, Sun 11-7. *T* (212) 489-0390. Low prices for trendy clothing, makeup, and accessories at this Swedish import. Other branches. S E,V to Fifth Ave-53rd St

Rockefeller Center
Paul Manship *Prometheus* (1934)
in front of the GE Buidling

Rockefeller Center, Fifth Ave to Sixth Ave around East 50th St. The centerpiece of this urbanely planned space is the building complex leading from Fifth Ave via the Channel Gardens (between La Maison Française and the British Empire Building) to the GE Building (formerly the RCA Building). The Center is rich in Art Deco architecture and decoration. Its most famous piece of sculpture, Paul Manship's gilded *Prometheus*, overlooks the sunken plaza at the foot of the gardens. Check out the artwork in the lobby of the GE Building (self-guided tour leaflet at desk or check the website: www.rockefellercenter.com). Lee Lawrie's *Atlas* faces Fifth Ave opposite St Patrick's Cathedral, his back to the International Building. A trip up and down the escalator in the black marble lobby of the International Building offers a great view of the cathedral's façade.

Other Rockefeller Center options: There's a backstage tour of the **NBC Studios**; tours leave daily from the NBC Experience Store on 49th St (Fifth/Sixth Aves), *T* (212) 664-3700. NBC's *Today Show* broadcasts live on weekdays from 7am to 9am. Stand on the sidewalk and peer in the windows of the glassed-in studio at the southwest corner of 49th St and Rockefeller Plaza. (Other people will have the same idea, so arrive early for a front row view.) *S* B, D, F, V to 47th-50th Sts-Rockefeller Center

Museum of Arts & Design, 40 West 53rd St (Fifth/Sixth Aves), open daily 10-6, Thurs until 8; Thurs 6-8 pay what you wish. *T* (212) 956-3535, www.americancraftmuseum.org. Formerly the American Craft Museum. Exhibitions explore contemporary three-dimensional art in clay, fiber, metal, glass, wood, and other media. Occasional historical exhibitions. At some time in the not-too-far-distant future the museum plans to move to Columbus Circle. *S* E, V to Fifth Ave-53rd St; B, D, F to 47th-50th St-Rockefeller Center

Museum of Television and Radio, 25 West 52nd St (Fifth/Sixth Aves), open Tues-Sun noon 6, Thurs until 8. Closed Mon. *T* (212) 621-6800 for recorded information or (212) 621-6600 for an operator; www.mtr.org. Philip Johnson designed the building; here you can view selections from an archive of more than 100,000 radio and TV shows, commercials, and other pop pleasures. Radio listening room, special programs, educational seminars. Sometimes crowded. *S* B, D, F, V to 47th-50th St-Rockefeller Center; E, V to Fifth Ave-53rd St

Radio City Music Hall, 1260 Sixth Ave (50th St), box office open Mon-Sat 10-8, Sun 11-8. *T* (212) 247-4777, www.radiocity.com. The Music Hall is equally famous as a monument of Art Deco splendor and as the home of the leggy, high-kicking Rockettes. To see the interior without attending a show, join a tour: *T* (212) 631-4345. *S* B, D, F, V to 47th-50th Sts-Rockefeller Center; E, V to Fifth Ave-53rd St

St Patrick's Cathedral, Fifth Ave between 50th/51st Sts, open daily 6:30am-9:30pm. *T* (212) 753-2261. Completed 1888, St Patrick's is the home of the archdiocese of New York, the largest Catholic cathedral in the US, and the 11th largest in the world. The façade, one of the city's famous landmarks, presents monumental doors whose sculptural figures represent St Joseph (patron of the church) and several American saints. Visit the Lady Chapel (east end of the nave) conceived in the 13c French Gothic style. Call for tour information. *S* B, D, F, V to 47th-50th Sts-Rockefeller Center; E, V to Fifth Ave-53rd St

Saks Fifth Avenue, 611 Fifth Ave (49th/50th Sts), open Mon-Sat 10-7, Thurs until 8pm, Sun 11-7. *T* (212) 753-4000. One of the city's grandest department stores, as elegant and glamorous as it was in 1924, when it opened with its show windows displaying a pigskin trunk ($3000) and a selection of raccoon coats ($1000). *S* B, D, F, V to 47th-50th Sts-Rockefeller Center

commercial galleries

Galleries are clustered along 57th St near Fifth Ave and also run northward along Madison Ave. Most are well-established and traditional; some of the shows are museum-quality. Usually open Tuesday-Saturday from 10-11 am until 5-6 in the evening. Call for summer hours.

Berry-Hill, 11 East 70th St (Fifth Ave), *T* (212) 744-2300, www.berry-hill.com. American painting and sculpture from 18c to early-20c, also contemporary painting. *S* 6 to 68th St-Hunter College

Mary Boone, 745 Fifth Ave (57th/58th Sts), *T* (212) 752-2929, www.maryboonegallery.com. Boone gained notoriety in 1999 when she was arrested and charged with illegal distribution of ammunition; the bullets were souvenirs from a show, whose artwork included handmade guns. Also a Chelsea branch. *S* E, F, N, R to Fifth Ave

Galerie St Etienne, 24 West 57th St (Fifth/Sixth Aves), *T* (212) 245-6734. Founded in 1939 by Otto Kallir, who fled Vienna leaving behind his successful Neue Gallerie. German and Austrian Expressionism, Self-Taught and Outsider Art, including "Grandma Moses" (Anna Mary Robertson). *S* E, F, N, R to Fifth Ave

Knoedler & Company, 19 East 70th St (Fifth Ave), *T* (212) 794-0550, www.knoedlergallery.com. Founded in 1846, almost a quarter century before the Metropolitan. Post-War and contemporary art, especially the New York School; estates of Milton Avery, Nancy Graves, Richard Poussette-Dart, and living artists Sean Scully, David Smith, Frank Stella, Donald Sultan. *S* 6 to 68th St

Laurence Miller, 20 West 57th St (Fifth Ave), *T* (212) 397-3930, www.laurencemiller.com. Modern and contemporary art photography. Historical surveys, one-person shows. *S* E, F, N, R to Fifth Ave

PaceWildenstein, 32 East 57th St (Madison Ave), *T* (212) 421-3292, www.pacewildenstein.com. Contemporary and modern art. Also in this building are other divisions of the dealership, showing photography, prints, primitive art. *S* N, R to Fifth Ave; 4, 5, 6 to 59th St

Michael Werner, 4 East 77th St (Madison/Fifth Aves), *T* (212) 988-1623, www.artnet.com/mwerner.html. The New York branch of a Cologne gallery, American and European artists, especially Germans: Georg Baselitz, Sigmar Polke, Marcel Broodthaers. *S* 6 to 77th St

Jay Davis *Accumulation* (2002; Mary Boone Gallery, Fifth Avenue)

eating and drinking

AT THE MUSEUMS
THE WHITNEY MUSEUM

Sarabeth's Restaurant is a branch of the popular Madison Ave restaurants. Sandwiches, light meals, beverages, desserts. Closed Mon, Tues. *T* (212) 570-3670. Also a bare bones café with sandwiches (also by Sarabeth's), fruit, cookies, and beverages.

ASIA SOCIETY

The **Asia Society** has a glass-enclosed café serving lunch and tea, also dinner on Fri, when the museum has extended hours. Closed Mon and major holidays; restricted summer hours. Reserve 24 hours in advance: *T* (212) 570-5202.

SURROUNDING AREA

Most of the restaurants that follow are located between Madison and Second Aves, 57th and 77th Sts. If you want to venture a little further, look at the restaurant section for Metropolitan Museum and Museum Mile.

$ **Afghan Kebab House**, 1345 Second Ave (70th/71st Sts), *T* (212) 517-2776. Meat and fish grilled over charcoals, also vegetable dishes, pilafs. Other locations. Open Sun. *S* 6 to 68th St

Annie's, 1381 Third Ave (78th/79th Sts), *T* (212) 327-4853. Neighborhood restaurant, open for breakfast. American food plus a few dishes from elsewhere. Weekend brunch is crowded. *S* 6 to 77th St

Brother Jimmy's BBQ, 1485 Second Ave (77th/78th Sts), *T* (212) 288-0999. Boisterous crowd chowing down on Southern food, fried chicken, ribs and wings. Open late. *S* 6 to 77th St

Dallas BBQ, 1265 Third Ave (72nd/73rd Sts), *T* (212) 772-9393. Plate-filling portions of chicken, ribs; also burgers. Low prices, little atmosphere. Chain restaurant. *S* 6 to 68th St

EJ's Luncheonette, 1271 Third Ave (73rd St), *T* (212) 472-0600. Breakfast, lunch, or dinner at retro luncheonette with blue-plate specials. Cash only. *S* 6 to 77th St

Googie's Italian Diner, 1491 Second Ave (77th/78th Sts), *T* (212) 717-1122. Diner fare plus basic Italian-American. Opens for breakfast at 9. Sunday brunch; cash only. *S* 6 to 77th St

Pamir, 1437 Second Ave (74th/75th Sts), *T* (212) 734-3791. Neighborhood Afghan. Lamb and kebabs. *S* 6 to 77th St

Patsy's Pizzeria, 206 East 60th St (Third Ave), *T* (212) 688-9707. Part of an expanding chain of pizzerias serving classic thin-crust pizza. *S* 4, 5, 6 to 59th St

$$ **Atlantic Grill**, 1341 Third Ave (76th/77th Sts), *T* (212) 988-9200. Big, popular, sometimes noisy, seafood restaurant serves large portions. *S* 6 to 77th St

Bistro Le Steak, 1309 Third Ave (75th St), *T* (212) 517-3800. Open late, dinner only. Steak and frites are reliable, tables are close in this casual neighborhood place. *S* 6 to 77th St

Due, 1396 Third Ave (79th/80th Sts), *T* (212) 772-3331. Neighborhood regulars at longtime Northern Italian restaurant. Cash only. Open late. *S* 6 to 77th St

Henry's Evergreen, 1288 First Ave (69th/70th Sts), *T* (212) 744-3266. A little further east. Cheerful Chinese, with dim sum, appetizers, and regular menu. The surprise is the wine list. *S* 6 to 68th St

Persepolis, 1423 Second Ave (74th/75th Sts), *T* (212) 535-1100. Simple, friendly Persian restaurant. Open late weekends. *S* 6 to 77th St

Rain East, 1059 Third Ave (62nd/63rd Sts), *T* (212) 223-3669. Pan-Asian with touches of Vietnamese, Japanese, Korean, and Thai. Draws young crowd and neighborhood types. Also a West Side branch. *S* F to Lexington Ave-59th St; 4, 5, 6 to 59th St

Rouge, 135 East 62nd St (Park/Lexington Aves), *T* (212) 207-4601. Townhouse decked out in red; mainly French with Asian and Italian accents. *S* F to Lexington Ave-59th St; 4, 5, 6 to 59th St

Sel et Poivre, 853 Lexington Ave (64th/65th Sts), *T* (212) 517-5780. Pleasant atmosphere, bistro food. Well-priced prix fixe menus at lunch and dinner. *S* F to Lexington Ave-63rd St; 6 to 68th St

Ulrika's, 115 East 60th St (Lexington/Park Aves), *T* (212) 355-7069. Swedish restaurant with home-style cooking. Aquavit and herring. Scandinavian décor. *S* F to Lexington Ave-63rd St. 4, 5, 6 to 59th St

$$$ Aureole, 34 East 61st St (Madison/Park Aves), *T* (212) 319-1660. One of the city's finest; sophisticated, elegant, and very very expensive New American food with worldly touches. Two-level townhouse setting. *S* F to Lexington Ave-63rd St; N, R, W to Lexington Ave-59th St

Brasserie 360, 200 East 60th St (Third Ave), *T* (212) 688-8688. Newish restaurant with French-Belgian brasserie downstairs, sushi bar upstairs. An odd combination, but both serve good food. *S* 4, 5, 6 to 59th St

Circus, 808 Lexington Ave (62nd St), *T* (212) 223-2965. Upscale and innovative Brazilian cuisine. Feijoada on weekends. Casual and elegant. Open late. *S* F to Lexington Ave-63rd St; 6 to 68th St

Coco Pazzo, 23 East 74th St (Fifth/Madison Aves), *T* (212) 794-0205. The oldest of the trend-setting regional Italian restaurants by Pino Luongo. Very expensive but still popular. *S* 6 to 77th St

Daniel, in the Mayfair Hotel, 60 East 65th St (Park/Madison Aves), *T* (212) 288-0033. Daniel Boulud's masterpiece; luxurious setting, inspired French cuisine with cosmopolitan influences, beautifully presented. High prices. *S* F to Lexington Ave-63rd St; 6 to 68th St

Il Monello, 1460 Second Ave (76th/77th Sts), *T* (212) 535-9310. Upscale Northern Italian back in business with a new chef; good wine list. *S* 6 to 77th St

Jo Jo, 160 East 64th St (Lexington/Third Aves), *T* (212) 223-5656. Old favorite recently revived. Intimate dining rooms in romantic townhouse setting. Haute French bistro cooking. *S* F to Lexington Ave-63rd St

Orsay, 1057 Lexington Ave (75th St), *T* (212) 517-6400. Formerly Mortimer's, beloved of the beautiful, and still a hot spot for people-watching. French bistro-brasserie with hickory-chip smoker. *S* 6 to 77th St

Payard Pâtisserie, 1032 Lexington Ave (73rd/74th Sts), *T* (212) 717-5252. Mirrored and muted. Bistro menu, melt-in-your-mouth pastries and desserts. Lunch, sandwiches, afternoon tea. *S* 6 to 77th St

rm, 33 East 60th St (Park/Madison Aves), *T* (212) 319-3800. The initials stand for Rick Moonen, celebrity chef, famous for his way with seafood. Small, shipshape restaurant with two dining rooms. Inventive fish specialties and some vegetarian dishes. Dinner only. *S* N, R, W to Fifth Ave/59th St

Shopping

The Manhattan neighborhood between 57th and 79th Sts from Fifth Ave to Third Ave is one of the most upscale shopping areas in the world. Even a casual stroll down Madison Ave here has the potential to seriously damage your bank account. Designer boutiques and high-end clothing, jewelry, and shoe stores loom on every corner, not to mention several of New York's best-known department stores (Barneys, Bergdorf's, and Bloomies). Stores are open Sunday unless otherwise indicated.

ACCESSORIES

Alain Mikli Optique, 880 Madison Ave (71st/72nd Sts), *T* (212) 472-6085, www.mikli-nyc.com. Closed Sun. Modern, upscale French eyeglass frames. *S* 6 to 68th St

Hermès, 691 Madison Ave (62nd/63rd Sts), *T* (212) 751-3181, www.hermes.com. Closed Sun. Home of the legendary Kelly Bag. Silk scarves, ties, handbags, clothing, and fragrances from this well-known French company. *S* N, R to Fifth Ave

Judith Leiber, 987 Madison Ave (76th/77th Sts), *T* (212) 327-4003, www.judithleiber.com. Closed Sun. Like no other handbags, these creative, glittery collectors' items are pieces of art. *S* 6 to 77th St

ANTIQUES

Linda Horn Antiques, 1015 Madison Ave (78th/79th Sts), *T* (212) 772-1122, www.lindahorn.com. Closed Sun. Warm, welcoming shop; 19c antiques and Horn's own collection of "re-creations." *S* 6 to 77th St

BABIES & KIDS

La Petite Étoile, 746 Madison Ave (64th/65th Sts), *T* (212) 744-0975, www.lapetiteetoile.com. Sun 12-5. Tasteful, European-made children's clothes. Features lines by Lilli Gauffrette and Tetine. *S* 6 to 68th St

Oilily, 870 Madison Ave (70th/71st Sts), *T* (212) 628-0100, www.oililyusa.com. Brightly colored clothing from the Netherlands. The miniature backpacks are hard to resist. *S* 6 to 68th St

CLOTHING

BCBG Max Azria, 770 Madison Ave (65th/66th Sts), *T* (212) 717-4225, www.bcbg.com. BCBG stands for Bon Chic Bon Genre (good style, good attitude), which you'll find here with Max Azria's sophisticated work and weekend wear. *S* 6 to 68th St

Burberry, 9 East 57th St (Fifth/Madison Aves), *T* (212) 371-5010, www.burberry.com. The plaid that seems to be everywhere is here in full force; items for men and women, including the famous trench coat. *S* N, R to Fifth Ave

Calvin Klein, 654 Madison Ave (60th/61st Sts), *T* (212) 292-9000. Sun 12-6. This white-walled flagship space perfectly complements Calvin's sleek, minimalist designs for men and women. Don't miss his collections for the home, including tableware and linens. *S* N, R to Fifth Ave

Calypso, 935 Madison Ave (74th/75th Sts), *T* (212) 535-4100. Feel yourself transported to a Caribbean climate as you discover colorful, flouncy skirts, peasant blouses, and straw totes. *S* 6 to 77th St

Chanel, 15 East 57th St (Fifth/Madison Aves), *T* (212) 355-5050, www.chanel.com. Closed Sun. Running low on the ever-popular No. 5? Replenish your supply and check out the latest suits, dresses, and cosmetics from Karl Lagerfeld. *S* N, R to Fifth Ave

Diesel, 770 Lexington Ave (60th/61st Sts), *T* (212) 308-0055, www.diesel.com. Two floors of their famous denim, watches, belts, shoes, bags, and fragrances. *S* 4, 5, 6 to 59th St; N, R to Lexington Ave

DKNY, 655 Madison Ave (60th/61st Sts), *T* (212) 223-3569, www.dkny.com. Donna Karan captures the spirit of New York City with her apparel. Three levels for men and women; gifts. *S* N, R to Fifth Ave

Nicole Miller, 780 Madison Ave (66th/67th Sts), *T* (212) 288-9779, www.nicolemiller.com. Closed Sun. Evening dresses, sportswear, and separates for women of all ages, plus accessories. *S* 6 to 68th St

Niketown, 6 East 57th St (Fifth/Madison Aves), *T* (212) 891-6453, www.niketown.nike.com. Full line of Nike products at this 57th Street giant. *S* N, R to Fifth Ave

Oilily, 820 Madison Ave (68th/69th Sts), *T* (212) 772-8686, www.oililyusa.com. Just two blocks from the children's shop of the same name; women can grab a full-size bag or sweater. *S* 6 to 68th St

Paul & Shark, 772 Madison Ave (66th/67th Sts), *T* (212) 452-9868,
www.paulshark.it. High-quality clothing from Italy, hi-tech fabrics
for people who spend their days sailing the high seas. *S* 6 to 68th St

Polo Ralph Lauren, 867 Madison Ave (71st/72nd Sts), *T* (212) 606-2100,
www.polo.com. A spectacular retail space in a renovated mansion,
the perfect setting for Lauren's preppy, classic designs for men and
women. You'll find the Polo Sport Line across the street at 888
Madison Ave. *S* 6 to 68th St

Prada, 841 Madison Ave (69th/70th Sts), *T* (212) 327.4200,
www.prada.com. Closed Sun. Moneyed fashionistas (and partners)
shop here for the latest look. Exceptional clothing, shoes and bags
from Italy. *S* 6 to 68th St

Scoop, 1275 Third Ave (73rd/74th Sts), *T* (212) 535-5577,
www.scoopnyc.com. Label-of-the-moment staples for the young and
well-to-do. *S* 6 to 77th St

Searle, 609 Madison Ave (57th/58th Sts), *T* (212) 753-9021,
www.searlenyc.com. Stylish women's clothes for work and leisure.
Cashmere, great selection of skirts and pants. *S* N, R to Fifth Ave.
Also 805 Madison Ave (67th/68th Sts), *T* (212) 628-6665.
S 6 to 68th St

Timberland, 709 Madison Ave (62nd/63rd Sts), *T* (212) 754-0436,
www.timberland.com. Outerwear and waterproof footwear for men,
women, and kids who love the great outdoors. *S* N, R to Fifth Ave

TSE, 827 Madison (68th/69th Sts), *T* (212) 472-7790. Open Sun during
holiday season. Cashmere, cashmere, cashmere. *S* 6 to 68th St

DEPARTMENT STORES

Barneys New York, 660 Madison Ave (60th/61st Sts), *T* (212) 826-8900,
www.barneys.com. Pricey designer togs on lower floors; for trendy,
less expensive lines, try the Co-op department. *S* N, R to Fifth Ave

Bergdorf Goodman, 754 Fifth Ave (57th/58th Sts), *T* (212) 753-7300.
Closed Sun. Upscale merchandise and a lot of it. Outstanding
loungewear, women's suits, a Manolo Blahnik footwear boutique,
and can't-miss tableware and stationery on 7. *S* N, R to Fifth Ave

Bloomingdale's, 1000 Third Ave (59th St/Lexington Ave), *T* (212) 355-
5900, www.bloomingdales.com. Bloomies is the third most visited
tourist attraction after the Statue of Liberty and Empire State
Building. Something for everyone! *S* 4, 5, 6 to 59th St; N, R to
Lexington Ave

HEALTH & BEAUTY

Caron, 675 Madison Ave (61st/62nd Sts), *T* (212) 319-4888. Très Parisien! This parfumier produces scents for all occasions and adds the finishing touch of a Baccarat crystal bottle. *S* N, R to Fifth Ave

Clyde's, 926 Madison (73rd/74th Sts), *T* (212) 744.5050. Sun 10-6. Oodles of hair accessories. High-end and standard European and domestic pharmacy products. *S* 6 to 77th St

Face Stockholm, 687 Madison Ave (61st/62nd Sts), *T* (212) 207-8833, www.facestockholm.com. Sun 12-7. Two hundred lip shades and 150 eye shadows to choose from. Let the helpful, professional staff give you a "real-life" make-up lesson that promises not to leave you wondering whose face is staring back at you from the mirror. *S* N, R to Fifth Ave

HOUSEWARES

Adrien Linford, 927 Madison Ave (73rd/74th Sts), *T* (212) 628-4500. Unusual, moderately-priced housewares; beautiful photo albums and frames, painted bowls, linen napkins, jewelry, and handmade cards. *S* 6 to 77th St

Mackenzie-Childs of New York, Ltd, 824 Madison Ave (68th/69th Sts), *T* (212) 570-6050, www.mackenzie-childs.com. Closed Sun. Whimsical hand-painted glassware, funky frames, napkin rings. *S* 6 to 68th St

Marimekko, 1262 Third Ave (72nd/73rd Sts), *T* (212) 628-8400, www.kiitosmarimekko.com. Open Sun during holiday season. Colorful, distinct designs from Finland; fabric by the yard, tablecloths, towels, totebags, and a clothing line. *S* 6 to 68th St

Pierre Deux, 625 Madison Ave (58th/59th Sts), *T* (212) 521-8012, www.pierredeux.com. French country printed fabrics, Cordon Bleu foods, Quimper ware, and soft-sided fabric totebags. *S* N, R to Fifth Ave

JEWELRY

Agatha, 611 Madison Ave (57th/58th Sts), *T* (212) 758-4301, www.agatha.fr. Sun 12-6. From Paris, reasonably-priced pendants, earrings, rings, charms, belts, and necklaces. *S* N, R to Fifth Ave

Cartier, 828 Madison Ave (69th/70th Sts), *T* (212) 472-6400, www.cartier.com. Closed Sun. Famous for watches, but also has glamorous jewelry and accessories. *S* 6 to 68th St

David Yurman, 729 Madison Ave (63rd/64th Sts), *T* (212) 752-4255, www.davidyurman.com. Closed Sun. These bold, chunky designs are on every New York woman's wish list. *S* N, R to Fifth Ave

Tiffany & Co., 727 Fifth Ave (56th/57th Sts), *T* (212) 755-8000, www.tiffany.com. Closed Sun. Wandering tourists and security personnel abound on the first floor where wedding bands and other high-priced items are displayed. Visit the second floor for Elsa Peretti's works in sterling and designs by Paloma Picasso. *S* N, R to Fifth Ave

LINGERIE

La Perla, 777 Madison Ave (66th/67th Sts), *T* (212) 570-0050, www.laperla.com. Closed Sun. Luxurious, lacy, and priced like no other undergarments you've ever seen! *S* 6 to 68th St

Wolford, 619 Madison Ave (58th/59th Sts), *T* (212) 688-4850, www.wolford.com. Closed Sun. Bodysuits, hosiery. Try them once and no other brand will ever compare. *S* N, R to Fifth Ave

SHOES

Christian Louboutin, 941 Madison Ave (74th/75th Sts), *T* (212) 396-1884. Closed Sun. High-end, red-soled, Parisian heels for women; expensive, but exquisite. *S* 6 to 77th St

J.M. Weston, 812 Madison Ave (67th/68th Sts), *T* (212) 535-2100, www.jmweston.com. Impeccable shoes for men that (with re-soling) will last a lifetime. Hand-made in France since 1891. *S* 6 to 68th St

Robert Clergerie, 681 Madison Ave (61st/62nd Sts), *T* (212) 207-8600. Classic elegant shoes you can actually walk in; platform sandals, comfortable boots from this French designer. *S* N, R to Fifth Ave

Stuart Weitzman, 625 Madison Ave (58th/59th Sts), *T* (212) 750-2555, www.stuartweitzman.com. Beautifully-made shoes and boots for women in timeless styles. *S* N, R to Fifth Ave

Unisa, 701 Madison Ave (62nd/63rd Sts), *T* (212) 753-7474, www.unisa.com. Reasonably priced shoes and bags for women. Sexy, yet practical, great sandals. *S* N, R at Fifth Ave

SPECIALTY

Art of Shaving, 141 East 62nd St (Lexington/Third Aves), *T* (212) 317-8436, www.artofshaving.com. Closed Sun. Every shaving accessory imaginable. *S* 4, 5, 6 to 59th St or N, R to Lexington Ave

Clearly First, 980 Madison Ave (76th/77th Sts), *T* (212) 988-8242, www.clearlyfirst.com. Finely-crafted merchandise from Scandinavian designers. Stationery, glass, clothing, and more. *S* 6 to 77th St

Dylan's Candy Bar, 1011 Third Ave (60th/61st Sts), *T* (646) 735-0078, www.dylanscandybar.com. Just steps away from Bloomingdale's, this candy heaven has ice cream flavors like Central Park Zoo (complete with animal crackers) and a rainbow of M&Ms, Skittles, and jellybeans in help-yourself bins. *S* 4, 5, 6 to 59thSt or N, R to Lexington Ave

ItoEn, 822 Madison Ave (68th/69th Sts), *T* (212) 988-7111, www.itoen.com. Open Sun during holiday season. Teas and teaware from around the globe. Sample tea at the Sencha Bar. *S* 6 to 68th St

Tender Buttons, 143 East 62nd St (Lexington/Third Aves), *T* (212) 758-7004. Closed Sun. Cash only. Lose a button off your vintage coat? Find a replacement at this charming shop; buttons of all colors, sizes, styles. *S* 4, 5, 6 to 59th St; N, R to Lexington Ave

TOYS

FAO Schwarz, 767 Fifth Ave (58th/59th Sts), *T* (212) 644-9400, www.fao.com. A New York City legend; amazing selection of toys (especially stuffed animals) guaranteed to send any child into a frenzy! *S* N, R to Fifth Ave

WINE

Sherry-Lehmann, 679 Madison Ave (61st/62nd Sts), *T* (212) 838-7500, www.sherry-lehmann.com. Closed Sun. Madison Ave landmark, huge selection of wines from everywhere in all price ranges. *S* N, R to Fifth Ave

CHELSEA &
THE MEATPACKING
DISTRICT

Chelsea is the 1990s' answer to SoHo, the center of the gallery scene. There are no museums with permanent collections on view here (as at the Metropolitan), but you haven't seen the scene if you haven't been to Chelsea. Visit between September and mid-June if you can. Many galleries and Dia: Chelsea are closed at some point during the summer months.

Dia: Chelsea

OPEN	Early Sept–mid-June Wed–Sun 12–6
CLOSED	Summers (mid-June and early-Sept), 1/1 and 12/25
CHARGES	$6 full price; $3 seniors and students with ID; free for children under 10. Free to members. Admission price includes both buildings
TELEPHONE	(212) 989-5566
WWW.	diacenter.org
MAIN ENTRANCE	548 West 22nd St (Tenth/Eleventh Aves). Second exhibition space at 545 West 22nd St
SUBWAY	C, E to 23rd St. Walk west or take the 23rd St crosstown bus to Eleventh Ave
DISABLED ACCESS	Accessible to disabled visitors with the exception of the site-specific installation on the roof
SHOPS	The bookshop (open Wed–Sun 11–6), is one of the city's best sources of art books, with titles on contemporary art and videos
EATING	Rooftop café and video salon

In addition to its changing exhibitions, Dia offers poetry readings, video, special events, lectures.

Dia: Chelsea (formerly Dia Art Center), an exhibition space devoted to contemporary art, is one of the main reasons the art world has set up shop in Chelsea. In 1974 Philippa de Menil, (whose grandfather was founder of Schlumberger, the

multinational oil exploration engineering firm) and her husband Heiner Friedrich, an art dealer, founded the Dia Art Foundation. Both were committed to Conceptual, Minimal, and Earth Art. They sponsored site-specific art in unusual places and they offered grants to artists to support unusual projects. In 1987 when Chelsea was only beginning to emerge from its past as a neighborhood of lackluster industrial buildings, slum housing, and taxi garages, Dia opened this four-story building. The name "dia" comes from the Greek root meaning "through," and suggests the center's role in enabling projects that might not be possible in traditional museums.

THE BUILDING

The main exhibition space, built as a warehouse, was converted by Gluckman Mayner Architects, who later did the exhibition spaces for the nearby Mary Boone and Gagosian Galleries. Jorge Pardo designed the bookstore and lobby as part of an installation project in 2002. On the roof is a small-scale urban park that includes an architectural glass pavilion with a mirrored cylinder inside, and a shed that has been remodeled as a café and video salon. Dan Flavin's untitled site-specific installation (1996) illuminates two windowed staircases with fluorescent lights, which are visible at night from the street. Outside, on West 22nd St, the 23 pairs of basalt columns alternating with trees form part of an installation entitled *7000 Oaks*, the work of Joseph Beuys. The installation began in Kassel, Germany, at the 1982 Documenta Festival, the world's biggest contemporary art fair, and was intended to continue as a worldwide tree-planting project.

EXHIBITION PROGRAM

Dia: Chelsea is famous for its long-term single artist, site-specific exhibitions. Artists usually get a full floor of space and a full year of viewing time, so that visitors can come back again and again. Recent shows have included Bruce Nauman's "Mapping the Studio," a multimedia exhibit almost six hours long, during which seven DVD's projected views of Nauman's studio from different angles; the minimalist works of Jo Baer; and Belgian artist-inventor Panamarenko's giant cocoon-blimp patched together with plastic and tape.

Memorable past shows include Robert Irwin's scrim installations in which the artist divided one floor of the building into square cells, walled with semitransparent scrim and lit with natural and fluorescent light. Equally compelling was Tropos, Ann Hamilton's 1993 installation, in which she altered the surface of the factory floor so that it was no longer flat and covered it entirely with horsehair. In the center sat a single performer, a woman at a desk, who read and burned the pages of a book line by line.

NOTE Although works from the permanent collection sometimes go on view at Dia: Chelsea, the permanent collection is shown primarily in Beacon, New York, about 60 miles up the Hudson River from New York City. You can get to Beacon via MetroNorth from Grand Central Terminal. For information, *T* (845) 440-0199.

Dia: Beacon occupies a recycled industrial plant, ideal for large-scale works like the Andy Warhol's 434-foot painting, *Shadows*, Richard Serra's monumental sculptures, and all 1590 panels of Hanne Darboven's *Kulturgeschichte 1880-1983*. This latter work traces 100 years of history and culture using postcards, magazine covers, reproductions of art works, etc. This is the sort of thing Dia likes and the factory at Beacon can accomodate monumental works.

Yeshiva University Museum

OPEN	Tues, Wed, Thurs, Sun 11-5
CLOSED	Mon, Fri, Sat, Jewish holidays

CHARGES	$6 full price; seniors and students with current valid ID $4.00; children 5-16 $4.00; children under 5 free
TELEPHONE	(212) 294-8330
WWW.	yumuseum.org
MAIN ENTRANCE	15 West 16th St
SUBWAY	F, V to 14th St; N, R, Q, W to 14th St-Union Sq
SHOPS	Shop with Judaica, books, jewelry crafted by local and Israeli artists, recorded music including Klezmer and Sephardic music, archival recordings, sheet music, collectibles, Passover gifts, postcards, Jewish sports memorabilia. Open Mon-Thurs 10-6, Sun 9-5
EATING	Café

Changing exhibitions, guided tours, special events, family programs

The Center for Jewish History, on the far east of Chelsea, is an umbrella organization for five Jewish institutions: The Yeshiva University Museum, the Leo Baeck Institute, the American Jewish Historical Society, the American Sephardi Federation, and YIVO Institute for Jewish Research. Each of them examines a different aspect of Jewish experience, and several are scholarly in their orientation. Yeshiva University Museum has its main exhibition space at the Center, and there is always historical and contemporary Jewish art on display.

THE COLLECTION

The permanent collection of Yeshiva University Museum includes folk art, archaeological and ceremonial artifacts, clothing and textiles, documents, books, and manuscripts, which document 2000 years of Jewish art and culture. Highlights include a letter by Thomas Jefferson affirming religious freedom and denouncing anti-Semitism; a Torah scroll that belonged to the 18c founder of the Hassidic movement; ceremonial objects for religious rituals; examples of textiles and clothing - an embroidered Ottoman wedding dress and a child's Czechoslovakian national costume made just before World War II - and architectural models of historic 13c-19c synagogues. Fine art includes paintings, graphics and sculpture: Robert Indiana's *Dutch Masters in the Rose Room* and Reuven Rubin's *New Colony*. The museum shows the permanent collection through changing exhibitions, usually two running simultaneously; one historical and the other focused on living artists.

on route

Lobby of the Chelsea Hotel

Chelsea Hotel, 222 West 23rd St (Seventh/Eighth Aves), a landmarked hotel. Thomas Wolfe, Arthur Miller, Tennessee Williams, and Vladimir Nabokov stayed here. So did Jackson Pollock and Willem de Kooning; Andy Warhol used the hotel for background in his 1967 film *Chelsea Girls*. Sid Vicious, bass player for the punk rock Sex Pistols, was indicted for murdering his girlfriend Nancy Spungen with a hunting knife in Room 100. (He died of a heroin overdose the night after he was freed on bail and so never stood trial.) Check out the cast-iron sunflowers decorating the balconies and the art in the lobby. **S** C, E, 1, 9 to 23rd St

Chelsea Market, 75 Ninth Ave (15th/16th Sts). A full block of inspiration for foodies: wholesale and retail, breads, specialty groceries, restaurant supplies, and a food court for the gods. The Oreo cookie was reputedly "invented" here in 1912, when Nabisco occupied part of the site. **S** A, C, E to 14th St

Chelsea Piers Sports Complex, West 23rd St at the Hudson River. **T** (212) 336-6500, www.chelseapiers.com. Where once transatlantic liners dropped their hawsers, you can now swing at a golf ball, hoist yourself up a climbing wall, or repair your frazzled nerves in the day spa. Open to the public on a fee-per-activity basis; day passes ($50) to the health club. **S** C, E to 23rd St

Exit Art/The First World, 475 Tenth Ave (36th St). Gallery open 7 days, café open Wed-Sun; **T** (212) 966-7745, www.exitart.org. A SoHo veteran relocated on the northern fringe of Chelsea (a block east of the Javits Center), this not-for-profit shows young and emerging artists and has boosted the careers of David Hammons, Adrian Piper, David Wojnarowicz; exhibitions have featured underground comics, performance art from Iron Curtain countries, record jackets, multidisciplinary art - take a look at the website. **S** A,C,E to 34th St-Penn Station

The Kitchen, 512 West 19th St (Tenth/Eleventh Aves), **T** (212) 255-5793, www.thekitchen.org. Center for video, performance, dance, music, and film has a full schedule of events and also an art gallery. It was founded in 1971 in the kitchen of a now defunct hotel and came to Chelsea from SoHo two years before Dia: Chelsea. **S** A, C, E to 14th St

The Museum at FIT, Seventh Ave at 27th St, closed Sun, Mon, **T** (212) 217-5800, www.fitnyc.edu. The Fashion Institute of Technology's high-style museum; changing exhibits on every aspect of fashion including its place in society. Recent exhibitions have looked at "Fashion Italian Style" (terrific shoes!), Scaasi gowns for the rich and famous, and sexual politics as expressed in the styles of fin-de-siècle Paris. **S** 1, 9 to 18th St

Printed Matter, 535 West 22nd St (Tenth/Eleventh Aves), **T** (212) 925-0325, www.printedmatter.org. A prime venue for artists' books. Also exhibitions, readings, book launches, and signings. Founded in 1976, Printed Matter arrived from SoHo in 2001. **S** C, E to 23rd St

THE FIFTH AVENUE CORRIDOR:
42ND STREET TO 23RD STREET

Fifth Avenue cuts a swathe along Manhattan's midline from the Harlem River to Washington Square. Between the southern boundary of the Silk Stocking District and the northern edge of Chelsea, it passes by some of the borough's most famous cultural and architectural landmarks as well as some of its historic commercial establishments.

These sights along Fifth Avenue and close to it are arranged from north to south. For the northern continuation of this section see Silk Stocking District p 108.

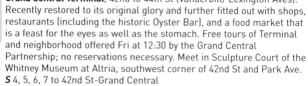

Grand Central Terminal, 42nd to 44th St (Vanderbilt/ Lexington Aves). Recently restored to its original glory and further fitted out with shops, restaurants (including the historic Oyster Bar), and a food market that is a feast for the eyes as well as the stomach. Free tours of Terminal and neighborhood offered Fri at 12:30 by the Grand Central Partnership; no reservations necessary. Meet in Sculpture Court of the Whitney Museum at Altria, southwest corner of 42nd St and Park Ave. **S** 4, 5, 6, 7 to 42nd St-Grand Central

Chrysler Building, 405 Lexington Ave (42nd St), open during business hours. At 1048 feet, it was briefly the world's tallest building (bested by the Empire State Building) and still is one of its most famous. The stainless steel spire and crown make it instantly recognizable. Walk through the lobby, whose opulent polished wood, marble, and chrome décor shows what money could buy back in 1930. **S** 4, 5, 6, 7 to 42nd St-Grand Central

New York Public Library, Fifth Ave at 41st St, open Thurs-Sat 10-6, Tues, Wed 11-7:30; due to budget cuts the library is closed Mon. **T** (212) 869-8089, www.nypl.org. This beautiful Beaux Arts building with the famous stone lions outside today contains research collections for the humanities and social sciences. Guided tours at 11 and 2. Don't miss the renovated Public Catalogue Room and Main Reading Room, which rank among the city's great interiors. Interesting exhibitions in the first floor exhibition hall and elsewhere throughout the library. **S** B, D, F, V to 42nd St; 7 to Fifth Ave

Bryant Park, 40th to 42nd St, Fifth to Sixth Aves. Open 7am until evening-11pm in summer, earlier in winter. Behind the Library more than 9 acres of lawns, gardens, and promenades (some bordered with London plane trees), offer office workers a choice lunch spot and everyone else a chance to stroll, sit, buy a snack or meal, and take in the passing scene. **S** B, D, F, V, to 42nd St/Bryant Park; 7 to Fifth Ave

Lord &Taylor, 424 Fifth Ave (38th/39th Sts), open Mon-Fri 10-8:30, Sat 10-7, Sun 11-7. Classic department store with a long New York history, elegant and relaxed, less trendy than some but not dowdy either. **S** B, D, F, V, to 42n St; 7 to Fifth Ave

Empire State Building, 350 Fifth Ave (33rd/34th Sts). Observatories open Mon-Fri 10am-midnight, Sat-Sun 9:30am-midnight. Last tickets sold fifteen minutes before closing. Cash only. **T** (212) 736-3100, www.esbnyc.com. Since the building opened in 1931, more than 110 million people have elevatored up to the 86th floor for panoramic views of the city from the glassed-in observatory and/or outdoor promenade. (Crowds and long waiting times have closed the small 102nd floor tower to the public.) Lights illuminate the exterior at night, the colors chosen to celebrate holidays, special events (Queen Elizabeth's Golden Jubilee, Fire Department Memorial Day, German Reunification Day), and worthy causes (Breast Cancer Awareness, Child Abuse Prevention). The lights are turned off sometimes during the spring and fall migration seasons when too many birds are flying too near the building. The NY Skyride, a film simulating a helicopter ride swooping past New York sights (Statue of Liberty, Times Square) is located on the second floor; open 365 days, 10am-10pm; separate charge from admission to Observatory. The film is short, vertiginous, and fairly expensive. **S** B D F N Q R V W to 34th St

Chrysler Building (left) and Empire State Building

Museum of Sex, 233 Fifth Ave (27th St). Adults only (18 and over); closed Wed; **T** (212) 689-6337; www.museumofsex.com. Opened in 2002; educational, kitschy, and sufficiently hard core to draw the fire of the Catholic League for Religious and Civil Rights. Changing exhibits of photography, artifacts, film clips, etc. **S** N, R, W to 23rd St

The Flatiron Building, Broadway and Fifth Ave at 23rd St. New York's tallest skyscraper (285 feet) when it was built (1902) and one of the first anywhere to be hung on a steel skeleton. Named for the triangular plot on which it stands, it is the work of Daniel H. Burnham, a pioneer in construction methods and an influential city planner. The building remains a symbol of New York at the turn of the 20c; its haunting beauty has inspired such photographers as Edward Steichen and Alfred Stieglitz. **S** N, R, W and 6 to 23rd St

commercial galleries

A recent count tallied more than 150 galleries in Chelsea. Most are open Tuesday-Saturday 10-6; many close during the late summer. Galleries are concentrated in the 20s between Tenth and Eleventh Aves, but exhibition spaces reach uptown as far as 29th St and downtown to 13th St, officially part of the Meat Packing District. This list only scratches the surface.

MEATPACKING DISTRICT

Alexander and Bonin, 132 Tenth Ave (18th/19th Sts), *T* (212) 367-7474. Contemporary American and European artists. *S* A, C, E to 14th St

Axis Gallery, 453 West 17th St (Ninth/Tenth Aves), *T* (212) 741-2582, www.axisgallery.com. African art, South African artists and photographers. *S* A, C, E to 14th St

Casey Kaplan Gallery, 416 West 14th St (Ninth/Tenth Aves), *T* (212) 645-7335, www.caseykaplangallery.com. Well-regarded gallery; contemporary artists, film video, photography, sculpture. *S* A, C, E to 14th St

Rare Gallery, 435 West 14th St (Ninth/Tenth Aves), *T* (212) 268-1520, www.rare-gallery.com. Founded 1998 to promote emerging artists concerned with contemporary issues. Photography, video, sculpture, painting, installations; combinations thereof. *S* A, C, E to 14th St

Sperone Westwater, 415 West 13th St (Ninth Ave/Washington St), *T* (212) 999-7337, www.speronewestwater.com. Contemporary artists and Italian neo-Expressionists including Sandro Chia and Francesco Clemente. Bruce Nauman and Susan Rothenberg have been with the gallery from its beginning in 1975. *S* A, C, E to 14th St

White Columns, 320 West 13th St (entrance on Horatio St between Hudson St/Eighth Ave), *T* (212) 924-4212, www.whitecolumns.org. Open Wed-Sun 12-6. New York's oldest (1969) alternative art space. Alice Aycock, William Wegman, Act-Up, and Ashley Bickerton got their first big New York exposure here. Closed Aug. *S* A, C, E to 14th St

David Zwirner, 525 West 19th St (Tenth/Eleventh Aves), *T* (212) 727-2070, www.davidzwirner.com. First opened (1993) in SoHo. Focuses on emerging American and international artists; also shows contemporary and modern masters. *S* A,C, E to 14th St

Nathan Carter *I'm trying to read the road signs but they keep changing languages...looks dodgy around here* (2003; Casey Kaplan Gallery)

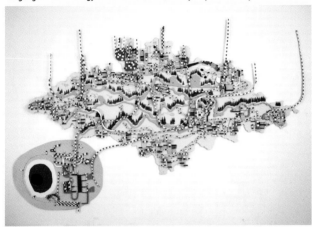

WEST 22ND STREET AREA

Paula Cooper, 534 West 21st St and 521 West 21st St (Tenth/Eleventh Aves), *T* (212) 255-1105, www.paulacooper.com. Cooper opened SoHo's first gallery in 1968, her first show benefitting the Student Mobilization Committee to End the War in Vietnam. Later she mounted groundbreaking exhibits of Elizabeth Murray, Jackie Winsor, Robert Gober, Jennifer Bartlett. Cooper still focuses on Conceptualists and Minimalists including Donald Judd, Tony Smith, Carl Andre, Jonathan Borofsky. *S* C, E to 23rd St

Matthew Marks, 522 West 22nd St and 523 West 24th St (Tenth/Eleventh Aves), *T* (212) 243-0200, www.matthewmarks.com. Respected Chelsea pioneer (1994); world-famous contemporary American and European artists - Willem De Kooning, Lucian Freud, Roni Horn, Ellsworth Kelly - as well as works on paper. Two stellar spaces. *S* C, E to 23rd St

Max Protetch Gallery, 511 West 22nd St (Tenth/Eleventh Aves), *T* (212) 633-6999, www.maxprotetch.com. Contemporary art, Chinese artists, artists involved with public sculpture. Ceramics, painting, architectural drawings. *S* C, E to 23rd St

Brent Sikkema, 530 West 22nd St (Tenth/Eleventh Aves), **T** (212) 929-2262, www.brentsikkema.com. Contemporary and sometimes controversial. Josiah McElheny, Arturo Herrera, Kara Walker. **S** C, E to 23rd St

Sonnabend, 536 West 22nd St (Tenth/Eleventh Aves), **T** (212) 627-1018. Ileana Sonnabend, long known as the "Mom of Pop" was married to legendary dealer Leo Castelli and opened her first gallery with him in their Upper East Side living room. The two established the reputations of such art stars as Andy Warhol, Jasper Johns, and Robert Rauschenberg. Today the gallery shows Ashley Bickerton, John Baldessari, Haim Steinbach, and Gilbert & George. **S** C, E to 23rd St

WEST 24TH STREET AREA

Mary Boone, 541 West 24th St (Tenth/Eleventh Aves), **T** (212) 989-7074, www.maryboonegallery.com. The downtown space of this onetime SoHo pioneer, who got her start as a protégé of Leo Castelli; A-list contemporary painters. Also a branch on Fifth Avenue. **S** C, E to 23rd St

Charles Cowles, 537 West 24th St (Tenth/Eleventh Aves), **T** (212) 925-3500. Founded in 1980; contemporary and modern painting, sculpture, ceramics; represents 20 artists including Howard Ben Tré, Beverly Pepper, Al Souza, Toshika Takeazu, Peter Voulkos. **S** C, E to 23rd St

Gagosian Gallery, 555 West 24th St (Tenth/Eleventh Aves), **T** (212) 741-1111, www.gagosian.com. Enormous gallery capable of accommodating large-scale works. Represents artists (Anselm Kiefer, Andy Warhol, Damien Hirst) who command towering prices. Also on Madison Ave. **S** C, E to 23rd St

Barbara Gladstone Gallery, 515 West 24th St, (Tenth/Eleventh Aves), **T** (212) 206-9300, www.gladstonegallery.com. Founded 1979, contemporary American and European art, represents Vito Acconci, Matthew Barney, Jan Dibbets, Mario Merz, Richard Prince, Rosemarie Trockel, James Turrell. **S** C, E to 23rd St

Yossi Milo Gallery, 552 West 24th St, **T** (212) 414-0370, www.yossimilogallery.com. Small upstairs gallery, photography. **S** C, E to 23rd St

FURTHER UPTOWN

Paul Kasmin Gallery, 293 Tenth Ave (27th St), **T** (212) 563-4474, www.paulkasmingallery.com. Modern painting: Donald Baechler, Anthony Caro, Caio Fonseca, Robert Indiana, Morris Louis, Frank Stella, Andy Warhol. **S** C, E to 23rd St

Sean Kelly, 528 West 29th St (Tenth/Eleventh Aves), *T* (212) 239-1811, www.skny.com. British born curator-gallerist shows contemporary American, international artists; installations, group shows, photography. Roster includes Marina Abramovic, Ann Hamilton, Rebecca Horn, Iran do Espirito Santo, Callum Innes. *S* A, C, E to 34th St

Gary Snyder Fine Art, 601 West 29th St (Eleventh/Twelfth Aves), *T* (212) 871-1077, www.modernamericanart.com. Skylit exhibition space, gallery focuses on modern American art (1920s through the 1960s), a period in which Snyder is an acknowledged expert. Snyder represents the the estate of German expatriate artist, Hilla Rebay, Solomon Guggenheim's art guru. Also contemporary artists. *S* A, C, E to 34th St

eating and drinking

AT THE MUSEUMS
DIA: CHELSEA
The **rooftop café** at Dia: Chelsea serves beverages.

YESHIVA UNIVERSITY MUSEUM
Date Palm Café (kosher) serves vegetarian and dairy sandwiches, salads, soups, pasta, pizza, baked goods, Mediterranean specialties; open Sun-Thurs 11-4:30

SURROUNDING AREA
$ **Amy's Bread**, 75 Ninth Ave (15th/16th Sts, in Chelsea Market), *T* (212) 462-4338. One of three locations; serves breads, baked goodies and sandwiches; cramped quarters, so grab and go. *S* A, C, E to 14th St; L to 8th Ave

Bright Food Shops, 216 Eighth Ave (21st St), *T* (212) 243-4433. Minimalist former diner serves Asian/TexMex fusion, beer and wine. Cash only. *S* C, E to 23rd St

The Dish, 201 Eighth Ave (20th/21st Sts), *T* (212) 352-9800. American diner serves up way-above-average diner food with people-watching to match. Serves late. *S* C, E to 23rd St

F & B, 269 West 23rd St (Seventh/Eighth Aves), *T* (646) 486-4441. Hot dogs and sausages (think Hamburg, not Hebrew National), frites (served with v. Chelsea toppings like aioli and black truffle oil); go with the beignets if you're around for breakfast. Cash only. *S* C, E, 1, 9 to 23rd St

Grand Sichuan, 229 Ninth Ave (24th St), *T* (212) 620-5200. Chain of not-your-average Chinese; hot and spicy fare at very reasonable prices; the book-length menu provides plenty of information on regional cuisine, and ensures everyone will find something to please. *S* C, E to 23rd St

Gus's Figs Bistro, 250 West 27th St (Seventh/Eighth Aves), *T* (212) 352-8822. Fashionistas-in-training from FIT (the Fashion Institute of Technology) frequent this appealing Mediterranean bistro on the far western side of Chelsea. Open late. Closed Sunday. *S* 1, 9 to 28th St

Maroons, 244 West 16th St (Seventh/Eighth Aves), *T* (212) 206-8640. Big portions at this small Southern/Jamaican crowd pleaser; laid-back atmosphere, comfy lounge, and friendly staff. Serves late. *S* A, C, E, 1, 2, 3, 9 to 14th St

Petite Abeille, 107 West 18th St (Sixth/Seventh Aves), *T* (212) 604-9350. Tiny, crowded, cheerful Belgian café; sandwiches, moules frites, waffles. Breakfast, lunch, and dinner. *S* 1, 9 to 18th St

Riazor, 245 West 16th St (Seventh/Eighth Aves), *T* (212) 727-2132. Bohemian décor and old-style Spanish menu at this tucked-away spot; classics like chorizo and shrimp are best; sangria. Cash and American Express only. *S* A, C, E, 1, 2, 3, 9 to 14th St

Rocking Horse Café, 182 Eighth Ave (19th/20th Sts), *T* (212) 463-9511. Popular Chelsea spin-on-the-old-standards Mexican; sidewalk tables make for excellent people watching in nice weather. *S* C, E to 23rd St

Rue des Crepes, 104 Eighth Ave (15th/16th Sts), *T* (212) 242-9900. The décor's a bit kitschy, but it's worth overlooking for the tasty crepes. Interesting savory combinations come in buckwheat crepes, but save room for the sweet ones, like the traditional lemon and butter. *S* A, C, E to 14th St; L to Eighth Ave

La Taza de Oro, 96 Eighth Ave (14th/15th Sts), *T* (212) 243-9946. Huge portions served at this established, authentic Puerto Rican; regulars come for the café con leche, reportedly the best north of San Juan. Cash only. Breakfast. *S* A, C, E to 14th St

Le Zie 2000, 172 Seventh Ave (20th St), *T* (212) 206-8686. Oft-crowded neighborhood favorite; hearty portions of pasta and excellent Venetian dishes. Cash only. **S** 1, 9 to 23rd St

$$ **L'Acajou**, 53 West 19th St (Fifth/Sixth Aves), **T** (212) 645-1706. Some say this bistro on the far east of Chelsea could use sprucing up, but regulars applaud the consistent Alsatian food and impressive wine list. Closed Sun. **S** F, V, N, R, W to 23rd St

La Belle Vie, 184 Eighth Ave (19th/20th Sts), **T** (212) 929-4320. French bistro standards (steak au poivre, escargots) at reasonable prices; in nice weather linger over weekend brunch at one of the sidewalk tables. **S** C, E to 23rd St; 1, 9 to 18th St

Bottino, 246 Tenth Ave (24th/25th Sts), **T** (212) 206-6766. This charming Italian restaurant, smack dab in the middle of the Chelsea gallery scene, features an extensive wine list; for a quick bite stick with the excellent appetizers. In nice weather, escape to the outdoor garden. Dinner only. **S** C, E to 23rd St

Cafeteria, 119 Seventh Ave (17th St), **T** (212) 414-1717. Fancy comfort food served to the beautiful-and-they-know-it; open round the clock. **S** 1, 9 to 18th St

Empire Diner, 210 Tenth Ave (22nd St), **T** (212) 243-2736. One-time late-night favorite for party kids and Wall Street types alike, this Chelsea landmark still serves above-average classic diner fare. Good for a late night bite, and people watching. **S** C, E to 23rd St

Monster Sushi, 158 West 23rd St (Fifth/Sixth Aves), **T** (212) 620-9131. Gigantic portions of quality sushi make this Manhattan chain a good value. **S** F, V, 1, 9 to 23rd St

Moran's Chelsea, 146 Tenth Ave (19th St), **T** (212) 627-3030. Cozy, comfortable upscale Irish pub; traditional pub fare, plenty of ale on tap, and friendly service. **S** C, E to 23rd St; 1, 9 to 18th St

Nisos, 176 Eighth Ave (19th St), **T** (646) 336-8121. Airy, pleasant Mediterranean featuring fresh grilled fish. Open late. **S** C, E to 23rd St

The Red Cat, 227 Tenth Ave (23rd/24th Sts), **T** (212) 242-1122. Comfortable, relaxed American bistro; good wine list with plenty to choose from, even by the glass. **S** C, E to 23rd St

$$$ **Arezzo**, 46 West 22nd St (Fifth/Sixth Aves), **T** (212) 206-0555. Unflashy Italian featuring seasonal specialties (many from the coal-burning oven). Closed Sun. No lunch Sat. **S** F, V, N, R, W to 23rd St

AZ, 21 West 17th St (Fifth/Sixth Aves), *T* (212) 691-8888. Slick Asian fusion where the décor (swanky bar, sleek silver elevator, retractable glass roof) vies with the creative New American fare. *S* F, V to 14th St; 9 to 18th St

Chelsea Bistro & Bar, 358 West 23rd St (Eighth/Ninth Aves), *T* (212) 727-2026. Unassuming bistro serving up reliable, classic French fare and a cozy atmosphere. *S* C, E to 23rd St

Da Umberto, 107 West 17th St (Sixth/Seventh Aves), *T* (212) 989-0303. Noisy neighborhood favorite serving authentic, excellent Northern Italian. Closed Sun. *S* F, V to 14th St; 1, 9 to 18th St

Frank's Restaurant, 85 Tenth Ave (15th St), *T* (212) 243-1349. Bigger than big portions at this old fashioned steakhouse in the Meatpacking District. A neighborhood fixture since 1912 when they really packed meat nearby. No lunch weekends. *S* A, C, E to 14th St

Gasgogne, 158 Eighth Ave (17th/18th Sts), *T* (212) 675-6564. Romantic bistro serving authentic Southern French; in warm weather, head out to the garden. *S* 1, 9 to 18th St

Man Ray, 147 West 15th St (Sixth/Seventh Aves), *T* (212) 929-5000. Surprisingly interesting French-Asian fusion served to a young, hip crowd in equally hip setting; you might even spot a celeb or two. *S* F, V, 1, 2, 3, 9 to 14th St

Old Homestead, 56 Ninth Ave (14th/15th Sts), *T* (212) 242-9040. Long-running Meatpacking District steakhouse with outsized portions. Bring you appetite and a couple friends. *S* A, C, E to 14th St

BARS

Bongo, 299 Tenth Ave (27th/28th Sts), *T* (212) 947-3654. Retro-hip hangout serves 1950s style cocktails (read sweet) and swanky bar food. Closed Sun. *S* C, E to 23rd St; 1, 9 to 28th St

Flight 151, 151 Eighth Ave (17th/18th Sts), *T* (212) 229-1868. Decorated with airplane parts, this neighborhood bar serves just-OK bar food and reasonably priced drinks to a young crowd. *S* A, C, E to 14th Sts

Glass, 287 Tenth Ave (26th/27th Sts), *T* (212) 904-1580. High-concept bar/lounge (bamboo garden, two-way mirror in the bathroom) caters to the Chelsea art scene. *S* 1, 9 to 28th St

The Half King, 505 West 23rd St (Tenth/Eleventh Aves), *T* (212) 462-

4300. Upscale Irish pub serving early (homemade scones) and late (shepherd's pie); arty crowd. **S** C, E to 23rd St

Kanvas Bar & Lounge, 219 Ninth Ave (23rd/24th Sts), **T** (212) 727-2616. Spacious, modern bar serves creative mixed drinks and decent bar food. **S** C, E to 23rd St

Open, 559 West 22nd St (Tenth/Eleventh Aves), **T** (212) 243-1851. Airy, minimalist space blends well with the gallery scene; good light eats, flowing red wine; it's like an opening without the art. **S** C, E to 23rd St

Slate, 54 West 21st St (Fifth/Sixth Aves), **T** (212) 989-0096. Upscale billiards and snacks in a relaxed, trendy atmosphere. **S** F, N, R, W to 23rd St

Trailer Park Lounge & Grill, 271 West 23rd St (Seventh/Eighth Aves), **T** (212) 463-8000. American rec-room kitsch (Elvis, tiki) decorates this white-trash themed hang; the crazy concoctions match the décor, better than average bar food. **S** C, E to 23rd St

shopping

Chelsea - the neighborhood of Manhattan between 14th and 26th Sts, from Fifth Ave to the West Side Highway - has morphed from its industrial past into one of the city's artistic hot spots. With its large gay population, Chelsea is a center of contemporary design, offering trendy clothing boutiques for men and women, as well as furniture and home stores. On its southwestern fringe you'll discover the gritty appeal of the Meatpacking District where high-end designer clothing stores stand side-by-side with meat warehouses. Don't miss the Chelsea Wholesale Flower Market, The Annex Antique Fair & Flea Market, and one of Chelsea's peerless poster shops. Shops are open Sunday, unless otherwise indicated.

ACCESSORIES

Ellen Christine Millinery, 255 West 18th St (Seventh/Eighth Aves), *T* (212) 242-2457, www.ellenchristine.com. Closed Mon. Hats of all kinds, including custom-made and vintage. *S* 1, 2 to 18th St

Fossil, 103 Fifth Ave (17th/18th Sts), *T* (212) 243-7296, www.fossil.com. Stylish and reasonably-priced watches, bags, and wallets. *S* N, R, W, L, 4, 5, 6 to 14th St-Union Square

Innovation Luggage, 670 Sixth Ave (20th/21st Sts), *T* (212) 243-4720, www.innovationluggage.com. Great luggage, reasonable prices: Tumi, Samsonite, High Sierra, and Kipling. *S* F to 23rd St

ANTIQUES

The Annex Antique Fair & Flea Market, Sixth Ave (25th/26th Sts), *T* (212) 243-5343. Sat & Sun only, 9-5. You never know what you might find! Clothes, furniture, and some surprises as well. *S* F to 23rd St

The Garage Antique Shop, 112 West 25th St (Sixth/Seventh Aves), *T* (212) 647-0707. Sat & Sun only, 9-5. Two floors of trash or treasure to paw through. *S* 1, 2 to 23rd St

BABIES & KIDS

Books of Wonder, 16 West 18th St (Fifth/Sixth Aves), *T* (212) 989-3270, www.booksofwonder.com. An amazing selection of new and used kids' books. Lots of rare editions. *S* 1, 2, 3, F, V, L to 14th St

Buy Buy Baby, 270 Seventh Ave (25th/26th Sts), *T* (917) 344-1555, www.buybuybaby.com. A huge selection of everything for baby. Clothes from such labels as Marimekko and Carter's, plus other baby supplies. *S* 1, 2 to 23rd St

CLOTHING

Alexander McQueen, 417 West 14th St (Ninth/Tenth Aves), *T* (212) 645-1797, www.alexandermcqueen.com. London style in the Meatpacking District. Pricey designs for women from a true original. *S* A, C, E, L to 14th St-Eighth Ave

Barney's Co-op, 236 West 18th St (Seventh/Eighth Aves), *T* (212) 593-7800, www.barneys.com. Young, trendy designs. *S* 1, 2 to 18th St

Comme des Garçons, 520 West 22nd St (Tenth/Eleventh Aves), *T* (212) 604-9200. Closed Mon. High-end fashion designer Rei Kawakubo's boutique. Her pants, shirts, jackets, skirts, and dresses. *S* A, C to 23rd St

Eileen Fisher, 166 Fifth Ave (21st/22nd Sts), *T* (212) 924-4777, www.eileenfisher.com. Loose-fitting and comfortable, these designs flatter women of all ages. *S* N, R, W to 23rd St

Gerry's, 110 Eighth Ave (15th/16th Sts), *T* (212) 243-9141. Trendy shirts, track suits, and Cavalli jeans for him and her. *S* N, R, W, L, 4, 5, 6 to 14th St-Union Sq

Jeffrey New York, 449 West 14th St (Ninth/Tenth Aves), *T* (212) 206-1272. One of the hottest designer boutiques in Manhattan. Don't miss the shoes! *S* A, C, E, L to 14th St-Eighth Ave

Kenneth Cole, 95 Fifth Ave (16th/17th Sts), *T* (212) 675-2550, www.kennethcole.com. Sleek, urban shoes and bags for men and women, dependably stylish clothes. *S* N, R, W , L, 4, 5, 6 to 14th St-Union Sq

Paul Smith, 108 Fifth Ave (15th/16th Sts), *T* (212) 627-9770, www.paulsmith.co.uk. British menswear with pizzazz. *S* N, R, W , L, 4, 5, 6 to 14th St-Union Sq

Parke & Ronen, 176 Ninth Ave (20th/21st Sts), *T* (212) 989-4245; www.parkeandronen.com. Neighborhood boutique with stylish basics for men and women. *S* A, C to 23rd St

Stella McCartney, 429 West 14th St (Ninth/Tenth Aves), *T* (212) 255-1556, www.stellamccartney.com. Young women worldwide were banging down the doors while Stella McCartney was at Chloé and now she's out on her own. *S* A, C, E, L to 14th St-Eighth Ave

Weiss & Mahoney, 142 Fifth Ave (19th/20th Sts), *T* (212) 675-1915. Reproduction military gear. Jackets, hats, rough-and-tumble clothing from Carhaart. *S* N, R, W to 23rd St

CONSIGNMENT & VINTAGE

The Family Jewels, 130 West 23rd St (Sixth/Seventh Aves), *T* (212) 633-6020, www.familyjewelsnyc.com. Since 1980 has offered vintage clothing and accessories, all in excellent condition. *S* F to 23rd St

Rags-A-Go-Go, 218 West 14th St (Seventh/Eighth Aves), *T* (646) 486-4011, www.ragsagogo.com. Secondhand clothing at great prices. *S* A, C, E, L to 14th St-Eighth Ave

Reminiscence, 50 West 23rd St (Fifth/Sixth Aves), *T* (212) 243-2292, www.reminiscence.com. Reasonably priced boas, poodle skirts, shoes, lunch boxes, and more. *S* N, R, W to 23rd St

DISCOUNT CLOTHING

Daffy's, 111 Fifth Ave (18th/19th Sts), **T** (212) 529-4477, www.daffys.com. Discount chain, clothes for men, women, and kids. Wide selection, especially underwear, shoes. **S** N, R, W, L, 4, 5, 6 to 14th St-Union Sq

Find Outlet, 361 West 17th St (Eighth/Ninth Aves), **T** (212) 243-3177. Thurs-Sun 12-7. Closed Mon-Wed. A small selection of trendy designer clothes for young women, at about half price. **S** 1, 2 to 18th St

Loehmann's, 101 Seventh Ave (16th/17th Sts), **T** (212) 352-0856, www.loehmanns.com. Five floors of clothing for men and women; accessories, swimwear, evening wear, designer finds. **S** 1, 2 to 18th St

FLOWERS & GARDENS

Chelsea Wholesale Flower Market, 75 Ninth Ave (15th/16th Sts), **T** (212) 620-7500, www.chelseaflowersny.com. One of New York's hidden treasures, open to everyone. Quality fresh flowers. Plants, too. **S** A, C, E, L to 14th St-Eighth Ave

Prudence Design, 228 West 18th St (Seventh/Eighth Aves), **T** (212) 691-1541, www.prudencedesigns.net. Closed Sun. Tiny shop; gorgeous arrangements in clever containers. **S** 1, 2 to 18th St

HEALTH & BEAUTY

Jo Malone, 949 Broadway (22nd/23rd Sts), **T** (212) 673-2220, www.jomalone.co.uk. Beautiful fragrances created with avocado, aloe, apricot, eucalyptus, mint, and other natural ingredients. **S** N, R, W to 23rd St

Origins, 175 Fifth Ave (22nd/23rd Sts), **T** (212) 677-9100, www.origins.com. Pamper yourself, from head to toe, with these light, gloriously-scented products. **S** N, R, W to 23rd St

Sephora, 119 Fifth Ave (19th/20th Sts), **T** (212) 674-3570, www.sephora.com. Perfume from around the world, cosmetics, many top-of-the-line companies. **S** N, R, W to 23rd St

HOUSEWARES

ABC Carpet & Home, 881 & 888 Broadway (18th/19th Sts), **T** (212) 473-3000, www.abchome.com. Open until 8 weekdays. Renowned for their selection of high-end carpets and rugs, also fine home products from European makers. **S** N, R, W to 23rd St

Bodum, 413-415 West 14th St (Ninth/Tenth Aves), *T* (212) 367-9125, www.bodum.com. Colorful, modern products for the kitchen; many coffee-related items. *S* A, C, E, L to 14th St-Eighth Ave

La Cafetière, 160 Ninth Ave (19th/20th Sts), *T* (646) 486-0667. Closed Mon. French accessories for the kitchen and the home. *S* A, C to 23rd St

Details, 142 Eighth Ave (16th/17th Sts), *T* (212) 366-9498. Open late. Funky, fun items for the home, especially the bathroom. Shower curtains, towels, soaps, and more. *S* A, C, E, L to 14th St-Eighth Ave

Fishs Eddy, 889 Broadway (18th/19th Sts), *T* (212) 420-9020, www.fishseddy.com. Tableware to brighten any home at great prices. Patterns range from colorful fruits and vegetables to baseball equipment to black-and-white Eiffel Towers. *S* N, R, W to 23rd St

Jensen-Lewis, 89 Seventh Ave (15th/16th Sts), *T* (212) 929-4880, www.jensen-lewis.com. Stylish, contemporary furniture, tables, lamps, mirrors, and unique wine racks. *S* 1, 2, 3, F, V, L to 14th St

New York Cake & Baking Supply, 56 West 22nd St (Fifth/Sixth Aves), *T* (212) 675-2253. Closed Sun. Molds, serving platters, decorating kits, edible toppings (including lifelike flowers made of sugar), cookie cutters, fillings, utensils, cookbooks, and much more. *S* F to 23rd St

MUSIC

Academy Records & CDs, 12 West 18th St (Fifth/Sixth Aves), *T* (212) 242-3000, www.academy-records.com. CDs and vinyl for jazz and classical lovers. *S* 1, 2, 3, F, V, L to 14th St

Jazz Record Center, 236 West 26th St (Seventh/Eighth Aves), Room 803, *T* (212) 675-4880, www.jazzrecordcenter.com. Closed Sun. Rare and out-of-print CDs, DVDs, videos, and books. *S* 1, 9 to 28th St

POSTERS

Carrandi Gallery, 138 West 18th St (Sixth/Seventh Aves), *T* (212) 206-0499. Closed Sun and Mon. Specializes in vintage prints from the 1890s to the 1940s. *S* 1, 2 to 18th St

Chisholm Larsson Gallery, 145 Eighth Ave (17th/18th Sts), *T* (212) 741-1703, www.chisholm-poster.com. Closed Mon. Collectible, high-end, foreign-movie and vintage advertisement posters. *S* A, C, E, L to 14th St-Eighth Ave

J. Fields Gallery, 55 West 17th St (Fifth/Sixth Aves), sixth Floor, *T* (212) 337-0162, www.avidcollectorposters.com. Closed Sun. Original film posters as well as restoration services. *S* 1, 2 to 18th St

Jerry Ohlinger's Movie Material Store, Inc., 242 West 14th St (Seventh/Eighth Aves), *T* (212) 989-0869, www.moviematerials.com. Daily 1-7.45. Movie buffs will enjoy flipping through binders of posters and chatting with knowledgeable staff. *S* A, C, E, L to 14th St-Eighth Ave

Movie Star News, 134 West 18th St (6th/7th Aves), *T* (212) 620-8160, www.moviestarnews.com. Closed Sun. Movie posters from your favorite films, whether from the 1970s or last month. The posters here are reproductions and prices are reasonable. *S* 1, 2 to 18th St

SHOES

Giraudon New York, 152 Eighth Ave (16th/17th Sts), *T* (212) 633-0999, www.giraudonnewyork.com. Open late Mon, Tues, Fri, Sat. Shoes for men and women that appear way too stylish to be so comfortable. *S* A, C, E, L to 14th St-Eighth Ave.

Medici, 24 West 23rd St (Fifth/Sixth Aves), *T* (212) 604-0888. The perfect place to find *the* pair of the season. For young, trendy females only. *S* N, R, W to 23rd St

Sacco, 94 Seventh Ave (15th/16th Sts), *T* (212) 675-5180 and 14 East 17th St (Fifth Ave/Broadway), *T* (212) 243-2070, www.saccoshoes.com. Designer styles, affordable price tags. *S* 1, 2, 3, F, V, L to 14th St

Skechers, 150 Fifth Ave (19th/20th Sts), *T* (212) 627-9420, www.skechers.com. Comfortable, trendy sneakers, boots and other shoe styles for men and women. *S* N, R, W , L, 4, 5, 6 to 14th St-Union Sq

SPECIALTY

Abracadabra, 19 West 21st St (Fifth/Sixth Aves), *T* (212) 627-5194, www.abracadabrasuperstore.com. Magic and costume warehouse; an unbelievable selection of masks. *S* N, R, W to 23rd St

Beads of Paradise, 16 East 17th St (Fifth Ave/Broadway), *T* (212) 620-0642. Daily, from 11-7:30. Beautiful beads in all colors, shapes and sizes. Worth a look, whether you're creating something new or are simply looking to restring your own old beads. *S* N, R, W , L, 4, 5, 6 to 14th St-Union Square

SOHO

The New Museum of Contemporary Art

OPEN	Tues-Sun 12-6, Thurs 12-8
CLOSED	Mon, Jan 1, Thanksgiving, Dec 25; store open on Mon
CHARGES	$6.00 general; $3.00 students, seniors, and Thurs from 6 pm-8 pm. Free for visitors 18 and under. Media Lounge always free during museum hours
TELEPHONE	(212) 219-1222
WWW.	**newmuseum.org**
MAIN ENTRANCE	583 Broadway (Houston/Prince Sts)
SUBWAY	6 train to Spring St or Bleecker St; NR to Prince St; C or E to Spring St; F or S to Broadway/Lafayette
SHOPS	Shop with books and limited-edition prints, catalogues, arty T-shirts, hats

Lectures, visitors' programs, seminars, publications, catalogues. No café.

Founded in 1977 by Marcia Tucker, formerly a curator of painting and sculpture at the Whitney Museum of American Art, the New Museum of Contemporary Art is a major venue for contemporary art in the city and the only institution with a gallery specifically devoted to new media. Tucker believed that art cannot be separated from its political and social contexts, so the art on view here usually has a statement to make. It's no surprise that it was the first institution in the city to show such now-established names as Jenny Holzer and David Hammons. It also gave major solo shows early on to Martin Puryear, John Baldessari, and Leon Golub, whose work has entered the collections of major institutions.

THE BUILDING

The museum is presently located in a landmarked cast-iron building, dating from 1896, designed by the firm of Cleverdon & Putzel for John Jacob Astor, whose fortune owed a great deal to speculation in New York real estate. However, in the next few years the museum hopes to move to a new and larger building on the Bowery, the city's historic Skid Row, between Rivington and Stanton Sts. The architects Kazuyo Sejima and Ryue Nishizawa of Tokyo were chosen in a limited competition to design the new building, which is expected to open at the end of 2005.

THE COLLECTION

The permanent collection is far from the most important thing about the New Museum; in fact, you can't count on seeing any of it when you visit.

Throughout most of its 25-year history, the museum kept itself at the cutting edge by means of a semi-permanent collection of works that were acquired and then sold after a specified time period. In 2000 the museum received, as a gift, the **Altoids Curiously Strong Collection**, which had been started in 1998. Every year the company that makes the famous mints, invites a group of artists, curators, dealers, and other professionals to suggest emerging artists whose work is "curious," "strong," and "original." The search committee then chooses about 20 new works, which are eventually donated to the New Museum, another tactic to keep the museum up-to-date.

José Antonio Hernández-Diez
Marx (2000)

EXHIBITION PROGRAM

The exhibition program is at the heart of the New Museum's activities. The museum's first exhibition (1977) explored early work of several artists whose careers were clearly established, but the New Museum really appeared on the artworld's radar screen with a show called **"Bad" Art** (1978). The show

Carroll Dunham *The Sun* (1999)

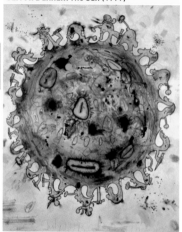

included work by Neil Jenney, William Wegman, and others showcasing work that mixed kitsch with traditional images, and personal fantasies with bits and pieces from "high" and "low" culture. In **The Living Paintings** show (1988) three spray-painted artists hung from their own paintings six hours a day and discussed art with gallery goers. For a period of seven years, performance artist Linda Montano, appeared in the Mercer Street Window on specified dates to discuss life and art with museum visitors. Montano was a sculptor and former nun perhaps best-known at the time for having been tied by a rope to another artist for a year without the two touching one another.

More recent exhibitions of note have included the first major museum survey (2003) of the paintings of the now-influential Carroll Dunham, who began painting colorful abstract blobs and bleeps in the 1980s and morphed into doing cartoonish paintings, often of an eyeless box-headed man with a stovepipe hat and a grimace of rage. More bizarre, surely, was Belgian artist's Wim Delvoye's *Cloaca* (2002), a much-larger-than-life contraption that recreated the human digestive system. It was built from laboratory glassware, electric pumps, plastic tubing, a computer and glass jars with the necessary digestive acids and micro-organisms. It "ate" food supplied by several restaurants, digested it, and converted it into feces. Gastroenterologists, computer scientists and engineers collaborated in creating this extraordinary piece of technology.

on route

Artists Space, 38 Greene St (corner Grand St), third floor. **T** (212) 226-3970, www.artistsspace.org. One of New York's most venerable (1977) not-for-profit art spaces, where thousands of young artists have gotten a helping hand. Some recent highly regarded exhibitions have had an international focus; other exhibitions have been entertaining, subversive, or wacky. Occasionally there's an Artists Selects show, in which an established artist selects the work of an unknown. Tues-Sat 11-6. **S** C, E to Spring St; J, M, N, R, W, 6, 1, 9 to Canal St

Bishop's Crook Lamppost, in front of 515 Broadway (near Spring St). The city used to have thousands of these lampposts, decorated with tendrils, acanthus leaves (the kind on Corinthian columns) and scroll work. Fewer than 50 originals remain. They were designed by Richard Rodgers Bowker and introduced around 1896. **S** N, R, W to Prince St

Broken Kilometer, 393 West Broadway (Spring/Broome Sts), mid-Sept until mid-June, Wed-Sun, noon-6 pm (closed 3-3:30 pm). Closed in summer. This 18.75-ton work of Conceptual art by Walter De Maria consists of 500 polished brass rods, each 2 meters long, laid out in 5 parallel rows of 100 rods each. The spaces between the rows increase by increments of 5mm. The work is a companion piece to De Maria's 1977 *Vertical Earth Kilometer* at Kassel, Germany, a brass rod inserted 1000 meters into the ground. *Broken Kilometer* has been on view since 1979 and was commissioned by the Dia Center for the Arts (see Chelsea). **S** A, C, E to Canal St

Cast-Iron Architecture, everywhere in SoHo. In 1973, 26 blocks of the neighborhood were designated a Historic District to protect the cast-iron architecture, until then considered expendable. These buildings have masonry cores but are clad with cast-iron façades designed to imitate marble or limestone. Any kind of decoration - fluted Corinthian columns, floral swags, scrolls, even blocks of stone - could be cast from iron, then bolted onto the fronts of buildings, and painted to look like stone.

Dean & DeLuca, 560 Broadway (Prince St). **T** (212) 431-1691, www.deandeluca.com. One of the city's most famous and opulent gourmet stores, a long-term SoHo resident. Gorgeous food at extravagant prices. **S** N, R, W to Prince St

The Drawing Center, 35 Wooster St (Broome/Grand Sts), Tues-Fri 10-6,

SoHo sidewalk and building art

Sat 11-6. Closed Sun, Mon, holidays, Aug. *T* (212) 219-2166, www.drawingcenter.org. The nation's only not-for-profit institution to focus on drawing as a major art form; historical and contemporary shows of great interest and quality. *S* N, R, W, J, M, Z, 6, A, C, E, 1, 9 to Canal St

Grey Art Gallery, 100 Washington Square East (Washington Sq), closed Sun, Mon, part of summer. *T* (212) 998-6780, www.nyu.edu/greyart. New York University's exhibition space. Intelligent, sometimes offbeat, changing exhibitions; permanent collection focuses on American painting from 1940 to the present, contemporary Asian and Middle Eastern Art. *S* A, C, E, F, V, S to West Fourth St; N, R to Eighth St; 6 to Astor Pl; 1, 9 to Christopher St

The New York Earth Room, 141 Wooster St (Houston/Prince Sts), Wed-Sun, noon-6 pm (but closed 3-3:30 pm); closed in summer. Walter De Maria's only surviving Earth Room; its German predecessors in Munich and Darmstadt have long since been dug up and carted away. The Earth Room consists of 250 cubic yards (140 tons) of moist earth covering the gallery floor to a depth of 22 inches. It has been on view since 1980, commissioned by the Dia Center for the Arts (see Chelsea). *S* F, V, S to Broadway-Lafayette St; N, R, W to Prince St

Prada Store, 575 Broadway (Prince St), *T* (212) 324-8888. This store opened (2001) in the space formerly occupied by the Guggenheim's SoHo branch, redesigned by Rem Koolhaas. If you're not in the market for wearables, you can ride up and down in the glass elevator and admire the architecture. *S* N, R, W to Prince St

Swiss Institute, 495 Broadway (Spring/Broome Sts), third floor, Tues-Sat 11-6. *T* (212) 925-2035. Swiss culture in the USA, art exhibitions, also jazz and classical concerts, lectures and readings, dance performances, film and video screenings. *S* J, M, N, Q, R, W, Z, 6 to Canal St

commercial galleries

For three decades, SoHo was where it happened, the center of everything new and exciting in contemporary art. That has changed. It has become apparent that in real estate, art is quickly followed by commerce. Back in the early 1990s an influx of expensive stores and boutiques pushed SoHo rents upward, but chain stores and less chic establishments followed, depressing the area's cachet quotient. Galleries have moved out, many of them to Chelsea. Several museums and alternative art spaces have also departed. Where once you could buy art, you can now buy accessories. This does not mean, however, that a day in SoHo is a day without art.

 Most galleries are open Tuesday-Saturday from 10 or 11 until 5-6. In the summer they are open only on weekdays and some close in August.

Janet Borden Gallery, 560 Broadway (Prince St), *T* (212) 431-0166, wwww.janetbordeninc.com. Veteran SoHo gallery shows contemporary photography: Jan Groover, Sandy Skoglund, Lee Friedlander, Oliver Wassow. *S* 6 to Spring St

Deitch Projects, 76 Grand St (Wooster/Greene Sts), *T* (212) 343-7300. An old-timer but young in spirit, consistently innovative. Regular exhibits of art stars; a second space at 18 Wooster St for performance art, installations. One of the best. **S** A, C, E, J, M, Z, N, R, W, or 6 to Canal St

Gallery 292, 120 Wooster St (Spring/Prince Sts), **T** (212) 431-0292, www.gallery292.com. 20c and contemporary photography, rare photography books. Chris Steele-Perkins' photojournalistic studies of 1950s' British teddy-boys were a hit in 2003. **S** N, R, W to Prince St

Susan Inglett, 100 Wooster St (Spring/ Prince Sts), **T** (212) 343-0573. Conceptualists, Minimalists and contemporary artists include Dan Asher, Robin Kahn, Annette Lemiux, Sol LeWitt, Erika Rothenberg, Allan Ruppersburg, Lawrence Weiner and others. **S** N, R, W to Prince St

Phyllis Kind, 136 Greene St (Houston/Prince Sts), **T** (212) 925-1200. www.phylliskindgallery.com. In SoHo for more than 30 years, the gallery emphasizes Art Brut, outsider art and the work of self-taught artists or those in these traditions. Shows Robert Colescott, Alison Saar, Howard Finster, Russell Gillespie. **S** B, D, F, Q to Broadway-Lafayette; N, R, W to Prince St; 6 to Bleecker St

Nolan/Eckman, 560 Broadway (at Prince St), sixth floor, **T** (212) 925-6190. Small, well-respected gallery shows emphasizes works on paper by contemporary American and European artists. **S** N, R, W to Prince St; 6 to Spring St

eating and drinking

AT THE MUSEUMS

The museums in SoHo do not have restaurants or cafés.

SURROUNDING AREA

$ **Baluchi's**, 193 Spring St (Sullivan/Thompson Sts), **T** (212) 226-2828. Moderately priced chain of restaurants serving good North Indian food. **S** C, E to Spring St

Biny, 8 Thompson St (Canal St), **T** (212) 334-5490. Japanese food, sushi, and karaoke after 10pm. Sushi, shashimi, noodles, teriyaki. Also take out. **S** A, C, E to Canal St

Ear Inn, 326 Spring St (Greenwich/Washington Sts), **T** (212) 226-9060. One of the city's oldest bars; good bar food, burgers, chowder, other simple fare. **S** 1, 9 to Canal St; C, E, to Spring St

Le Gamin, 132 West Houston St (MacDougal/Sullivan Sts), **T** (212) 673-4592. Sandwiches, salads, and especially crepes at this café; other locations. Open for breakfast. Cash only. **S** 1, 9 to Houston St

Hampton Chutney, 68 Prince St (Crosby/Lafayette Sts), **T** (212) 226-9996. Tiny restaurant serving dosas, Indian flat breads filled with traditional Indian and updated stuffings. The name comes from the Long Island Hamptons where the owners have another restaurant. **S** F, S, V to Broadway-Lafayette St

Hoomoos Asli, 100 Kenmare St (Lafayette St), **T** (212) 966-0022. Very small basic eatery serving kosher Israeli food, fresh salads, hummus, falafel, other Middle Eastern specialties. Cash only. Open late. **S** 6 to Spring St

Housing Works Used Book Café, 126 Crosby St (Houston/Prince Sts), **T** (212) 334-3324. Sandwich spot with soups, baked goods. The profits go to Housing Works, a charity for homeless people with HIV. Beer and wine with the books. Open for breakfast if you eat at 10am. **S** 6 to Bleecker St; N, R, W to Prince St; F, V, S, to Broadway-Lafayette St

Kelley and Ping, 127 Greene St (Houston/Prince Sts), **T** (212) 228-1212. Noodle shop and retail store (Asian groceries) with cafeteria-style service. **S** N, R, W to Prince St; 6 to Spring St; F, V, S to Broadway-Lafayette St

Lombardi's, 32 Spring St (Mott/Mulberry Sts), **T** (212) 941-7994. Slightly east of SoHo. A classic coal-burning-brick-oven pizzeria (claims to be America's oldest) that turns out the genuine thin-crust article. No surprise that it's busy. Grab a seat on the breezy deck on hot summer days. Cash only. **S** 6 to Spring St

Spring Street Natural, 62 Spring St (Lafayette St), **T** (212) 966-0290. Vegetarian plus some fish and poultry dishes. Good soups, salads, and sandwiches. Woodsy atmosphere. Open late weekends. **S** 6 to Spring St

$$ **Bistro Les Amis**, 180 Spring St (at Thompson St), **T** (212) 226-8645. Cozy corner café with fair prices and good food. In nice weather, choose one of the sidewalk tables. Thanks to the waitresses' thick accents you'll think you're in Paris rather than SoHo. Open late. Brunch on weekends. **S** C, E to Spring St

Blue Ribbon, 97 Sullivan St (Prince/Spring Sts), *T* (212) 274-0404. Eclectic bistro with excellent food; busy and noisy, but open until 4am and known for attracting famous chefs on the way home. Includes vegetarian dishes. Not open for lunch. *S* C, E to Spring St

Blue Ribbon Sushi, 119 Sullivan St (Prince/Spring Sts), *T* (212) 343-0404. Japanese avatar of Blue Ribbon family of restaurants. (The original Blue Ribbon in SoHo, the eclectic Blue Ribbon Bakery in Greenwich Village and a Brooklyn version in Park Slope.) Good sushi, beautiful décor, no reservations, crowded. *S* C, E to Spring St

Canteen, 142 Mercer St (Prince St), *T* (212) 431-7676. Open late Thurs-Sat. Big space down under Prada, with high tech décor and good upscale comfort food. Good people-watching for the see-and-be-seen crowd. Sister establishment to MercBar across the street (see Bars). *S* N, R, to Prince St

Country Café, 69 Thompson St (Broome/Spring Sts), *T* (212) 966-5417. Small, established Moroccan-French place. Casual atmosphere, lunch specials. *S* C, E to Spring St

The Cupping Room Café, 359 West Broadway (Broome/Grand Sts), *T* (212) 925-2898. Pleasant SoHo old timer serves up goodly portions of reliable food. Opens early (think breakfast), stays open late. *S* A, C, E to Canal St

Ideya, 349 West Broadway (Broome/Grand Sts), *T* (212) 625-1441. Head here for a caipirinha or mojito. Caribbean and South American food and drinks, Brazilian jazz and salsa bands. *S* A, C, E or 1, 9 to Canal St

Herban Kitchen, 290 Hudson St (Spring St), *T* (212) 627-2257. Organic food highlights seasonal cooking, including many vegetarian specialties in attractive, simple setting. *S* C, E to Spring St; 1, 9 to Canal St

Jerry's, 101 Prince St (Greene/Mercer Sts), *T* (212) 966-9464. Popular and convenient; good American comfort food has kept this restaurant going through the ups and downs of SoHo. Opens at 9am on weekdays. *S* N, R, W to Prince St

La Jumelle, 55 Grand St (West Broadway/Wooster St), *T* (212) 941-9651. Belgian-French bistro food at reasonable prices. Stripped down menu with comfortable favorites. Open late. *S* A, C, E, N, R, W to Canal St

Kin Khao, 171 Spring St (Thompson St/West Broadway), *T* (212) 966-3939. Trendy Thai, with some of the gloss worn off. *S* C, E to Spring St

Lucky Strike, 59 Grand St (West Broadway/Wooster St), *T* (212) 941-0772. Not as hot as formerly, but still crowded and still reliable for bistro food and a late night bite. *S* A, C, E to Canal St

Lupa, 170 Thompson St (Bleecker/Houston Sts), *T* (212) 982-5089. Just north of the border (i.e. Houston St). Immensely popular trattoria with excellent food and convivial atmosphere. *S* A, C, E, V, S, F to West Fourth St

Woo Lae Oak, 148 Mercer St (Houston/Prince Sts), *T* (212) 925-8200. Attractive reincarnation of midtown Korean restaurant that burned in 1994; smokeless grill, creative cooking. *S* N, R, W to Prince St; 6 to Bleecker St

$$$ Aquagrill, 210 Spring St (Sixth Ave), *T* (212) 274-0505. Stellar SoHo seafood; with raw bar. Good service. Reserve early or arrive late. Closed Mondays. Good brunch on weekends. *S* C, E to Spring St

Balthazar, 80 Spring St (Broadway/Crosby St), *T* (212) 9675-1414. A favorite with beautiful people and ordinary mortals. Very good brasserie food, noisy bar scene, great brunch on weekends and even breakfast during the week. *S* N, R, W to Prince St

Downtown Cipriani, 376 West Broadway (Broome/Spring Sts), *T* (212) 343-0999. It's see-and-be-seen for celebs and other movers and shakers at Harry Cipriani's SoHo counterpart. The menu is a little less formal here than at the flagship uptown rendition in the Sherry Netherland Hotel, but you can count on the same consistent continental fare. Open for lunch and late-night dinner. Outdoor seating in nice weather. *S* C, E to Spring St

Fiamma Osteria, 206 Spring St (Sullivan St/Sixth Ave), *T* (212) 653-0100. Two-level townhouse restaurant with fine Italian food. Long wine list. Closed Mondays. *S* C, E, to Spring St

Honmura An, 170 Mercer St (Houston/Prince Sts), *T* (212) 334-5253. Serene upscale Japanese noodle restaurant. The specialty is soba (buckwheat noodles) but there are also other kinds of noodle dishes, duck, fish, and shrimp. Not to mention sake. Closed Mon. No lunch Tues. *S* F, S, V to Broadway-Lafayette St; N, R, W to Prince St; 6 to Bleecker St

Mercer Kitchen, 99 Prince Street (Mercer/Greene Sts), *T* (212) 966-5454. Jean-George Vongerichten's downtown outpost. Though A-listers have moved on, fans still come for the consistently good Provençal-inspired fare. Breakfast daily, weekend brunch. Open late. *S* N, R, W to Prince

Savore, 200 Spring St (Sullivan St), **T** (212) 431-1212. Sophisticated northern Italian in elegant setting. Many daily specials. **S** C, E to Spring St

Zoë, 90 Prince St (Mercer St/Broadway), **T** (212) 966-6722. Updated American food with hints of the Pacific rim. Handsome large dining room (can be noisy), long wine list. Bar has good drinks, snacks, and bar food. **S** N, R, W to Prince St

BARS

Biny, 8 Thompson St (Grand/Canal Sts), **T** (212) 334-5490. Restaurant with karaoke bar after 10pm. **S** A, C, E to Canal St

Bar 89, 89 Mercer St (Broome/Spring Sts), **T** (212) 532-0989. Come to admire the bathrooms, whose glass stall doors become cloudy when you latch the door. Good bar food. Expensive drinks. **S** N, R, W to Spring St

Broome St Bar, 363 West Broadway (Broome St), **T** (212) 925-2086. Beer-and-burger bar has survived the ups and downs of SoHo. **S** C, E to Spring St

Ear Inn, 326 Spring St (Greenwich/Washington Sts), **T** (212) 226-9060. Some say it's New York's oldest bar. The neon window sign used to read "Bar" but the "B" got broken. See also Eating, p 153

Fanelli, 94 Prince St (corner of Mercer St), **T** (212) 226-9412. One of SoHo's (and the city's) oldest, harking back to 1872, when the neighborhood was industrial. Casual pub with good bar food. **S** N, R, W to Prince St

Grand Bar & Lounge, in the SoHo Grand Hotel, 310 West Broadway (Canal/Grand Sts), **T** (212) 965-3000. Elegant, expensive, beautifully designed; unsurprisingly, it attracts beautiful people. **S** A, C, E or 1, 9 to Canal St

MercBar, 151 Mercer Street (Houston/Prince Sts), **T** (212) 966-2727. Laid-back hunting-lodge atmosphere for the downtown crowd. **S** N, R, W to Prince St

Naked Lunch, 17 Thompson St (Grand Street), **T** (212) 343-0828. Club-bar with a Moroccan vibe. It has nothing to do with the Burroughs novel, but well-dressed yuppie types come here to meet more of the same. **S** A, C, E to Canal

Pravda, 281 Lafayette St (Houston/Prince Sts), **T** (212) 226-4696. Dozens of vodka varieties, plus great Russian appetizers including blini, zakouski, and caviar. **S** N, R, W to Prince St

Sway, 305 Spring St (Greenwich/Hudson Sts), **T** (212) 620-5220. Lounge with good sound system, comfortable couches, Moroccan décor. Open until 4am. **S** 1, 9 to Canal St; C, E to Spring St

Thom, 60 Thompson St, in 60 Thompson Hotel, **T** (212) 219-2000. Second-floor lounge with two large rooms, fireplace. Good appetizers. There's a restaurant next door but the bar's a better bet. **S** C, E to Spring St

V Bar & Café, 225 Sullivan Street (Bleecker/W. 3rd Sts), **T** (212) 253-5740. A little further afield (try it on your way north to the Gray Gallery) is this neighborhood favorite. Sandwich café by day, cozy wine bar at night. Good selection of wines by the glass. **S** A, C, E; B, D, F, V, S to W. 4th St

Void, 16 Mercer St (Howard St), **T** (212) 941-6492. Multimedia lounge tucked away at the southeast corner of SoHo. Draws graphic designers, computer types, the electronic music set. Online access, video. Cash only. **S** J, M, Z, N, Q, R, W, or 6 to Canal St

shopping

SoHo - Manhattan between Houston and Canal Sts, from Sixth Ave to Lafayette St - is a shopper's paradise. The old, narrow streets are lined with boutiques of the city's hottest designers. Spend an afternoon scoping out the clothing, beauty products, housewares, and jewelry. If you don't have a lot of time, stroll along Prince and Spring Sts to get the flavor of the area. Many shops are open Sunday afternoons.

ACCESSORIES

Anya Hindmarch, 115 Greene St (Spring/Prince Sts), **T** (212) 343-8147; www.anyahindmarch.com. One of the hottest designers in handbags today, classic leather totes. **S** N, R, W to Prince St

Il Bisonte, 120 Sullivan St (Spring/Prince Sts), **T** (212) 966-8773, www.ilbisonte.com. Chic Italian leather bags. **S** C, E to Spring St

Girlprops.com, 153 Prince St (Thompson St/West Broadway), *T* (212) 505-7615, www.girlprops.com. Inexpensive, irresistible accessories. Rings, necklaces, barrettes, bags. *S* C, E to Spring St

The Hat Shop, 120 Thompson St (Spring/Prince Sts), *T* (212) 219-1445, www.hatny.com. All shapes, styles, fabrics, and colors. *S* C, E to Spring St

Kate Spade, 454 Broome St (Greene/Mercer Sts), *T* (212) 274-1991, www.katespade.com. The undisputed queen of the classy nylon tote. Second shop around the corner (59 Thompson St) carries luggage and paper products. *S* N, R, W to Prince St

Morgenthal-Frederics, 399 West Broadway (Broome/Spring Sts), *T* (212) 966-0099, www.morgenthal-fredericsny.com. The latest in eyeglass frames, on-site optician. *S* C, E to Spring St

Tag Heuer SoHo Boutique, 422 West Broadway (Spring/Prince Sts), *T* (212) 965-5304, www.tagheuer.com. Expensive Swiss watches since 1860. *S* C, E to Spring St

BOOKS

Housing Works Used Book Café, 126 Crosby St (Prince/Houston Sts), *T* (212) 334-3324, www.housingworksubc.com. Well-stocked used book store and café with current titles and older editions. Your money will benefit Housing Works, an HIV/AIDS advocacy organization active in New York City. *S* 6 to Spring St

CLOTHING

Anna Sui, 113 Greene St (Spring/Prince Sts), *T* (212) 941-8406, www.annasuibeauty.com. Street-smart women's clothes with an Asian flare. Handbags, shoes, and cosmetics, too. *S* N, R, W to Prince St

Beau Brummel, 421 West Broadway (Spring/Prince Sts), *T* (212) 219-2666, www.beaubrummel.com. High-end Italian suits for men. *S* C, E to Spring St

Big Drop, 174 Spring St (Thompson St/West Broadway), *T* (212) 966-4299. Also 425 West Broadway (Spring/Prince Sts), *T* (212) 226-9292. These boutiques cater to well-off young women; the latest from designers like Rebecca Taylor and Seven Jeans. *S* C, E to Spring St

Catherine Malandrino, 468 Broome St (Greene/Mercer Sts), *T* (212) 925-6765, www.catherinemalandrino.com. Upscale, feminine pieces for celebrity drop-ins and mere mortals alike. *S* N, R, W to Prince St

Cynthia Rowley, 112 Wooster St (Spring/Prince Sts), *T* (212) 334-1144, www.cynthiarowley.com. Flirty but tasteful designs, with appealing accents of beads, ruffles, or fabric trim. *S* N, R, W to Prince St

D&G, 434 West Broadway (Spring/Prince Sts), *T* (212) 965-8000, www.dolceandgabbana.it. Young trendsetters will fawn over Dolce & Gabbana's less expensive designs. *S* C, E to Spring St

H&M, 558 Broadway (Spring/Prince Sts), *T* (212) 343-0220, www.hm.com. This Swedish store has taken New York by storm. Trendy, inexpensive fashions for both sexes. *S* N, R, W to Prince St

John Varvatos, 149 Mercer St (Prince/Houston Sts), *T* (212) 965-0700, www.johnvarvatos.com. Stylish suits and casual wear. Jimmy Fallon of "Saturday Night Live" was spotted sitting in the front row of this designer's show. *S* N, R, W to Prince St

Laundry by Shelli Segal, 97 Wooster St (Spring/Prince Sts), *T* (212) 334-9433. Basics with that extra something. Great dresses. *S* N, R, W to Prince St

Marc Jacobs, 163 Mercer St (Prince/West Houston Sts), *T* (212) 343-1490, www.marcjacobs.com. High-end, casual designs for women and men that almost make you believe that looking good is effortless. Shoes, too. *S* N, R, W to Prince St

Marianne Novobatzky Couture, 65 Mercer St (Broome/Spring Sts), *T* (212) 431-4120. Closed Sun. Elegant, classic, expensive clothes. Any of these beautifully-made pieces can be tailored for a perfect fit. Exceptional jackets and gowns. *S* N, R, W to Prince St

Miu Miu, 100 Prince St (Mercer/Greene Sts), *T* (212) 334-5156, www.miumiu.it. Miuccia Prada's secondary line is a younger take on the original. Extraordinary coats and shoes. *S* N, R, W to Prince St

Nanette Lepore, 423 Broome St (Crosby/Lafayette Sts), *T* (212) 219-8265, www.nanettelepore.com. Lepore designs sets of pieces (top, skirt, pants, and dress) in coordinating fabrics. *S* 6 to Spring St

Phat Farm, 129 Prince St (West Broadway/Wooster Sts), *T* (212) 533-7428, www.phatfarm.com. Russell Simmons, rap music mogul, knows his stuff when it comes to street fashions. Hip-hop styles for men and women. Lots of shirts and sweatsuits. *S* N, R, W to Prince St

Triple Five Soul, 290 Lafayette St (Houston/Prince Sts), *T* (212) 431-2404, www.triple5soul.com. Skate gear and streetwear, all emblazoned with the "555" logo. *S* B, D, F, Q to Broadway-Lafayette

CONSIGNMENT & VINTAGE

Alice Underground, 481 Broadway (Grand/Broome Sts), *T* (212) 431-9067, www.aliceundergroundnyc.com. Vintage pants, t-shirts, and leather for men and women; formalwear. Reasonable prices. *S* N, R, W to Canal St

Eye Candy, 329 Lafayette St (Bleecker/Houston Sts), *T* (212) 343-4275. Tiny shop with vintage accessories. Lots of sparkly jewelry, bags and suitcases, gloves, boots, hats, and shoes. *S* 6 to Bleecker St

Ina, 101 Thompson St (Spring/Prince Sts), *T* (212) 941-4757. Nearly-new designer finds at less than half of the original price. Exceptional shoes by Prada, Celine, etc. *S* C, E to Spring St

Transfer International, 594 Broadway (Prince/West Houston Sts), Suite 1002, *T* (212) 941-5472, www.rag-nation.com. Current designer fashions as consignments; barely-worn top-of-the-line labels. *S* B, D, F, Q to Broadway-Lafayette St

HEALTH & BEAUTY

Armonie Naturali-Perlier/Kelemata, 436 West Broadway (Spring/Prince Sts), *T* (877) 737-5353, www.perlierusa.com. Great creams from Italy for body and the bath; many made with honey. *S* C, E to Spring St

H2O+, 460 West Broadway (Prince/West Houston Sts), *T* (212) 505-3223, www.h2oplus.com. Water-based beauty products that won't break the bank. Don't miss the Aquafirm line. *S* V, S, F, 6 to Houston St

Ricky's, 590 Broadway (Prince/West Houston Sts), *T* (212) 226-5552, www.rickys-nyc.com. Cosmetics superstore: hair products, totebags, wigs, hosiery, even photo developing. *S* V, S, F, 6 to Houston St

Shu Uemura, 121 Greene St (Prince/West Houston Sts), *T* (212) 979-5500, www.beauty.com. Great make-up, great packaging, 70 shades of eyeshadow, famous mascara. *S* N, R, W to Prince St

HOUSEWARES

The Apartment, 101 Crosby St (Spring/Prince Sts), *T* (212) 219-3661, www.theapt.com. Mon, Tues by appt. only; other days open afternoons. Everything, and they mean everything, is for sale in this store, which is designed to look like a fully-furnished apartment. *S* N, R, W to Prince St

Artemide Soho, 46 Greene St (Grand/Broome Sts), *T* (212) 925-1588, www.artemide.com. Closed Sun. Modern lamps for the office and home. **S** A, C, E to Canal St

Broadway Panhandler, 477 Broome St (Wooster/Greene Sts), **T** (212) 966-3434, www.broadwaypanhandler.com. High-end pots and pans at competitive prices. **S** A, C, E to Canal St

Cappellini Modern Age, 102 Wooster St (Spring/Prince Sts), **T** (212) 966-0669, www.cappellininewyork.com. Closed Sun. Modern designs in bright colors and prints. Chairs, lamps, couches, even cupboards. **S** N, R, W to Prince St

Global Table, 107 Sullivan St (Spring/Prince Sts), **T** (212) 431-5839, www.globaltable.com. Closed Mon. Brightly-colored tableware from around the globe. **S** C, E to Spring St

Kartell, 45 Greene St (Grand/Broome Sts), **T** (212) 966-6665, www.kartell.com. Closed Mon. Who would have thought that plastic furniture could look warm and welcoming? Pieces for the home and office. **S** A, C, E to Canal St

Rooms & Gardens, Inc., 7 Mercer St (Canal/Grand Sts), **T** (212) 431-1297, www.roomsandgardensantique.com. Closed Sun. Traditional French furniture from the 19c to 20c. **S** N, R, W to Canal St

JEWELRY

Fragments, 116 Prince St (Wooster/Greene Sts), **T** (212) 334-9588, www.fragments.com. The work of more than 40 designers; new, well-established, expensive, and moderate. **S** N, R, W to Prince St

Kokopelli, 152 Prince St (Thompson St/West Broadway), **T** (212) 925-4411. An impressive collection of Native American jewelry. One-of-a-kind pieces are priced to match. **S** N, R, W to Prince St

Versani, 152 Mercer St (Prince/Houston Sts), **T** (212) 941-9919, www.versani.com. Sterling silver designs at reasonable prices. Outstanding rings. **S** N, R, W to Prince St

SHOES

Camper, 125 Prince St (Wooster/Greene Sts), **T** (212) 358-1842, www.camper.es. This Spanish company makes comfortable shoes for men and women. Perfect for walking around all day and then heading out for the night. **S** N, R, W to Prince St

John Fluevog, 250 Mulberry St (Prince St), **T** (212) 431-4484, www.fluevog.com. On the eastern fringes of SoHo. Flaunt your fashion sense on casual Friday with this funky footwear. Moderately upscale shoes for men and women. **S** 6 to Spring St

Steve Madden, 540 Broadway (Prince/Spring Sts), **T** (212) 343-1800. www.stevemadden.com. Boots, strappy stilettos, platforms, and sneakers. **S** V, S, F to Broadway-Lafayette; 6 to Spring St; N, R, W to Prince St

Otto Tootsi Plohound, 413 West Broadway (Spring/Prince Sts), **T** (212) 925-8931.Uptown at 38 East 57th St, **T** (212) 231-3199. Great downtown shoe styles at upscale prices; men and women. **S** C, E to Spring St; N,R to Prince St

Sacco, 111 Thompson St (Prince/Spring Sts), **T** (212) 925-8010. www.saccoshoes.com. Stylish shoes and boots at comfortable prices. Designed for Sacco and crafted in Italy. **S** C, E to Spring St

Skechers, 530 Broadway (Spring St), **T** (212) 431-8803, www.skechers.com. Comfortable, affordable, stylish. Other locations. **S** 6 to Spring St

Stephane Kélian, 158 Mercer St (Prince/Houston Sts), **T** (212) 925-3077, www.stephane-kelian.fr. High-end leather shoes and boots for men and women. Loafers, gorgeous bags, too. **S** N, R, W to Prince St

SPECIALTY

Chess Forum, 219 Thompson St (Bleecker/West Third Sts), **T** (212) 475-2369, www.chessforum.com. Daily until midnight. Chess sets for the serious or playful personality; sets with pop culture themes (the Simpsons, the Wizard of Oz). **S** B, D, Q, F to Broadway-Lafayette St

Pearl Paint, 308 Canal St (Mercer St/Broadway), **T** (212) 431-7932, www.pearlpaint.com. Five floors of art supplies, willing and knowledgeable staff. **S** N, R, W to Canal St

Pop Shop, 292 Lafayette St (Houston/Prince Sts), **T** (212) 219-2784, www.haring.com. T-shirts, posters, towels, and baby clothes bearing the signature images Keith Haring, 1980s Pop artist. Profits benefit AIDS-related charities and children's organizations. **S** 6 to Bleecker St

THE MUSEUM
OF MODERN ART
IN QUEENS

The Museum of Modern Art (MoMA)

Until 2005, the Museum of Modern Art will remain at its temporary home in Long Island City, Queens (MoMA QNS), while its landmark building at 11 West 53rd St in Manhattan undergoes a major expansion and renovation. Thereafter the Queens facility will become storage and study space.

OPEN	Mon, Thurs, Sat, Sun 10–5; Fri 10-7:45
CLOSED	Tues, Wed, Jan 1, Thanksgiving, Dec 25
CHARGES	Adults $12; students (with current identification) and seniors (65 and older) $8.50; children under 16 accompanied by an adult free; Fri 4-7.45, pay what you wish
TELEPHONE	**(212) 708-9400**
WWW	**moma.org**
ENTRANCE	33rd Street at Queens Blvd, Long Island City
SUBWAY	7 *local* train to 33 St in Queens. The 7 express does not stop near MoMA QNS. E or V to 23 St/Ely Ave, Queens; follow the signs to the 7 local to 33 St. N or W train to Queensboro Plaza; transfer to the 7 local train to 33 St
BUS	From Manhattan, take the Q32 from Madison Ave (stops between 32nd and 59th Sts) to Queens Blvd/33rd St. Or take the Q60 from 60th St between First and Second Aves to Queens Blvd/33rd St Artlink shuttle service operates Sat and Sun 10-5 between Manhattan and several Queens museums. Catch the bus on West 53rd St between Fifth and Sixth Aves in Manhattan to MoMA QNS. A second Artlink bus travels from MoMA QNS to P.S.1 and other Queens cultural destinations. For further information call **(212) 708-9750** or visit www.queensartlink.org
SHOPS	Design store with books, contemporary products including desktop, tabletop, stationery, and toys. MoMA Design Stores, with a larger selection of furniture, lighting, and items in the museum's design collection, are located in Manhattan: in SoHo at 81 Spring St, **T (646) 613-1367** and in midtown at 44 West 53 St, **T (212) 767-1050**
EATING	Small café

The Museum of Modern Art in Queens

Changing exhibitions, lectures, gallery talks. Until 2005, MoMA's extensive film and media programs are screened at the Gramercy Theatre, 127 East 23rd St (Lexington Ave) in Manhattan: box office T (212) 777-4900.

The Museum of Modern Art (1929) has one of the world's greatest collections of late 19c-20c European and American painting and sculpture, as well as outstanding examples of film and media, photography, architecture and design, drawings, prints, and illustrated books.

THE BUILDING

In 2002, museum opened temporarily in the raw industrial space of a former stapler factory. Michael Maltzan, a Los Angeles-based architect designed the entrance lobby using angled ramps and jutting galleries. The exterior is bright blue stucco. On the roof, visible from the elevated subway, black panels display the letters MoMA, which come briefly into readable alignment as the train pulls into the station. The letters replace a stapler-shaped sign that for more than 30 years flashed the words, "Easy Loading," in glorious neon against the skyline. By coincidence, Jack Linsky, who made his fortune selling Swingline staplers, spent a lot of it on art. In 1982 he and his wife donated to the Metropolitan Museum a collection valued at about $90 million, now installed in galleries bearing the Linsky name.

THE COLLECTION

MoMA's permanent collection - 100,000 paintings, sculptures, drawings, prints, photographs, architectural models and drawings, and design objects, plus some 19,000 films and four million film stills - summarizes European and American art from the Post-Impressionist period of the late 19c through the mid-20c. The museum has world-famous examples of work by Cézanne, Seurat, Gauguin, and van Gogh. It has outstanding work by Picasso and Matisse (in fact many of the paintings and sculptures in the blockbuster "Matisse Picasso" exhibition of 2003 came from

MoMA's own holdings), as well as masterworks by Braque, and Mondrian. It is also one of the best places in the world to see the work of avant-garde American Abstract Expressionists, who were working in New York in the 1940s and 1950s.

For exhibition in its temporary space, the museum chose some 100 core works, which it felt represented the chronological and aesthetic range of its massive permanent collection. Highlights from this core group are rotated through the galleries in an informal manner so you can't be sure exactly what you will see when you arrive, but some of MoMA's most celebrated works will surely be on view. Here, as in the building on 53rd St, the collection is installed more or less chronologically, but because of the space restrictions of the temporary space, the art is telescoped, so that familiar masterworks hang near recent creations by artists born in the mid- to late-20c.

HIGHLIGHTS

Paul Cézanne, *The Bather*

Vincent van Gogh, *The Starry Night, The Olive Trees*

Henri Rousseau, *The Dream, The Sleeping Gypsy*

Piet Mondrian, *Broadway Boogie Woogie*

René Magritte, *The False Mirror*

Jackson Pollock, *One (Number 31, 1950)*

Andy Warhol, *Gold Marilyn Monroe*

Picasso's **Les Demoiselles d'Avignon**, one of MoMA's most famous painting, is undergoing conservation work and will not be on display until 2005.

Among the museum's trademark masterpieces are **Paul Cézanne**'s early painting, *The Bather* (c 1885). Cézanne was shy, a man with so many 19c inhibitions that he rarely worked directly from a nude model. Since he insisted that his portrait subjects keep as still as the fruit in his still lifes through perhaps 100 sittings, it is not surprising then that he often worked from photographs of professional models. **Vincent van Gogh** is represented in the core collection by *The Olive Trees* (1889) and *The Starry Night* (1889), an exalted and tumultuous vision of the night sky, which is one of the museum's most-loved paintings. **Paul Gauguin**'s *The Seed of the Areoi* (1892) shows the artist's Polynesian mistress seated in a pose in which critics have detected Egyptian, Javanese, and Western elements.

The Dream (1910) and *The Sleeping Gypsy* (1897) by **Henri Rousseau** are other museum favorites. Rousseau claimed he had done military service in Mexico, but the exotic foliage of this painting came from his imagination and from visits to the Botanical Garden in Paris.

Pablo Picasso is represented in the collection by work from all periods of his long career. His melancholy *Boy Leading a Horse* (1905-6), one of the earliest works by this artist in the collection, depicts the subject a flattened, simplified landscape. *Les Demoiselles d'Avignon*, only a year later (1907), is a pivotal work in 20c painting; its jarring use of perspective, anatomical distortions, and slashing brushwork represent a revolutionary break with painting that preceded it. Also in the collection are important examples of his Analytical Cubism, a radical style developed largely by Picasso and Georges Braque. The forms of these works have been analyzed into their geometrical components and are usually rendered in subdued grays, browns, and black. *"Ma Jolie"* (1911-2), *Still Life with Liqueur Bottle* (1909), *Woman's Head (Fernande)*, painted in 1909, and *Girl with a Mandolin [Fanny Tellier]*, dating from 1910, belong to this period. There is also a *Guitar* (1912-3), a sculpture, constructed of sheet metal and wire.

In addition to Picasso's early Cubist works are paintings from his Synthetic Cubist style, about a decade later. *Three Musicians* (1921) has reminded some observers of the Cubist technique of collage. The year before Picasso painted this work, he designed costumes for Stravinsky's *Pulcinella*, a ballet based on the *commedia dell' arte*; the harlequin and pierrot (playing the clarinet) are drawn from this tradition. Also, *Three Women at the Spring*, a

Visitors to the MoMA viewing **Vincent van Gogh**'s *The Starry Night* (1889)

Neoclassical group of monumental figures painted the same year. *Seated Bather* (1930) is a hard distorted female figure with a mantis-like head. During this period Picasso's marriage to his first wife, Olga, was strained, as he had already begun a relationship with Marie-Thérèse Walter, who would become his second. *Girl Before a Mirror* (1932) is a variation on a traditional "vanity" picture in which a woman gazing at her reflection in a mirror sees instead a skull. The woman is Marie-Thérèse.

MoMA is also fortunate in its holdings of **Henri Matisse**. *The Red Studio* (1911) depicts the artist's workspace with paintings on which he was working placed around the room. *View of Notre-Dame* (1914) shows the spare outline of the cathedral rising above the waters of the Seine. Probably the most famous of Matisse's works is the joyous and energetic *Dance* (1909), a study commissioned by the Russian collector, Sergei Shchukin, who had seen Matisse's *Joy of Life* in Paris. *Piano Lesson* (1916) shows Matisse's son playing on a Pleyel piano; the green triangle is the garden visible through the window. The painting behind the boy is *Woman on a High Stool* (1914), which the museum also owns. Some viewers have seen in its geometry a commentary on Cubism. Probably Matisse's best-known sculpture is *The Back* (1909-31), a series of four reliefs in which detail is stripped away and the figure is pared down to its underlying forms.

German Expressionist works on view may include **Gustav Klimt**'s *Hope II* (1907-8), a stylized yet erotic image of a pregnant woman, and **Ernst Ludwig Kirchner**'s *Street, Dresden* (1908), painted in intense, nightmarish colors.

The Futurists, fiercely anti-traditionalist artists active in Italy during the early years of the 20c, are represented by **Giacomo Balla**, **Gino Severini**, *Dynamic Hieroglyphic of the Bal Taberin* (1912) and **Umberto Boccioni**, whose bronze *Unique Forms of Continuity in Space* (1913) suggests the forceful energy of a striding figure. Vassily Kandinsky's *Four Panels, Nos. 1-4* (1914) were painted for the New York apartment of a collector.

"To Be Looked At," the title of the exhibit of core works from the permanent collection, takes its name from a work by **Marcel Duchamp**, *To Be Looked At (From the Other Side of the Glass) with One Eye, Close To, for Almost An Hour* (1918), a construction of glass, wire, silver leaf, and oil paint. The museum also owns *The Passage from Virgin to Bride* (1912) and *Bicycle Wheel* (1951), a wheel mounted on a kitchen stool, remade after the original (1913) was lost. It was Duchamp's first "ready-made," a mass-produced object he chose randomly and displayed as a work of art. *Fresh Widow* (1920), currently on display, is a miniature French window, its glass panels covered with black leather.

Among the museum's signature Surrealist works is *The False Mirror* (1928) by **René Magritte**, a stylized eye with a patch of sky replacing the iris, a reversal that replaces external environment with internal vision. *The Persistence of Memory* (1931) by **Salvador Dalí** is equally famous: a dreamlike painting of soft watches and a blob of fetal protoplasm (Dalí said it was a self-portrait) in an arid landscape. Meret Oppenheim's *Object [Le Déjeuner en fourrure]* (1936), a fur-covered cup, saucer, and spoon, is certainly her best known work and one of the favorite images of Surrealism. Nearby is *The Hunter [Catalan Landscape]* (1923-4) by **Joan Miró**. André Breton, chief theorist of Surrealism, thought Miró 'the most Surrealist of all'. Though the Spanish artist's work often has a light-handedness that many of his fellow Surrealists lacked, it remains true to the Surrealist notion of releasing the unconscious forces of the mind.

The museum owns many works by the sculptor **Constantin Brancusi**, known for his ability to reduce natural forms to abstract simplicity. *Bird in Space* (1928?), a polished sweep of bronze, suggests the notion of flight; when it was brought to the United States for an exhibition, customs officials proposed to assess it as raw metal and charge duty. Also by Brancusi: *Socrates* (1923), carved of wood, and *Fish* (1930), a gray marble ovoid shape on a marble and limestone pedestal, and *The Blond Negress II* (1933).

    Three Women [Le Grand Déjeuner] (1921) by **Fernand Léger** shows the women as tubular forms with the polished finish of machinery. *Broadway Boogie Woogie* (1942-3) by **Piet Mondrian** abstracts the energy of the urban scene Mondrian encountered when he came to New York in 1940. Also by Mondrian, *Painting I* (1926), a black-and-white canvas in which the horizontals meet beyond the edges of the canvas.

    Other works from the years between the two World Wars in the collection include **Paul Klee**'s *Cat and Bird* (1928), Oskar Schlemmer's *Bauhaus Stairway* (1932), and *Departure* (1932-3) by **Max Beckmann**. The Nazis drove Beckmann from his academic job in Frankfurt in 1933, at which time he had begun working on this allegorical triptych, part of a series of nine that occupied him until his death in 1950. The paintings have been received either as a powerful comment on German culture and politics or as a statement of Beckmann's philosophy of life and his horror at human cruelty.

After World War II, the center of avant-garde painting shifted to New York. Not surprisingly, the museum's collection is rich in works from this period. **Jackson Pollock**'s *One (Number 31, 1950)*, a monumental painting, exemplifies Pollock's classic "drip" technique in which he dripped and splashed paint onto a canvas laid on the floor, a technique thought by painters and critics of the time to elude rational thought and reveal directly the unconscious impulses of the artist. Its flickering effect of the built-up surface with its whorls and loops of color has suggested to some viewers the energy of the modern city; others see in it the energy of nature. Also on view is **Mark Rothko**, *Number 10* (1950); Rothko started painting soft-edged rectangles in the late 1940s; their colors became more somber as time passed. **Willem de Kooning**, *Woman, I* (1950-2), an aggressive, predatory, but still humorous image.

Although not currently on display, the museum owns works by **Arshile Gorky** from the years before Abstract Expressionism blossomed as a movement, as well as early works by **Jackson Pollock**. *The She-Wolf* (1943) was the first of his paintings purchased by a museum and one of the first in which his own personal style begins to coalesce. The mythological subject refers to the foster mother of Remus and Romulus, founders of Rome.

Jasper Johns was one of the artists responsible for the shift from Abstract Expressionism to Pop Art, which briefly succeeded it. Johns' paintings of ordinary two-dimensional objects - targets, numbers, flags, and maps - have been seen by some as explorations of the relationship between art and reality. Jasper Johns, *Flag* (1954-5), one of his most famous motifs, continues the all-over tradition of Abstract Expressionism, while being both artificial and realistic.

Robert Rauschenberg's *Bed* (1955) was one of his first "combination" paintings, in which he incorporated three-dimensional objects, in this case a sheet, pillow, and quilt from his bed. The splashes of reddish and brownish paint on the fabric made some critics suggest that the bed looked as if an axe murder had been committed in it.

Andy Warhol's *Gold Marilyn Monroe* (1962), a silk screened image of the actress on a gold background, is one of many pictures of Monroe the artist produced after her suicide in 1962, but it is the only one that uses gold, a color traditionally used in Christian art for the halos surrounding the heads of saints. Also by Warhol, *Campbell's Soup Cans* (1962), thirty-two canvases each measuring 20 x 16 inches, each depicting a different flavor of Campbell's soup.

Also in the core collection is **Roy Lichtenstein**'s *Drowning Girl* (1963), one of his signature, blown-up, melodramatic, comic-strip paintings, executed in benday dots.

Claes Oldenburg's *Floor Cake* (1962), is a large soft sculpture made of canvas painted and filled out with foam rubber and cardboard boxes. In 1961, Oldenburg, a Yale-trained artist, opened The Store at 107 East 2nd St on the Lower East Side, in which he displayed painted plaster sculptures of consumer goods - food, articles of clothing - that he fabricated in the back room. He sold them at modest prices. Later Oldenburg moved The Store uptown to a gallery, where both the sculptures and the prices got larger than life. Later sculptures were made of vinyl, painted steel, and other materials.

Another kind of reaction to Abstract Expressionism can be seen in the work of **Frank Stella**, who came to New York in 1958. During the next year or so he executed a series of black paintings, for example *The Marriage of Reason and Squalor, II* (1959), whose pinstripes follow the shape of the canvas. The museum also owns some of Stella's shaped canvases and his aluminum and wire sculptures, painted in bright, splashy colors.

Roughly contemporary with the Pop artists were the Minimalists, whose work is represented by Carl Andre, *144 Lead Squares* (1969), Donald Judd, *Stack* (1967), a vertical installation of 12 lacquered iron boxes, and Tony Smith. More recent artists included in the core collection are Scott Burton, Martin Puryear, Joseph Beuys, Gerhard Richter, Anselm Kiefer, Sigmar Polke, Robert Gober, and Bill Viola.

on route

American Museum of the Moving Image (AMMI), 35th Ave at 36th St, Astoria, Tues-Fri 12-5, Sat and Sun 11-6; closed Mon, call about holiday hours, evening screenings Sat and Sun, 6:30. *T* (718) 784-0077, www.ammi.org. Housed in the former **Astoria Studios**, which once served as the East Coast production facilities of Paramount Pictures, AMMI has a blockbuster collection of artifacts relating to the history and technology of film, TV, and digital media. The core exhibition, **"Behind the Screen,"** has interactive exhibits that let you make a short animation or dub your voice into a movie soundtrack. Weekend screenings include retrospectives of major directors and actors as well as independent filmmakers. Red Grooms' installation, *Tut's Fever*, a mock movie palace of yesteryear, is a favorite. *S* R or G train to Steinway St; N train to Broadway (in Queens). Accessible via Artlink shuttle

Fisher Landau Center, 38-27 30th St, Long Island City, Thurs-Mon 12-5, *T* (718) 937-0727. One of Queens' little known art treasures. Installed in a rehabbed former parachute-harness factory, this exhibition space and study center contains part of the collection of Emily Fisher Landau, arts patron and philanthropist. Elegantly redesigned as gallery space by Max Gordon, architect of London's original Saatchi Gallery, the Center offers about two exhibitions chosen from the collection each year. The collection focuses on art from the 1960s to the present and includes important works by Jasper Johns, Robert Rauschenberg, Cy Twombly, John Baldessari, and others. Recent exhibitions have presented works by Ed Ruscha, Kiki Smith, Jasper Johns, and James Rosenquist. *S* N, W to 39th Ave

Gantry Plaza State Park, on the East River between 48th/49th Aves, west of the high-rise City Lights apartment building. At one time the gantry cranes that frame the entrance to the park transferred freight cars to and from barges in the river (the Sunnyside Train Yards are not far inland). The beautifully designed and landscaped two-and-one half acre park opened in 1998. *S* 7 local to Vernon Blvd/Jackson Ave; walk down 48th Ave to the river

Museum for African Art, 36-01 43rd Ave (third floor), Sunnyside, Mon, Thurs, Fri 10-5 ; Sat and Sun11-6. Closed Tues, Wed, Jan 1, Thanksgiving, Dec 25. *T* (718) 784-7700, www.africanart.org. One of only two museums in the USA dedicated to African art and culture, the museum offers excellent changing exhibitions that explore the contexts in which the art was created and also look at the purely aesthetic qualities of the works. This location in Queens is temporary, until its new home in Manhattan at Fifth Ave/110th St is ready (planned completion 2006). *S* 7 local to 33rd St in Queens. Also accessible via Artlink shuttle

Isamu Noguchi Garden Museum, 32-37 Vernon Blvd (33rd Rd), Long Island City, Thurs, Fri, Mon 10-5; weekends 11-6; closed Tues, Wed, Jan 1, Thanksgiving, Dec 25. *T* (718) 204-7088, www.noguchi.org. Sculptor Noguchi moved to this former photo-engraving plant (across Vernon Blvd from Socrates Sculpture Park) to be near his marble suppliers. The galleries display Noguchi's stone, metal, wood, and clay sculptures, models for public projects, and his famous Akari light sculptures. The garden is a serene walled space, where pieces of sculpture stand among stones and trees. *S* N, W to Broadway (Queens); walk eight blocks along Broadway toward the East River. Also accessible via artlink Shuttle

Former Pennsylvania Railroad Power Plant, 2nd St (50th/51st Aves). A great hulking industrial building with four towering smoke stacks. It dates back to 1909, when it was designed by the blue-ribbon firm of McKim, Mead, & White, architects to the Pennsylvania Railroad. They also designed the wantonly-destroyed and long-lamented Pennsylvania Station in Manhattan.

P.S. 1 Contemporary Art Center, 22-25 Jackson Ave (46th Ave), Long Island City, Thurs-Mon noon-6; closed Tues, Wed. *T* (718) 784-2084, www.ps1.org. One of the city's most famous venues for cutting-edge art, P.S. 1 was also a pioneer in the movement to reclaim alternative space for artistic uses. Now affiliated with MoMA, it offers changing exhibitions of painting and sculpture, installations, sound art, and photography. The name comes from the building, a former public school, most recently remodeled in 1997, with increased indoor space and a big outdoor gallery. *S* 7 to 45 Rd/Courthouse Sq. Exit onto Jackson Ave. Walk one block south to 46 Ave. G to 21 St/Van Alst. Accessible via Artlink shuttle

Queensboro Bridge, also known as the 59th St Bridge. It joins Long Island City, Queens, with midtown Manhattan by way of a link with Roosevelt Island. Historically, it is the third of the bridges to cross the East River, dating from 1909. Gustav Lindenthal, whose greatest work was the Hell Gate railroad bridge (1917) was the engineer; Henry Hornbostel, the architect, is responsible for the finials on top of the towers. In 1966 folk-rockers Paul Simon and Art Garfunkel made it famous far beyond the city limits with the song *The 59th Street Bridge Song (Feelin' Groovy)*.

SculptureCenter, 44-19 Purves St (near Jackson Ave), Long Island City, Thurs-Mon 12-6. **T** (718) 361-1750, www.sculpture-center.org. Founded as The Clay Club in 1928, SculptureCenter moved to Queens in 2002, settling into a former trolley repair shop redesigned by Maya Lin and architect David Hotson. Distinguished artists, from Isamu Noguchi and Louise Nevelson to Petah Coyne and Alison Saar have exhibited at SculptureCenter, whose focus remains on contemporary sculpture by less established artists. The 40-foot ceilings and an enclosed adjacent lot allow large-scale work. **S** E, V train, to 23rd St/Ely Ave in Queens; exit at front of train at the Citicorp Tower; turn left onto Jackson Ave, walk two blocks; turn right onto Purves St

Silvercup Studios, Queens Plaza South to 43rd Ave (21st/22nd Sts). New York's largest TV and film production facility, no tours, alas. The first studio opened in 1983 in the former flour silo of the landmark Silvercup Bakery. On top is the famous skyline Silvercup sign.

Socrates Sculpture Park, Broadway at Vernon Blvd, Long Island City, open all year 10-dusk. **T** (718) 956-1819, www.socratessculpturepark.org. Changing exhibitions of large-scale contemporary sculpture occupy this four-and-one half acre windswept patch of landfill once used for illegal dumping. The dramatic site directly on the East River looks west to the Manhattan skyline and east to the low-rise industrial landscape. **S** N or W to Broadway stop in Queens; walk 8 blocks along Broadway toward the river. Accessible via Artlink shuttle

commercial galleries

While Long Island City has attracted institutions needing exhibition space and artists needing low-rent studio space, the neighborhood has not yet seen an influx of commercial galleries.

Dorsky Gallery Curatorial Programs, 11-03 45th Ave (near 11th St), Long Island City, **T** (718) 937-6317. This nonprofit organization offers independent curators the chance to present shows of contemporary art with timely or historical themes. **S** E, V to 23rd St/Ely Ave; exit to the rear of train onto 21st St; walk one block south onto 45th Ave

Garth Clark Project Space, 45-46 21st St, Long Island City, *T* (718) 706-491, www.garthclark.com. Garth Clark is a leading dealer in ceramics, with a gallery on 57th St in Manhattan. Ceramics by full-time potters and artists better known as sculptors or painters. The roster includes Peter Vuolkos, Robert Arneson, Ruth Duckworth, Lucio Fontana. *S* 7 to 45th Rd Courthouse Sq. Exit on Jackson Ave, and walk a block south to 46th Ave

eating and drinking

AT THE MUSEUMS

The **American Museum of the Moving Image**, **P.S. 1** and **MoMA QNS**, and the newly renovated **Isamu Noguchi Garden Museum** all have cafés.

SURROUNDING AREA

NEAR MOMA QUEENS

$ **Ariyoshi Japanese Restaurant**, 41-13 Queens Blvd (41st St), Sunnyside, *T* (718) 937-3288. About eight blocks or one stop on the 7 local from MoMA. Spacious restaurant, with loyal clientele, sushi and traditional Japanese food. *S* 7 local to 40th St

Hemsin, 39-17/19 Queens Blvd (39th St), *T* (718) 937-1715. Turkish bakery and restaurant with Middle Eastern food including baklava baked on site. *S* 7 local to 40th St

New Thompson's Diner, 32-44 Queen's Blvd (Van Dam St/33rd St), *T* (718) 392-0692. The closest spot to MoMA, a half block from the museum. Classic 1950s'-style diner; regulars include Hispanic workers from nearby factories. Red beans and rice, roast pork, fried chicken, some leaner choices for the art crowd. *S* 7 local to 33rd St

$$ **Dazies**, 39-41 Queens Blvd (39th St), *T* (718) 786-7013. Established, family-run Italian restaurant, with dark wood, dark lighting, friendly service and a pianist during dinner (except Mon). Expensive for the area. *S* 7 local to 40th St

$$$ Water's Edge, East River at 44th Dr, Long Island City, **T** (718) 482-0033. Very upscale seafood restaurant, beautiful view, fine food. Private shuttle from 34th St pier on East River after 6pm. Closed Sun. **S** E, V to 23rd St-Ely Ave; 7 to 45th Rd-Court House Sq

NEAR P.S. 1

$$ La Vuelta, 10-43 44th Dr (11th St), Long Island City, **T** (718) 361-1858. Hip Latino restaurant with good food (some vegetarian dishes), affordable prices, and music on Sat night. Small back garden. **S** E or V to 23rd St/Ely Ave; G to Long Island City/Court Sq

Manducatis, 13-27 Jackson Ave, **T** (718) 729-4602. Good home-made Italian food in family-style restaurant, enjoyed for 20-plus years by staff and patrons of P.S. 1 Good wine list, unpromising decor. **S** 7 local to 45th Rd/Courthouse Sq

Manetta's, 10-76 Jackson Ave (49th Ave), **T** (718)786-6171. Thin-crust, brick-oven pizza, hero sandwiches, and salads. Spirited lunch crowd of nearby workers and occasional artgoers. **S** 7 local to Vernon Blvd/Jackson Ave

Tournesol, 50-12 Vernon Blvd (50th St), Long Island City, **T** (718) 472-4355. Probably LIC's first-ever French bistro. Friendly, well-reviewed food and ambiance. Moderately expensive. Brunch on Sun. **S** 7 local to Vernon Blvd/Jackson Ave

NEAR THE AMERICAN MUSEUM OF THE MOVING IMAGE

$$ S'Agapo Taverna Ouzeri, 34-21 34th Ave (34th St) Astoria, **T** 718-626-0303. Greek appetizers, whole grilled fish, lamb, Macedonian pork. **S** N or W to Broadway; G, R, V to Steinway St

Café Bar, 32-90 36th St (Broadway), Astoria, **T** (718) 204-5273. Mediterranean style food, sandwiches, and snacks in funky café. Daytime retreat for laptoppers, evening rendezvous for drink sippers. Slow service. **S** N to 36th Ave

shopping

Long Island City is an industrial area and doesn't offer many opportunities for recreational shopping.

entertainment

INFORMATION
TICKETS
CINEMA
THEATER, OPERA, DANCE
CONCERTS/MUSIC
CLUBS

INFORMATION

The best sources for up-to-date listings in paper or on the Web are:

New York Times (www.nytimes.com), especially Fri and Sun

Time Out New York (www.timeoutny.com)

The New Yorker (www.newyorker.com)

New York Magazine (www.newyorkmetro.com)

The Village Voice (www.villagevoice.com)

TICKETS

Tickets for Broadway shows, major sporting events, rock concerts, and musical events can be purchased through centralized ticket services using a major credit card. Expect to pay a per-ticket surcharge. For Broadway shows, ask about seat location when you buy the ticket; you cannot change seats later. Advertisements for events in the print media list the appropriate ticket service.

Telecharge, *T* (212) 239-6200, www.telecharge.com. Broadway and Off Broadway shows.

Ticketmaster, *T* (212) 307-7171. For Broadway productions, *T* (212) 307-4100; for Disney shows, *T* (212) 307-4747; www.ticketmaster.com. Theater tickets, sports, rock and pop concerts, family events. Buy by phone, online, or in person at outlets such as The Wiz, Tower Records, J&R Music World, HMV.

DISCOUNT TICKETS

TKTS Booth at Broadway and 47th St. Run by the **Theatre Development**

Fund, *T* (212) 221-0013, www.tdf.org. Discounted tickets for same day performances of Broadway and Off Broadway shows and some other cultural events including those at Lincoln Center (but not the Metropolitan Opera). Mon, Wed, Thurs, Fri and Sat for 8pm performances: 3pm-8pm; Tues for 7pm and 8pm performances: 2pm-7pm for 7 o'clock curtains and 2pm-8pm for 8 o'clock curtains. Wed and Sat for 2pm matinees: 10am-2pm; Sun for all performances: 11am-7pm. Long line sometimes, but discounts as high as 50 percent. Cash or travelers' checks only.

TKTS Lower Manhattan Theatre Centre,186 Front St at the South Street Seaport (the corner of Front and John Streets, the rear of the Resnick/Prudential Building). Open Mon-Sat 11am-6 pm and Sun for evening performances 11am-3:30pm. At this location matinee tickets must be purchased the day before the performance. Cash or travelers' checks only.

Theatre Development Fund, 1501 Broadway (43rd/44th Sts), *T* (212) 221-0013, www.tdf.org. Visitors from outside New York can buy a book of four ticket vouchers for $28 for Off-Off Broadway, music, and dance events. Call for information.

TICKET BROKERS

It's illegal in New York State to sell tickets for more than face value plus a service charge. However, out-of-state brokers will sell you tickets over the phone even for sold-out events (high prices). Brokers are listed under "Ticket Sales" in the Yellow Pages.

CINEMA

New York is a filmgoer's paradise. You can see popular movies at strategically located multiplexes, or you can visit a revival house or an art house to take in classic Hollywood, foreign, independent, or art films. Film societies and museums screen historic and contemporary movies.

For tickets - especially on weekends when lines can be long - you can use your major credit card to buy over the telephone using the automated 777-FILM system (service charge added). Or buy on the internet (well in advance): www.moviefone.com, www.fandango.com, or www.movies.com. When you arrive at the theater, swipe your credit card through the ticket machine to

Times Square

receive your tickets. First-run movies cost about $10 with discounts for seniors and children (sometimes restricted to weekday afternoons). Many theaters have listening devices for the hearing impaired.

Films are listed in the daily newspapers, weekly magazines, and online. Here is a list of important venues for film.

AMC Empire 25, 234 W. 42nd St (Eighth Ave), *T* (212) 398-3939. In Times Square; 25 screens on 11 floors in the former Empire Theater (1912).

Angelika Film Center, 18 W. Houston St (Mercer St), *T* (212) 995-2000. Six screens for (mainly) foreign and independent American films. Hang out at the café-pastry bar.

BAM Rose Cinemas, 30 Lafayette Ave (Flatbush Ave/Fulton St), Brooklyn, *T* (718) 623-2770. Brooklyn's finest (associated with Brooklyn Academy of Music) shows art films and first-run movies.

Clearview's Ziegfeld, 141 W. 54th (Sixth/Seventh Aves), *T* (212) 765-7600. Historic theater, now a movie palace (single screen), shows big-budget Hollywood movies, premieres. Reserved seating.

Sony Lincoln Square and IMAX Theatre, 1992 Broadway (68th St),
T (212) 336-5000. A dozen screens and an eight-story IMAX for high tech specials.

THEATER, OPERA, DANCE
BROADWAY AND OFF BROADWAY THEATER

Most of the 38 officially designated "Broadway" theaters are located north of Times Square between West 42nd and 53rd Sts. Tickets to Broadway productions cost up to $100. Off Broadway and Off-Off Broadway theaters are smaller in scale and more experimental in style. Tickets usually run between $20 and $60. The following list includes Off and Off-Off Broadway theaters as well as other venues.

Amato Opera Theatre, 319 Bowery (2nd St), *T* (212) 228-8200, www.amato.org. Small scale productions at low prices.
S F, V, S to Broadway-Lafayette St; 6 to Bleecker St

Atlantic Theater Company, 336 W. 20th (Eighth/Ninth Aves), *T* (212) 645-1242. Off Broadway, in former church. *S* C, E to 23rd St

Brooklyn Academy of Music, 30 Lafayette Ave (Flatbush Ave/Fulton St), *T* (718) 636-4100, www.bam.org. Opera, classical music, theater, and a great avant-garde festival in the fall. *S* C to Lafayette Ave; G to Fulton St; *S* M, N, R, W to Pacific St; Q, 1,2, 4,5, to Atlantic Ave

City Center Theater, 131 W. 55th St (Sixth/Seventh Aves), *T* (212) 581-7907, www.citycenter.org. Ballet, dance, and theater, revivals of musicals. *S* B, D, E to Seventh Ave

Jean Cocteau Repertory, 330 Bowery (Bond St), *T* (212) 677-0060.
S F, V, S to Broadway-Lafayette St; 6 to Bleecker St

The Kitchen, 512 W. 19th St (Tenth/Eleventh Aves), *T* (212) 255-5793. Experimental, dance, music, multimedia, video. Closed in summer.
S A, C, E to 14th St; L to Eighth Ave

Lincoln Center Theater, in Lincoln Center (W. 65th St at Columbus Ave), *T* (212) 239-6277 for tickets or (212) 362-7600 for general information, www.lincolncenter.org. Two venues - the Vivian Beaumont Theater and the much smaller Mitzi E. Newhouse Theater. New and classic plays often with famous actors. *S* 1, 2 to 66th St-Lincoln Center

La MaMa E.T.C., 74A E. 4th St (Bowery/Second Ave), *T* (212) 475-7710, www.lamama.org. Broadway. Ellen Stewart's East Village experimental performance space. *S* F, V to Lower East Side-Second Ave; 6 to Astor Pl

Metropolitan Opera House

Manhattan Theatre Club, City Center, 131 W. 55th St (Sixth/Seventh Aves), *T* (212) 399-3000, www.manhattantheatreclub.com. New and established playwrights. *S* B, D, E to Seventh Ave

Metropolitan Opera, Lincoln Center (W. 65th St/Columbus Ave), *T* (212) 362-6000, www.metopera.org. Opera and ballet on a grand scale. Standing room tickets on sale at box office Sat 10 am (line up early). Student discounts (2 tickets per performance), *T* (212) 362 6000 for availability. *S* 1, 2 to 66th St-Lincoln Center

New York State Theater, Lincoln Center (W. 65th St/Columbus Ave), *T* (212) 870-5570, wwww.nycopera.com. Opera and ballet, more innovative than the Met and less expensive. *S* 1, 2 to 66th St-Lincoln Center

New York Theatre Workshop, 79 E. 4th St (Bowery/Second Ave), *T* (212) 460-5475. Off Broadway. *S* F, V to Lower East Side-Second Ave; 6 to Astor Pl

Opera Orchestra of New York, Carnegie Hall, 154 W. 57th St (Seventh Ave), *T* (212) 799-1982, www.oony.org. Concert versions of unfamiliar operas. *S* A, B, C, D, 1, 2 to 59th St-Columbus Circle; N, Q, R W to 57th St

The Public Theater, 425 Lafayette St (Astor Pl/4th St); *T* (212) 539-8500. Joseph Papp's now-historic theater, new plays, classics, cabaret. *S* N, R to 8th St-NYU; 6 to Astor Pl

Second Stage Theatre, 307 W. 43rd St (Eighth Ave), *T* (212) 246-4422, www.secondstagetheatre.com. New American plays. *S* A, C, E to 42nd St-Port Authority; N, Q, R, W, S, 1, 2, 3, 7 to 42nd St-Times Sq

Vineyard Theatre, 108 E. 15th St (Union Sq East), *T* (212) 353-3366, www.vineyardtheatre.org. Musicals, new plays, revivals. *S* L, N, Q, R, W, 4, 5, 6 to 14th St- Union Sq

CONCERTS/MUSIC
CLASSICAL

Alice Tully Hall, Lincoln Center (65th St/Columbus Ave), *T* (212) 875-5050. Chamber music, recitals. *S* 1, 2 to 66th St-Lincoln Center

Avery Fisher Hall, Lincoln Center (65th St/Columbus Ave), *T* (212) 875-5030. Home of New York Philharmonic, also Great Performers series. *S* 1, 2 to 66th St-Lincoln Center

Bargemusic, Fulton Ferry Landing near Brooklyn Bridge, Brooklyn Heights, *T* (718) 624-4061, www.bargemusiccom. Chamber music on a barge with a view of the Manhattan skyline. *S* A, C to High St

Brooklyn Academy of Music, see above under Theater, Opera, Ballet.

Carnegie Hall, 154 W. 57th St (Seventh Ave), *T* (212) 247-7800, www.carnegiehall.org. Superb artists and orchestras. *S* A, B, C, D, 1, 2 to 59th St-Columbus Circle; N, Q, R W to 57th St

Metropolitan Museum of Art, Fifth Ave at 82nd St, *T* (212) 570-3949, www.metmuseum.org. Chamber music series. *S* 4, 5, 6 to 86th St

Merkin Concert Hall, 129 W. 67th St (Broadway/Amsterdam Ave), *T* (212) 501-3330, www.elainekaufmancenter.org. Early and avant-garde music. Also jazz. *S* 1, 2 to 66th St- Lincoln Center

JAZZ

Call ahead for cover charge and food/drink minimum.

BAMcafé, see Brooklyn Academy of Music, above. Lounge above lobby with jazz, blues, gospel.

Birdland, 315 West 44th St (Eighth/Ninth Aves), **T** (212) 581-3080. Not the place Charlie Parker played, big names. **S** A, C, E to 42nd St

Blue Note, 131 West 3rd St (Sixth Ave/MacDougal St), **T** (212) 475-8592; www.bluenote.net. Famous names, venerable club. **S** A, C, E, F, V, S to West 4th St

Iridium, 1650 Broadway (51st St), **T** (212) 582-2121, www.iridiumjazzclub.com. The legendary Les Paul plays Mon. **S** B, D, E to 7th Ave; 1, 9 to 50th St

Lenox Lounge, 288 Lenox Ave (aka Malcom X Blvd), 124th/125th Sts, **T** (212) 427-0253. Bop, traditional jazz. **S** 2, 3 to 125th St

Roulette, 228 West Broadway (White St), **T** (212) 219-8242, wwww.roulette.org. Avant-garde, electronic. **S** C, E, to Canal St; 1, 2 to Franklin St

Stanley H. Kaplan Penthouse, 1650 Broadway at Lincoln Center, tenth floor, **T** (212) 875-5050. Lincoln Center's smallest venue. **S** 1, 2 to 66th St-Lincoln Center

Tonic, 107 Norfolk St (Delancey/Rivington Sts), **T** (212) 358-7503. Jazz, pop, and rock, experimental. **S** F to Delancey St; J, M, Z to Delancey-Essex Sts

Village Vanguard, 178 Seventh Ave South (Perry St), **T** (212) 255-4037. Classic jazz, call to reserve. **S** A, C, E 1 2, 3 to 14th St

Zinc Bar, 90 Houston St (La Guardia Pl/Thompson St), **T** (212) 477-8337, www.zincbar.com. Jazz, Latin, African, salsa. **S** A, C, E, F, V, S to W. 4th St

POP AND ROCK

Beacon Theatre, 2124 Broadway (74th St), **T** (212) 496-7070. Landmark theater, big name rock groups, some gospel, world music. **S** 1, 2, 3 to 72nd St

The Bottom Line, 15 West Fourth St (Mercer St), **T** (212) 228-6300; www.bottomlinecabaret.com. Historic Village cabaret; folk-rock, bluegrass, jazz, comedy. Cash only. **S** N, R, to 8th St- NYU

Bowery Ballroom, 6 Delancey St (Bowery/Chrystie St), **T** (212) 533-2111, www.boweryballroom.com. One of the best; features touring groups, top indies, occasional local bands. **S** J, M to Bowery; 6 to Spring St

CBGB, 315 Bowery (Bleecker St), **T** (212) 982-4052, www.cbgb.com. Venerable venue, birthplace of 70s' punk. **SS** F, V, S to Broadway-Lafayette; 6 to Bleecker St

Fez, in the **Time Café**, 380 Lafayette St (Great Jones St), **T** (212) 533-2680.

Neo-Moroccan décor, lounge acts, cabaret, Mingus Big Band on Thurs, comedy. Arrive early. Cash only for drinks. **S** F, V, S to Broadway-Lafayette; 6 to Bleecker St

Irving Plaza, 17 Irving Pl (15th St), **T** (212) 777-6800; www.irvingplaza.com. Big-name acts on the way to arenas. Rock, pop, rap. Cash only. **S** L, N, Q, R, W, 4, 5, 6 to 14th St-Union Sq

Joe's Pub, 425 Lafayette St (Astor Pl/West 4th St), **T** (212) 539-8770. In the Public Theater; jazz, rock, pop, cabaret. **S** N, R to 8th St-NYU; 6 to Astor Pl

Knitting Factory, 4 Leonard St (Church St/Broadway), **T** (212) 219-3055, www.knittingfactory.com. Famous avant-garde club in TriBeCa. Four floors, four bars, experimental jazz, electronica, rock, poetry. **S** A, C, E to Canal St; 1, 2 to Franklin St

FOLK AND WORLD

S.O.B.'s (Sounds of Brazil), 204 Varick St (Houston St), **T** (212) 243-4940. Brazilian, Caribbean, West Indian. **S** 1, 2 to Houston St

Symphony Space, 2537 Broadway (95th St), **T** (212) 864-5400, www.symphonyspace.org. World music festivals, classical, jazz, spoken word; Wall to Wall series (free), has all-day Bach or Miles Davis. **S** 1, 2, 3 to 96th St

Town Hall, 123 W. 43rd St (Sixth/Seventh Aves), **T** (212)840-2824; www.the-townhall-nyc.org. Folk, world, classical music, cabaret. **S** B, D, F, V to 42nd St; N, Q, R W, S, 1, 2, 3, 7 to 42nd St-Times Sq

CLUBS

Centro-Fly, 5 W. 21st St (Fifth/Sixth Aves), **T** (212) 627-7770, www.centro-fly.com. Sophisticated Italian disco décor, guest DJs. **S** F, N, R to 23rd St

Étoile, 109 E. 56th St (Park/Lexington Aves), **T** (212) 750-5656. Hotel bar, dance club. Upper East Siders and retro tunes. **S** 4, 5, 6 to 59th St

Filter 14, 432 W. 14th St (Washington St), **T** (212) 366-5680. Small, friendly, diverse crowd. **S** A, C, E to 14th St

Lotus, 409 W 14th St (Ninth Ave/Washington St), **T** (212) 243-4420. Upscale restaurant-lounge-dance club. **S** A, C, E, 1, 2, 3 to 14th St

Webster Hall, 125 E. 11th St (Third/Fourth Aves), **T** (212) 353-1600; www.webster-hall.com. Several levels; disco, Latin, hip-hop, whatever. **S** L, N, Q, R , W , 4, 5, 6 to 14th St-Union Sq

planning

TOURIST OFFICES
GETTING THERE
GETTING AROUND
OTHER ESSENTIALS
PLACES TO STAY
ART CALENDAR

TOURIST OFFICES

The United States has no national tourist office.

IN NEW YORK

NYC & Company, 810 Seventh Ave (53rd St), *T* (212) 484-1222,
www.nycvisit.com. The city's official tourist organization; maps, street
finder, information on hotels, tours, entertainment, special offers,
restaurants. There is a second kiosk downtown at the southern end of
City Hall Park.

Times Square Visitors Center, 1560 Broadway (46th/47th Sts),
T (212) 768-1560, www.timessquarebid.org. Open 8am-8pm. In a
redesigned former movie theater. Information, theater tickets, discount
coupons, MetroCards, free internet access, ATM, post office, toilets,
maps, neighborhood restaurant guides.

GETTING THERE
BY AIR

Most international and many domestic flights arrive at John F.
Kennedy International Airport (JFK). The airport faces Jamaica
Bay in the borough of Queens, about 15 miles from midtown
Manhattan (60 minutes in moderate traffic). Many international
flights are channeled through Terminal 4, formerly the
International Arrivals Building. La Guardia Airport, also in
Queens, on the East River, about 8 miles (30-45 minutes) from
midtown, primarily serves domestic flights. Newark Liberty
International Airport, in Newark, New Jersey, is about 16 miles

(45-60 minutes) from midtown. Many international flights arrive there; its location makes it convenient for travelers headed for Manhattan's West Side.

John F. Kennedy International Airport (JFK), *T* (718) 244-4444

La Guardia Airport, *T* (718) 533-3400

Newark Liberty International Airport, *T* (973) 961-2000

IN NORTH AMERICA

Air Canada, *T* (888) 247-2262, www.aircanada.ca

American Airlines, *T* (800) 433-7300, www.aa.com

Continental Airlines, *T* (800) 525-0280, www.continental.com

Delta Airlines, *T* (800) 221-1212, www.delta.com

Midwest Express, *T* (800) 452-2022, www.midwestexpress.com

United Airlines, *T* (800) 241-6522, www.ual.com

U.S. Airways, *T* (800) 428-4322, www.usairways.com

FROM THE UK AND IRELAND

British Airways, **UK**, *T* (0845) 773 3377; **US**, *T* (800) 247-9297; www.british-airways.com

Virgin Atlantic, **UK**, *T* (01293) 747 747; **US**, *T* (800) 862-8621; www.virgin-atlantic.com

Aer Lingus, **Ireland**, *T* (00 353 1) 886 8844 (online booking helpdesk); reservations **Ireland**, *T* (0818) 365000; **UK**, *T* (0845) 084 4444, www.aerlingus.com

Continental Airlines, **UK**, *T* (0800) 776 464; www.continental.com

Delta Airlines, **UK**, *T* (0800) 414 767; **Ireland (except Dublin)**, *T* (01) 800 768080; **Dublin**, *T* 407 3165; www.delta.com

GETTING TO THE CITY FROM THE AIRPORTS

Information at **Ground Transportation counters** at all three major airports.

The Port Authority of New York and New Jersey operates a website (www.panynj.gov) with detailed information about ground transportation; they also have a telephone hotline, *T* (800) AIR-RIDE (247-7433). Live operator Mon-Fri 9am-5pm. Recorded information other times.

Public transportation - via city bus or subway - is available from La Guardia and JFK, but those who do not know the city well or who have heavy luggage, might opt for one of the alternatives below. From Newark, the **AirTrain monorail** connects the airport to the New Jersey Transit train system, which will take you into New York's Penn Station for $11.55.

Taxis to midtown are available at all three airports. During peak hours uniformed dispatchers will direct you to a cab; other times you must hail your own. Licensed taxis (the legal ones) are yellow and have medallion shields on the hood. Ignore offers of transportation from taxi hustlers, who may approach you in the terminal.

Taxis from Newark and La Guardia are metered. From Newark the ride to midtown costs around $45 plus tolls and tip.

Taxis from JFK are charged at a flat rate of $35 plus toll and tip.

Rental cars are available at the airports, but it makes no sense to rent a car unless you're going to travel out of the city.

Express bus This service is an inexpensive and comfortable option.

Express bus from JFK and La Guardia New York Airport Service, *T* (718) 875-8200 or (800) 872-4577, www.nyairportservice.com. The bus goes to the Port Authority Bus Terminal, Grand Central Terminal, and Penn Station. It runs every 15-30 minutes from 6am to midnight, less frequently later.

Express bus from Newark Airport Olympia Airport Express, *T* (212) 964-6233 in New York or (908) 354-3330 in New Jersey, www.olympiabus.com.

Car services Regulated by the city Taxi and Limousine Commission (TLC), these services can offer pre-arranged rides, but they can't be hailed on the street. Their license plates begin with the letter "T." At present the rates are competitive with taxis. **Carmel Limo**, *T* (212) 666-6666; **Tel Aviv**, *T* (212) 777-7777 or (800) 222-9888.

Super Shutttle offers a door-to-door shuttle van service 24 hours, 365 days; fare based on destination, about $15-$20 to/from airports. Unless you book exclusive service (about $75), the van will stop to pick up/drop off other passengers, so allow extra time. *T* (212) 258-3826, www.supershuttle.com

Gray Line Air Shuttle also offers van service to and from the airports; *T* (800) 451-0455 or (212) 315-3006, www.graylinenewyork.com

BY TRAIN

Penn Station (34th St/Eighth Ave) serves commuter lines to Long Island and New Jersey and also long-distance Amtrak trains; *T* (800) USA-RAIL, www.amtrak.com. High-speed Acela trains run between Boston and Washington, D.C. Book well ahead.

Grand Central Terminal (42nd St/Park Ave) serves commuter trains to areas north and east of the city.

Other useful telephone numbers are:

Long Island Rail Road, *T* (718) 217-5477

Metro-North Railroad, *T* 800-METRO-INFO (outside NYC), *T* (212) 532-4900 (in NYC)

BY BUS

Buses are relatively inexpensive but slow.

Greyhound Trailways, *T* (800) 231-2222; www.greyhound.com. The main long distance line, which runs nationwide.

Peter Pan has services across the northeast; *T* (800) 762-5100; www.peterpanbus.com

Port Authority Bus Terminal, 625 Eighth Ave (40th/42nd Sts), *T* (212) 564-8484. This is the main bus station.

GETTING AROUND

Buses and subways are run by the **Metropolitan Transit Authority**. Maps are posted in subway stations and on buses; you can also get them at Grand Central and in subway stations.

Metropolitan Transit Authority passenger information, *T* (718) 330-1234 (English speakers), (718) 330-4847 (non-English speakers). You can check schedules and download maps from their web site: www.mta.nyc.ny.us

TRAVEL PASSES AND TICKETS

MetroCard® Beginning in 2004, you must have a MetroCard (a fare card with a magnetic strip) to gain access to the subway system. The MetroCard is also the easiest way to pay the fare on public buses and will work on some privately operated bus systems within the city. (However, fare boxes on buses will accept exact change in coins - no pennies).

You can purchase MetroCards at toll booths or vending machines inside subway stations and at local merchants displaying the MetroCard logo. You must pay in cash at toll booths. Some MetroCard vending machines accept cash; all accept credit or ATM/debit cards. Transfers between subways and buses are free. Subway and local bus fare is $2.00; express buses cost $4.00.

MetroCards come in two forms, pay-per-ride (regular) cards and unlimited-ride cards.

Pay-per-ride MetroCards can be purchased in denominations from $2 to $80. Cards costing $10 or more entitle you to bonus rides: a $10 card will give you six rides for the price of five. You can share these cards with other people.

Unlimited-ride MetroCards are valid for specified periods: one day (the Fun Pass, $7, available at vending machines and neighborhood stores but not at subway toll booths); 7 days ($21); and 30 days ($70). These cards are good for unlimited rides on buses and subways, but can be used only once every 18 minutes in the same subway station or on the same bus line.

BY SUBWAY

Subways are fast and efficient. Trains are identified by numbers or letters; on subway maps the lines are indicated by colors. The train number and its terminal point are indicated on the front and side of the train. A free copy of the subway map is available at any subway station booth. Express and local trains sometimes run on the same track, but local trains stop at every station while express trains skip some stops. Uptown and downtown trains often have different entrances from the street; read the directional signs before you go through the turnstile. Entrances that are always open are marked with green globes; those that are sometimes closed have red globes.

The trains run 24 hours but service is less frequent late at night. During off-peak hours, wait in the designated area at the center of the platform, which is monitored by cameras; the conductor's car often stops there.

BY BUS

Buses, though slow, are often pleasant since you can view the passing scene. Stops are located at or near street corners. The route number and destination are indicated on the front of the bus. The fare ($2) is payable by silver coins or a MetroCard, which allows transfers from bus to bus or from bus to subway. If you've paid with coins, ask the driver for a paper transfer. Buses stop every two or three blocks (except for those marked "Limited"); between 10pm and 5am, you can ask the driver to let you off anywhere along your route.

Bus maps are available at NYC & Company, in subway stations, and at Grand Central Terminal. MTA Long Island Bus information is available by calling *T* (516) 766-6722

BY TAXI

There are 12,187 licensed taxis in New York City, so unless it's raining, snowing, or rush hour, you can probably find one. If the center light on top the cab is lit, the cab is available. Flag it down, get in, and tell the driver where you want to go. The rates are currently $2.00 plus $0.30 for each 1/5 mile, with an evening surcharge of $0.50 after 8pm. Although taxis by law are required to take you anywhere within the city limits, some drivers may be unwilling to take you to the far reaches of the outer boroughs.

Your driver may not speak fluent English and may drive imaginatively. It's a good idea to know more or less how to get to your destination, since drivers have been known to take unsuspecting tourists on long rides. Get a receipt in case you leave something in the cab or later want to make a complaint. There are about 200 taxi stands in the city, but most cabs cruise for passengers. "Gypsy" cabs operate in the outer boroughs and in Manhattan outside the central districts; they are not authorized to pick up passengers who hail them on the street, and are not recommended to visitors. Their fares are unregulated.

Taxi & Limousine Commission Report any problems to the Taxi & Limousine Commission, giving the driver's number (posted in the cab and on the receipt). To inquire about lost property or file a complaint, call the TLC at (212) 692-8294

OTHER ESSENTIALS

TRAVELERS WITH DISABILITIES

New York has become more accessible to disabled visitors since the passage of the Americans with Disabilities Act in 1990 mandated that any new construction include complete access. The airports have accessible restrooms, telephones, and restaurants, as well as parking spaces for the disabled close to the terminals. Check the website of the Port Authority of New York and New Jersey for detailed information: www.panynj.gov

TRANSPORTATION FROM THE AIRPORTS

Olympia Trails provides half-price bus service from Newark Airport for disabled travelers; you must purchase these discounted tickets ahead of time, since not all buses are equipped for wheelchairs; call ahead for the daily schedule of accessible buses, *T* (877) 894-9155 or (212) 964-6233, www.olympiabus.com

Gray Line Air Shuttle operates vans with lifts from JFK, La Guardia, and Newark airports to midtown hotels; you must reserve and arrange pickup 3 or 4 days in advance; *T* (800) 451-0455 or (212) 315-3006, www.graylinenewyork.com

Upward Mobility Limousine operates roll-in wheelchair vans for transportation from the airports or within the city. Book ahead. *T* (718) 645-7774

Public transit buses have wheelchair lifts and can "kneel," which lowers the steps. Not all subways are accessible, though some stations have been upgraded with elevators and other facilities.

New York City Transit, *T* (718) 596-8585, for information about stations or help routing a journey.

ACCESS

Hotels vary widely. Many of New York's older hotels have been upgraded, but bathrooms may be small. The online data base at www.access-able.com describes some hotels and other facilities.

Restaurants also vary in accessibility; dining rooms may be accessible, restrooms may not. Call ahead. The *New York Times Guide to New York City Restaurants*, revised yearly, includes wheelchair access in its ratings.

Big Apple Greeters offers free neighborhood visits guided by volunteers. Visitors with disabilities are especially welcome; guides are knowledgeable about facilities for the disabled. **T** (212) 669-8159, **TTY** (212) 669-8273, www.bigapplegreeter.org

Hospital Audiences publishes *Access for All*, a detailed guide to the accessibility of cultural institutions in the city, **T** (212) 575-7663. The information is also available online at www.hospaud.org/database. Some Broadway theaters have infrared devices for the hearing impaired.

Telecharge sells tickets for wheelchair locations in Broadway and other theaters, **T** (212) 239-6200

Theater Development Fund's Access Project offers services to the visually, physically, and hearing impaired, a ticket service to select events, and sign language interpretation and captioning for some shows; **T** (212) 221-1103, **TTY** (212) 719-4537, www.tdf.org

Hands On provides interpretive services for the hearing impaired, **T** (212) 822-8550, **TTY** (212) 627-1070, www.handson.org

CONSULATES
Australian Consulate General, 150 East 42nd St (34th floor), New York, NY 10017-5612, **T** (212) 351-6500

British Consulate-General, 845 Third Ave, New York, NY 10022, **T** (212) 745-0200

Canadian Consulate General, 1251 Ave of the Americas, New York, NY 10020-1175, **T** (212) 596-1628

Consulate General of Ireland, Ireland House, 345 Park Ave (17th floor), New York NY 10154-0037, **T** (212) 319-2555

New Zealand Consulate General, 780 Third Ave, Suite 1904, New York, NY 10017-2024, **T** (212) 832-4038

EMERGENCIES
Police, fire, ambulance, T 911

HEALTH
HOSPITAL EMERGENCY ROOMS
Bellevue Hospital Center, 462 First Ave (27th St), **T** (212) 562-4141. Adult emergency room, **T** (212) 562-3015; pediatric emergency room, **T** (212) 562-3025

Beth Israel Medical Center, First Ave at East 16th St, **T** (212) 420-2000. Emergency room, **T** (212) 420-2840

Cabrini Medical Center, 227 E. 19th St (Second/Third Aves),
T (212) 995-6120

Columbia Presbyterian Medical Center, 21 Audubon Ave (W. 166th St),
T (212) 305-2500; adult emergency room, *T* (212) 305-2255; pediatric
emergency room, *T* (212) 305-6628

New York Hospital Weill Cornell Center, 528 East 68th St (York Ave),
T adult emergency room, *T* (212) 746-5050; pediatric emergency room,
T (212) 746-3300

Roosevelt Hospital, 59th St (Ninth/Tenth Aves), *T* (212) 523-6800

St Vincent's Hospital, Seventh Ave at 12th St; emergency room,
T (212) 604-8000

LATE-NIGHT PHARMACIES
Most pharmacies are open Mon-Sat 9am-6pm (or later).

Duane Reade, Third Ave/74th St, *T* (212) 744-2668, W. 57th St/Broadway,
T (212) 541-9708, and Broadway/W. 91st St, *T* (212) 799-3172. Open
24-hours.

LOST OR STOLEN PROPERTY
If you've lost something on the street, contact the police.

New York City Transit Authority, *T* (212) 712-4500, for buses and
subways.

Taxis, *T* (212) 692-8294. (Yo-Yo Ma once left his cello in a cab and got it
back!)

LOST OR STOLEN CREDIT CARDS
American Express, *T* (800) 528-2122; for lost American Express travelers'
checks call the customer service center, *T* (800) 211-7282

Diners Club, *T* (800) 234-6377

Mastercard, *T* (800) 336-8472

Visa, *T* (800) 826-2181

OPENING HOURS
Banks usually open at 9am and close at 3pm, though some remain
open later on Thurs or Fri; a few have Sat morning hours. **Store
hours** are roughly Mon-Sat 9am-6pm, though department stores

open a little later. Many downtown shops stay open later. Many stores, including the major department stores, are open on Sun.

FEDERAL HOLIDAYS

New Year's Day	January 1
Martin Luther King Jr Day	third Monday in January
Presidents' Day	third Monday in February
Memorial Day	last Monday in May
Independence Day	July 4
Labor Day	first Monday in September
Columbus Day	second Monday in October
Election Day	first Tuesday after first Monday in November
Veterans' Day	November 11
Thanksgiving Day	fourth Thursday in November
Christmas Day	December 25

MUSEUM PASSES

In general museums offer reduced rates to the elderly, to students, and to children. Some museums have hours when you may pay what you wish.

CityPass There is no citywide museum pass, but CityPass allows you to visit six attractions within a 9-day period for about half price. The pass costs $45 and includes tickets to the Whitney Museum of American Art, the Intrepid Sea-Air-Space Museum, the Empire State Building, the Guggenheim Museum, the American Museum of Natural History, the Museum of Modern Art, and the Circle Line Harbor Tours. Buy the pass at the first of these attractions you visit.

SIGHTSEEING

BY BOAT

Staten Island Ferry Enjoy the Lower Harbor, Statue of Liberty, Ellis Island, and downtown skyline free (no narration) on this ferry (South St/Whitehall St), *T* (718) 727-2508, www.siferry.com

Bateaux New York, Chelsea Piers (23rd St/West Side Highway), Pier 61, *T* (212) 352-2022 or (866) 211-3806, www.bateauxnewyork.com. New York's answer to Paris' *bateaux mouches*. Dinner cruises (with dancing) in glass-covered boats, Memorial Day to Labor Day. Lunch cruises all year. Expensive.

Chelsea Screamer, Chelsea Piers, Pier 62 (23rd St/West Side Highway), *T* (212) 924-6262, www.chelseascreamer.com. Speedboat cruise (with narration) roars past the Statue of Liberty, Ellis Island, Brooklyn Bridge. Reservations not required.

Circle Line Cruises, Pier 83 at the foot of W. 42nd St, *T* (212) 563-3200, www.circleline.com. Cruises around Manhattan (with narration), evening cruises. Year-round.

New York Waterway, 38th St at West Side Highway, Pier 78, *T* (800) 533-3779, www.nywaterway.com. On weekends also at South St Seaport, Pier 17 (South/Beekman Sts). Circumnavigate Manhattan or cruise the waters around Lower Manhattan; twilight tours.

BY BUS

Gray Line, Port Authority Bus Terminal (Eighth Ave/42nd St), *T* (212) 397-2600, www.graylinenewyork.com. Narrated tours for every pocketbook and attention span.

BY BIKE

Bike the Big Apple, *T* (877) 865-2078, www.toursbybike. com. Half-day and full day tours of ethnic neighborhoods, bridges, parks, major tourist sights. Weekends, March through November. Cash only.

Time's Up!, *T* (212) 802-8212, www.times-up.org. An environmental group that promotes a less toxic city. Ride schedule posted on website or by phone; organized rides in Manhattan and the outer boroughs explore New York's natural setting and cultural environment.

Central Park Bike Tours, *T* (212) 541-8759, www.centralparkbiketour.com. Call to reserve. Tours of the major sights of Central Park; also Manhattan tours.

PLACES TO STAY

Luxury hotels charge more (sometimes much more) than $350 per night for a standard double room; moderately expensive, more than $200; moderate, more than $150; and budget, less than $150. In addition, New York hotels must tack on a city tax of 13.25 per cent and a per-room fee of $2.00. Unless otherwise indicated, hotel rooms have a private bathroom with a shower/bathtub.

The toll-free 800, 877, and 888 telephone numbers are for use within the United States; you can also try the Web: www.quikbook.com or www.hotwire.com. Hotels tend to reflect the neighborhoods where they're located. There are plenty of elegant hotels in the Silk Stocking District, and few in Chelsea. But since public transportation is so good in Manhattan, you can stay far from the sights you want to visit and whisk up and down on the subway.

MUSEUM MILE AND THE SILK STOCKING DISTRICT

Since these two districts merge, a hotel in either will be close to the major museums. While there are many East Side uptown hotels, the trick is finding one that will fit your pocketbook. Some are included here that are in midtown but convenient to the Upper East Side via public transportation.

$ **Habitat Hotel**, 130 E. 57th St (Lexington Ave), *T* (212) 753-8841 or (800) 255-0482, *F* (212) 829-9605, www.stayinny.com. Recently renovated budget hotel. *S* 4, 5, 6, to 59th St; N, R, W, to Lexington Ave/59th St

ThirtyThirty New York City, 30 E. 30th St (Madison/Park Aves), *T* (212) 689-1900, *F* (212) 689-0023. This hotel is the downtown sister of Habitat. It's not near the Upper East Side museums, but it is easy to get to them from here on the Lexington Ave subway. *S* 6 to 28th or 33rd St

Pickwick Arms, 230 E. 51st St (2nd/3rd Aves), *T* (212) 355-0300, (800) 742-5945, *F* (212) 755-5029. A budget hotel in a good location. Shared bathrooms. *S* 6 to 51st St; E, V to Lexington Ave/53rd St

$$ **The Franklin**, 164 E. 87th St (Lexington/3rd Aves), *T* (212) 369-1000, (877) 847-4444, *F* (212) 369-8000, www.franklinhotel.com. Simple hotel. *S* 4, 5, 6, to 86th St

Hotel Wales, 1295 Madison Ave (92nd St), *T* (212) 876-6000, (800) 607-4009, *F* (212) 860-7000, www.waleshotel.com. Smallish hotel in quiet neighborhood. *S* 6 to 96th St

Melrose Hotel, 140 E. 63rd St (Lexington Ave), *T* (212) 838-5700, (800), 635-7673 (MELROSE), *F* (212) 888-4721; www.melrosehotels.com. Formerly the Barbizon, a residence for white-gloved young ladies (Grace Kelly, Sylvia Plath). Some rooms are small; close to upscale shopping. **S** F to Lexington Ave/63rd St; N, R, W, 4, 5, 6, to 59th St

$$$$ **The Carlyle**, 35 E. 76th St (Madison Ave), **T** (212) 744-1600, (800) 227-5737, **F** (212) 717-4682. One of the city's most elegant and luxurious. **S** 6 to 77th St

The Mark, 25 E. 77th St (Madison Ave), **T** (212) 744-4300, (800) 843-6275, **F** (212) 472-5714, www.themarkhotel.com. Exceptional hotel with every amenity, $525 and up. **S** 6 to 77th St

The Sherry Netherland, 781 Fifth Ave, (59th/60th Sts), **T** (212) 355-2800, (800) 247-4377, **F** (212) 319-4306, www.sherrynetherland.com. Right at the corner of Central Park. Traditional elegance. **S** N, R, W to Fifth Ave/50th St; 4, 5, 6 to 59th St

The Stanhope ParkHyatt Hotel, 995 Fifth Ave (81st St), **T** (212) 774-1234, **F** (212) 517-0088, www.stanhopepark.hyatt.com. As close to the Metropolitan as you can get without being there. Luxury hotel. **S** 6 to 77th St

CHELSEA AND EAST

There are not many hotels in Chelsea proper, so this list includes a few further north and east. Chelsea's gallery district is on the far west side of the district in a neighborhood devoid of tourist hotels.

$ **Chelsea Lodge**, 318 W. 20th St (Eighth/Ninth Aves), **T** (212) 243-4499 or (800) 373-1116, **F** (212) 243-7852, www.chelsealodge.com. Small hotel (22 rooms) in handsome brownstone; excellent value; some shared bathrooms. **S** 1, 9 to18th St; C,E to 23rd St

Chelsea Savoy Hotel, 204 W. 23rd St (Seventh Ave), **T** (212) 929-9353, **F** (212) 741-6309, www.chelseasavoy.qpg.com. Basic rooms in a relatively new arrival (1997) on the scene. **S** 1, 9 to 23rd St

$$ **Chelsea Hotel**, 222 W. 23rd St (Seventh/Eighth Aves), **T** (212) 243-3700, **F** (212) 675-5531, www.chelseahotel.com. Historic, eccentric and atmospheric. Ask for a renovated room. **S** 1, 9 to 23rd St

Comfort Inn Manhattan, 42 W. 35th St (Fifth/Sixth Aves), **T** (212) 947-0200 or (800) 228-5150, **F** (212) 594-3047, www.comfortinnmanhattan.com. Small, family-friendly hotel; continental breakfast. **S** B, D, F, V, N, Q, R, W to 34th St-Herald Sq

Hotel Metro, 45 W. 35th St (Fifth/Sixth Aves), **T** (212) 947-2500 or (800) 356-3870, www.hotelmetronyc.com. Art Deco décor. **S** B, D, F, V, N, Q, R, W to 34th St-Herald Sq

La Quinta Manhattan, 17 W. 32nd St (Fifth Ave/Broadway), *T* (212) 736-1600 or (800) 531-5900, *F* (212) 563-4007. A little north of Chelsea, close to Empire State Building; rooms with themes. *S* B, D, F, N, Q, R, V, W to 34th St-Herald Sq

The Inn on 23rd St, 131 W. 23rd St (Sixth/Seventh Aves), *T* (212) 463-0330 or (877) 387-2323, *F* (212) 463-0302. A pleasant bed-and-breakfast; only about a dozen rooms, so reserve early. *S* 1, 9, F, V to 23rd St

Southgate Tower, 371 Seventh Ave (31st St); *T* (212) 563-1800, *F* (212) 643-8028, www.mesuite.com. Part of Manhattan East Suites chain. Near Penn Station. *S* 1, 2, 3, 9 to 34th St-Penn Station

$$$ **W Hotel - Union Square**, 201 Park Ave South (E. 17th St), *T* (212) 253-9119, (877) 946-8357, *F* (212) 253-9229, www.whotels.com. A luxury hotel in the remodeled Guardian Life Insurance Building. *S* N, Q, R, 4, 5, 6 to 14th St

SOHO

Hotels in SoHo are few and far between, though several upscale ones have opened recently. Reflecting SoHo's history, hotels are either quite basic or very expensive.

$ **Cosmopolitan Hotel**, 95 West Broadway (Chambers St), *T* (212) 566-1900 or (888) 895-9400, www.cosmohotel.com. Basic hotel in TriBeCa; recently refurbished. *S* A, C, 1, 2 to Chambers St

SoHo Bed and Breakfast, 167 Crosby St (Bleecker St), *T* (212) 925-1034, *F* (212) 226-9081. Good in this price range, but only 4 rooms. *S* 6 to Bleecker St

$$ **Holiday Inn Downtown/SoHo**, 138 Lafayette St (Canal/Howard Sts), *T* (212) 966-8898 or (800) 465-4329, *F* (212) 966-3933, www.holidayinn-nyc.com. Just south of SoHo in Chinatown, 227 rooms in this value-oriented chain hotel. *S* 6, N, R, Q, W, J, M to Canal St

$$$ **SoHo Grand Hotel**, 310 West Broadway (Canal/Grand Sts), *T* (212) 965-3000 or (800) 965-3000, *F* (212) 965-3244, www.sohogrand.com. Opened 1996 as first new SoHo hotel since the 19c. Architecturally interesting. Elegant, luxurious. *S* A, C, E, 1, 2 to Canal St

$$$$ **The Mercer Hotel**, 147 Mercer St (Prince St), *T* (212) 966-6060 or

(888) 918-6060, *F* (212) 965-3838, no web site. Small, stylish, luxury hotel. *S* N, R to Prince St

60 Thompson, 60 Thompson St (Broome/Spring Sts), *T* (212) 431-0400 or (877) 431-0400, *F* (212) 431-0200; www.60thompson.com. New building, some rooms with good views, many luxuries. *S* C, E to Spring St

ART CALENDAR

JANUARY
Winter Antiques Show Seventh Regiment Armory, Park Ave at 67th St, *T* (212) 628-0417, www.winterantiquesshow.com. High-end fair with fine and decorative art from Europe and Asia, and exceptional Americana. Shows lasts 10 days, mid-late Jan.

Outsider Art Fair The Puck Building, Houston/ Lafayette Sts, *T* (212) 777-5218, www.sanfordsmith.com. Self-taught and visionary artists, art brut; 30-40 exhibitors. Three days, late Jan.

FEBRUARY
National Black Fine Art Show Puck Building, Houston/Lafayette Sts, *T* (301) 263-0783, www.nationalblackfineartshow.com. African, Caribbean, and African-American art, from the marginal to the exceptional.

Art Show at the Armory Seventh Regiment Armory, Park Ave at 67th St, *T* (212) 766-9200, www.artdealers.org. Showcases some 70 dealers nationwide, works in all media from the 15c to the present.

MARCH
The Armory Show, International Fair of New Art Pier 90 (Hudson River at 50th St), *T* (212) 645-6440, www.thearmoryshow.com. Contemporary art; began 1999. In 2003 some 170 galleries exhibited.

International Art Expo Javits Convention Center, Eleventh Ave (34th-39th Sts), *T* (800) 331-570, www.artexpos.com. Huge show, more than 2400 artists.

Whitney Biennial Whitney Museum of American Art, 945 Madison Ave (75th St), *T* (212) 570-3600, www.whitney.org. The Whitney Museum's innovative and often controversial survey of who's who and what's what in contemporary American art. Late March-early June, even-numbered years.

Triple Pier Antiques Show Piers 88, 90, 92 at the Hudson River, Twelfth Ave, 48th-55th Sts, *T* (212) 255-0020. Posters, toys, jewelry, china, glassware, bakelite, luggage, and much, much more. Weekend event, also in Nov.

APRIL

International Asian Art Fair Seventh Regiment Armory, Park Ave at 67th St, *T* (212) 642-8572, www.haughton.com. Asian, East Asian, Middle Eastern Art. Sculpture, porcelain, textiles, painting.

New York Antiquarian Book Fair Seventh Regiment Armory, Park Ave at 67th St, *T* (212) 777-5218, www.sanfordsmith.com. Rare books, manuscripts, children's books, autographs; more than 150 dealers. Mid-April.

MAY

Washington Square Outdoor Art Exhibition Washington Square Park, *T* (212) 982-6255. Some 20 blocks in and around the park filled with arts and crafts. Memorial Day (last Mon) and next three weekends.

JUNE

Museum Mile Celebration Fifth Ave, 82nd-104th Sts, *T* (212) 606-2296, www.museummilefestival.org. Free admission to 9 museums, entertainment. Second Tues.

SEPTEMBER

Downtown Arts Festival Various downtown locations, *T* (212) 243-5050, www.downtownarts.org. Kicks off the fall season, with artists' projects, art walks, concerts, performances, all dedicated to the spirit of experimental art.

OCTOBER

International Antique Dealers' Show Seventh Regiment Armory, Park Ave at 67th St, *T* (212) 642-8572, www.haughton.com. Important antiques show; one week in mid-late Oct.

NOVEMBER

Triple Pier Antiques Fair Piers 88, 90, 92 at the Hudson River, Twelfth Ave, 48th-55th Sts. See March.

art glossary

Abstract Expressionism A movement in abstract art that developed in New York in the 1940s. The term was first used to describe the work of Jackson Pollock and Arshile Gorky. Although painters of widely varying styles were lumped under this name, most shared an outlook of rebellion against traditional styles. Most also rejected the notion of a finished art product that could be evaluated by traditional aesthetic rules and most expressed a strong desire for spontaneous freedom of expression, for example by gestural painting. In this they were influenced by the Surrealists who came to New York from Europe in the late 1930s-early 1940s.

Bauhaus Founded in Weimar, Germany, in 1919, as a state-supported school of architecture, design and art. Its philosophy emphasized the equality of craft and art and the importance of the craftsman-designer for industrial mass production, while also putting forth utopian aims based on design. The Bauhaus style was geometrical and cool, emphasizing technology and functionalism. When the Nazis shut down the Bauhaus in 1933, many faculty members (Josef Albers, Walter Gropius, Ludwig Mies van der Rohe, Lázló Moholy-Nagy) emigrated to the United States, where they became influential.

Biomorphism The use of shapes derived from organic rather than geometric forms.

Cézanne, Paul (1839-1906) One of the most important French Post-Impressionist painters, Cézanne was born into a successful bourgeois family. He was persuaded by his friend Émile Zola to study painting in Paris, where he met Camille Pissarro, who would later influence his art. During his lifetime, Cézanne moved from a darkly romantic style reflecting his esteem for Delacroix, to one that attempted to combine an interest in structure with naturalistic representation. His favorite subjects in later life were portraits of his wife, Hortense, still-lifes, and landscapes of his native Provence. Ignored or scorned for much of his life, Cézanne found critical acclaim in the last decades of the 19c. Since his death he has been recognized as an important influence on 20c art, especially Cubism.

Classical art In Greek art, refers to the time between the Archaic and Hellenistic periods, when Greek culture was at its peak. More generally the term "classical" refers to art or architecture that is descended, however indirectly, from the art of Greece and Rome.

Conceptualism Art in which the idea for the work is more important than the finished work itself (if there actually is one), which is seen as merely a vehicle for expressing the idea. Marcel Duchamp may have been the first Conceptualist ideologically, but the movement became widely popular in the 1960s. In many cases Conceptual artists try to make their work visually unremarkable, and in some cases the "artwork" does not exist outside of the artist's directions for creating it.

Constructivism A pre-Revolutionary Russian movement, dating from c 1913, whose aesthetic combined a belief in completely abstract geometric constructions with an interest in industrial materials, for example plastic. Vladimir Tatlin, founder of the movement, and Alexander Rodchenko, applied Constructivist principles to architecture and design. Constructivism became influential on the Bauhaus in Germany and De Stijl in the Netherlands.

Cubism The most important movement in painting and sculpture of the 20c; originating with Picasso and Braque, it departed from the notion of art as the imitation of nature, which had dominated Western thought since the Renaissance. Instead of resorting to the illusions of perspective, Cubism fragmented three-dimensional forms and reorganized them as overlapping planes of color. Cubism is usually considered to have two phases. The first, **Analytical Cubism** (c 1907-14), made use of geometrical forms of subdued, almost monochromatic, color. The later style, **Synthetic Cubism** (after 1914), used brighter colors and more decorative shapes, as well as such techniques as collage, and stenciling.

Dada A nihilistic artistic movement that revolted against established aesthetics. It originated in Zurich around 1915 with a group of writers and artists and spread through Europe and to

New York. Its adherents emphasized the illogical and the absurd in art and some Dadaist artists shocked and disrupted the bourgeoisie with provocative behavior. Among its most important practitioners were Marcel Duchamp, Francis Picabia, and Man Ray. Dada's emphasis on absurdity formed the basis of Surrealism and, later, its use of techniques involving accident in creating art influenced Abstract Expressionism.

Duchamp, Marcel (1887-1968) Although Duchamp's output was sparse, his ideas challenged the concept of aesthetic beauty and deeply influenced the course of 20c art. His *Nude Descending a Staircase* at the 1913 Armory Show brought him international notoriety. Thereafter he renounced painting that appealed only to the eye and began producing his "ready-mades," the most famous of which was a bicycle wheel mounted on a kitchen stool (though a urinal entitled *Fountain* comes in a close second). He also stated that an object becomes a work of art if the artist picks it out of a heap of other objects and declares it to be art. During the 1920s he built elaborate and useless mechanical gadgets. Later in life he more or less renounced making art altogether and became increasingly obsessed with chess.

Eakins, Thomas (1844-1916) Considered by many as the outstanding 19c American painter. Born in Philadelphia, he studied in Europe and later taught at the Pennsylvania Academy of Fine Arts, where he was attacked for his insistence on working from nude models and then forced to resign. His portraits are marked by their sense of characterization and inner truth. In his genre paintings, often of boating or swimming, he sought to reflect the "heart of American life." Only at the end of his life did he begin to receive recognition as a master of Realism.

The Eight A group of American painters active in New York after the turn of the 20c: Arthur B. Davies, Maurice Prendergast, Ernest Lawson, Robert Henri, George Luks, William J. Glackens, John Sloan, and Everett Shinn. They focused mainly on urban life and were important in developing a 20c American school of painting.

Expressionism A term used to describe art in which natural representation is less important than exaggerations of shape or color that express the artist's emotion. Van Gogh is sometimes considered the most important modern precursor of Expressionism, because of his distortions of line and heightened use of color; Gauguin is sometimes mentioned because of his interest in simplified forms, primitive civilizations, and folk art. Although artists have used expressive techniques for centuries, the term came into use with the Fauves (c 1911) and especially with the German Expressionists (c 1905-30) who used distortions and exaggerations to give shape to psychological truths and to express revulsion against the established social order.

Fauvism Avant-garde style of painting in France around the turn of the 20c. Henri Matisse, André Derain, Paul Signac, and Georges Rouault were among the most important practitioners of this short-lived movement. The Fauve painters developed a distinctive style of painting featuring flattened space, vivid and expressive colors, and bold patterns. The name, which means "wild beasts," came from a derogatory remark by a critic at their 1905 exhibition in the Salon d' Automne. Fauvism influenced German Expressionism.

Futurism An anti-traditional artistic movement with political overtones, founded in Italy by poet Filippo Tommaso Marinetti (1876-1944). In a manifesto, he summed up the movement's ideology with the famous statement that "a roaring car ... is more beautiful than the Victory of Samothrace."

Gauguin, Paul (1848-1903) French Post-Impressionist painter and printmaker. Born in Paris, Gauguin spent his childhood in Peru. In the early 1870s while working as a stockbroker, he began painting part-time and collecting works by the Impressionists. In 1883, he abandoned his job (and three years later his family) to paint. After working in France and traveling abroad, he left France for Tahiti in 1891, where he found visual and spiritual inspiration, reacting against the naturalism of the Impressionists and embracing the arts and styles of primitive peoples. Despite years of poverty and illness, he made his best paintings here, developing a style remarkable for its expressive use of color and simplified forms. Virtually ignored at the time of his death, he has been a major influence on the non-naturalistic direction of 20c art.

Genre painting Paintings depicting scenes from daily life, for example, the domestic scenes painted by 17c Dutch artists.

Gogh, Vincent van (1853-90) Dutch painter and draftsman, one of the most important Post-Impressionists. The son of a Protestant minister, van Gogh early exhibited the emotional instability and spiritual intensity that persisted throughout his life. He turned to painting c 1880, and worked intensively for the ten years that remained to him. In 1886, he moved to Paris, where he became interested in the expressiveness and symbolic power of color. He may have been influenced by Seurat's delicate pointillist brushwork, but eventually developed his own more slashing, swirling style. During his life he sold only one painting and was afflicted with poverty, hallucinations, and depression. Today, his influence on Expressionism, Fauvism, and early abstraction is considered enormous.

Goya, Franciso de (1746-1828) Spanish painter and graphic artist. After a successful early career in which he was made a court painter to King Charles IV, Goya suffered a mysterious illness (1792) that left him completely deaf. Thereafter he became increasingly occupied with morbid and sometimes bizarre themes. Among his most famous engravings are a series depicting the abuses of the Church and, toward the end of his life, a series which protested the cruelty and savagery of war. He was a prolific and technically original painter, famous in his time for his portraits (including those of the Spanish royal family); since his death he has been increasingly recognized for those works examining the dark side of life.

Hudson River School A group of American landscape painters, working c 1825-75; the first generation was led by Thomas Cole and Asher B. Durand. Inspired by the beauty of the American landscape, they painted unspoiled areas in the Hudson River Valley and the Catskill Mountains.

Impressionism Movement in painting that began in France about 1860. Among the first practitioners were Monet, Renoir, and Sisley, who as students together reacted against the narrowness of Academic training. They were joined in Paris by Cézanne, Pissarro, Berthe Morisot and later by Degas and Manet. When the

Salon rejected pictures by several members of this group, they decided to organize independent exhibitions. The group's name came from the title of a Monet painting, *Impression: Sunrise*, given by a journalist in derision, but accepted by the artists as descriptive of one aspect of their work. Although the artists within this group varied widely in technique and aim, in general the Impressionists rejected academic training, while remaining sympathetic with the Realist notion that the primary purpose of art is to record life or nature in an objective manner. Impressionist landscape painters (i.e. Monet) desired to capture the immediate and fleeting visual impression of a moment and so painted out of doors, trying to finish a picture before the light had changed. The Impressionists were at first scorned by the public and the art establishment, but began finding success in the 1890s. The influence of the Impressionists has been huge, both in terms of painters who developed their theories and those who reacted against them.

Klee, Paul (1879-1940) German painter and graphic artist. He was influenced by Kandinsky, with whom he had a lifelong friendship, and also by the Cubism of Braque and Picasso and by the luminous paintings of Robert Delaunay. In 1914 he went to Tunis, a journey that awakened him to possibilities of color. By 1915 he had developed the system of abstracted symbols and forms that characterized much of his later painting. After World War I, when he served in the German army, he taught painting at the Bauhaus and other schools in Germany, but in 1933 the Nazis forced him to abandon teaching and he fled to Switzerland. His works were included in the famous Degenerate Art exhibition in 1937. He was later afflicted with scleroderma, a rare and incurable degenerative disease, and his late work is increasingly dark. He is admired for his ability to work both abstractly and figuratively, and for his superb gifts of visual imagination. He was also a fine violinist, a poet, and an excellent music critic.

Manet, Édouard (1832-83) French painter and graphic artist. Born to a comfortable middle class family, Manet is remembered now as one of the founders of modern art. Throughout his career he admired the great painters of the past (particularly Velázquez), though he allied himself with the avant-garde of his day. He was rejected by the academy, and several of his paintings including *Déjeuner sur l'herbe* and *Olympia* provoked scandals on moral and aesthetic grounds. He was a complex artist, who painted many subjects and did not often repeat himself. His greatest paintings were on contemporary subjects: life as he saw it in the cafés and on the streets of Paris.

Matisse, Henri (1869-1954) Matisse, along with Picasso, was one of the foremost painters of the 20c. In 1891, he gave up a legal career to paint, and studied for several years with the academic painters Bouguereau and Moreau. In Paris he was receptive to various influences including the brilliant color of Fauvism and the geometric simplicity of African sculpture. By the 1920s he had settled on the kind of flat, luminous color and sinuous line that he used for the rest of his life. While he was recuperating from two operations for cancer, he used the technique of paper cutouts he had developed earlier and designed the decoration of the Chapel of the Rosary in Vence, France. Although he is best known for his painting and color cutouts, Matisse also made sculpture, designed the sets and costumes for Diaghilev ballets, and illustrated books, most famously *Jazz*.

Minimalism A movement in painting and sculpture that arose in the 1950s as a reaction against the emotionalism of Abstract Expressionism. It seeks to reduce art to elemental geometric forms, restricting the number of colors, values, shapes, lines and textures. Donald Judd and Carl Andre are among the best-known Minimalists.

Monet, Claude (1840-1926) French Impressionist painter; his painting *Impression, Sunrise* gave the movement its name. Monet developed his preference for painting out of doors from Eugène Boudin, whose work inspired him to become a painter. In 1862 he met Renoir, Sisley and Bazille with whom he formed the nucleus of the Impressionist group. During the Franco-Prussian War he went to England with Pissarro where he studied the work of Constable and Turner, painted the Thames, and met Paul Durand-Ruel, a dealer who championed Impressionism. After the war Monet moved to Argenteuil on the Seine near Paris, where Manet,

Renoir, and Sisley visited him (and also painted the local scenery). Eventually he bought a farm at Giverny, where he built a garden with a pond, a Japanese footbridge, trees and flowers, a kind of self-contained artistic world. He painted there from the 1890s through the 1920s, in an increasingly subjective and abstract manner, culminating in the *Waterlilies*.

Neoclassicism The reigning movement in European architecture and art from the late-18c to the mid-19c. It expressed a desire to revive the heroic spirit and moral values of ancient Greece and Rome, as well as the artistic style of antiquity. Archaeological discoveries in Herculaneum and Pompeii stimulated the movement, but Neoclassicism can also be seen as a reaction against the frivolities of the Rococo style.

Pollock, Jackson (1912-56) The outstanding figure of Abstract Expressionism. He studied painting under Regionalist painter Thomas Hart Benton, and painted in that style during the 1930s when he was employed by the Federal Art Project. By the end of World War II, he was painting abstractly and in style approaching the dripped and poured paintings for which he became famous. In the 1950s he continued painting in his All-over style and also began to make vaguely figurative works, often in black and white. Some critics supported his work, but he was popularly criticized for a style many did not understand. His personal life was generally unhappy, plagued by alcoholism. He died in a car crash when he was only 44, an accident that helped elevate him to legendary status.

Picasso, Pablo (1881-1973) One of the most versatile, prolific, and dominant artists of the 20c, Picasso was born in Malaga, Spain, the son of an artist. His first paintings were representational, often depicting poor people or social outcasts. After he moved to Paris in 1904, he joined an avant-garde circle of painters and writers, attracting critical attention of patrons and influential dealers. Between 1906 and 1909, he became interested in African art and also studied the work of Cézanne. Both these influences can be seen in *Les Demoiselles d'Avignon*, a pivotal work in his own development and an important one in the history of modern art. Along with Georges Braque and Juan Gris, Picasso was a prime developer of Cubism. Later in the 1920s he began to paint more violent and expressive works, including *Guernica*, perhaps his most famous painting, which expressed horror at the bombing of the Basque capital, Guernica, during the Spanish civil war. He was also a brilliant sculptor - one of the first to use found objects - as well as an inspired graphic artist, ceramist, and illustrator.

Post-Impressionism Styles of painting that developed from Impressionism or were in reaction against it, around 1880-1910. The most important painters of the group were Cézanne, Gauguin, and van Gogh. Post-Impressionist painters rejected the notion of depicting fleeting effects of light and color, but they differed in the manner of this rejection, emphasizing pictorial structure (Cézanne), scientific analysis of color (Seurat), or other aspects of painting.

Rembrandt Harmensz van Rijn (1606-69) Dutch painter, etcher, and draftsman, now considered his country's greatest artist, admired both for the emotional depth of his work and his mastery of technique. His early paintings were mainly figures, either old men depicted as philosophers or biblical figures or portraits of himself and family members. In the 1630s he became Amsterdam's most successful painter, receiving important commissions for portraits and also religious works. His most famous painting is *The Night Watch* (1642), incorrectly named in the 18c when its darkened varnish made it seem like a nocturnal scene; it is considered a culmination of the Dutch tradition of civic portraits. During the 1640s, Rembrandt's material success declined as his style became more introspective and his subject matter more spiritual. Biographers have explained the change as a response to the death of his first wife in 1642 and his mother two years earlier. In later life Rembrandt had financial difficulties (he was extravagant) and lived in reduced circumstances, though he was never destitute or reclusive. As he grew older, his style became looser and broader; one of his contemporaries noted that his paintings looked as if they had been laid on with a bricklayer's trowel.

Rubens, Peter Paul (1577-1640) Flemish painter, the most important northern European artist during the Baroque period.

Rubens visited Italy in 1600, where his style was formed. He returned to Antwerp upon the death of his mother and became immediately successful. He ran a large and efficient studio, turning out paintings on both religious and secular subjects. He was fortunate in his marriages (his first wife died in 1626) and his family life. Late in life he developed an interest in landscape painting, at which he also excelled. The later French painters Watteau, Delacroix, and Renoir were influenced by his work.

The Salon The official exhibition of the French Royal Academy of Painting and Sculpture, named for the Salon d'Apollon in the Louvre where the exhibitions were held. The first took place in 1667 and they were held annually after 1849. Because the Salons were for many years the only public exhibitions in Paris, the academic establishment - conservative in taste and hostile to the avant-garde - used them to control publicity and therefore financial success. Rival exhibitions began during the late 19c, for example the Salon des Réfusés in 1863, where Manet, Cézanne, and Pissarro exhibited. Although the work of these painters was ridiculed, the Salon des Réfusés helped undermine the power of the official Salons.

Seurat, Georges (1859-91) French painter. As a young man, he excelled at drawing, but was attracted to the colorist paintings of the Impressionists. Seurat studied scientific treatises on optics and developed his own theories and technique (later called pointillism) for achieving effects of vibrant color, placing small dots of unmixed color next to one another on a canvas rather than mixing them on a palette. His reputation was assured when *Sunday Afternoon on the Island of La Grande Jatte* was shown at the last Impressionist exhibition in 1886.

Surrealism A revolutionary movement in literature and art that started in France in the 1920s; it was characterized by interest in the bizarre and the irrational, though unlike Dada, it was positive in spirit. At its center was a belief that the unconscious and the spontaneous are superior to the rational and the controlled. André Breton, its chief theoretician, said that the movement would resolve dream states and reality into a "super-reality." Surrealist artists, for example Salvador Dalí, used such techniques as scrupulously painted scenes with hallucinatory subjects or constructions that brought together unrelated objects as a means of undermining rational thought.

Vermeer, Johannes (1632-75) Dutch painter, now ranked second only to Rembrandt. Not much is known about his life and only about 40 paintings by him are known to exist, probably because he earned most of his living by other means. He had a large family and significant financial difficulties; he is known to have left Delft, his native city, only once. Vermeer is recognized today for his beautifully composed, serene, but often enigmatic images of domestic life, usually one or two figures in a room, painted in cool colors, and illuminated from the left. More than any other Dutch genre painter, Vermeer is remarkable for his handling of light.

Author's acknowledgements

I'd like to thank Julie DeSarbo for researching and writing the shopping sections, Catherine Wright for her work on restaurants, and Mildred Marmur and Fred Wright for contributions they best understand.

Picture credits

Front and inside front cover: *Second Story Sunlight* by Edward Hopper, 1960 (detail on the front cover) reproduced by kind permission of the Whitney Museum of American Art, where the painting is held.

Back cover: The Solomon R. Guggenheim Museum, New York, courtesy of Gemma Davies.

Inside pictures: For permission to reproduce the pictures throughout the book, grateful thanks are due to the following: Bridgeman Art Library (pp 41, 45); Mary Boone Gallery (p 113); Casey Kaplan Gallery (p 133); The Chelsea Hotel (p 128); Gemma Davies (p 13); The Frick Collection (pp 75, 76, 77, 81, 82, 84, 85, 86, 89, 91, 92); The Guggenheim Museum (p 57); The Metropolitan Museum of Art (pp 12, 14, 21, 32, 38); New Museum (pp 147, 148); NYC & Comany (pp 7, 27, 53, 61, 95, 109, 110, 131, 150, 165, 169, 181, 183, 214); The Whitney Museum of American Art (pp 99, 102).

New York cabs

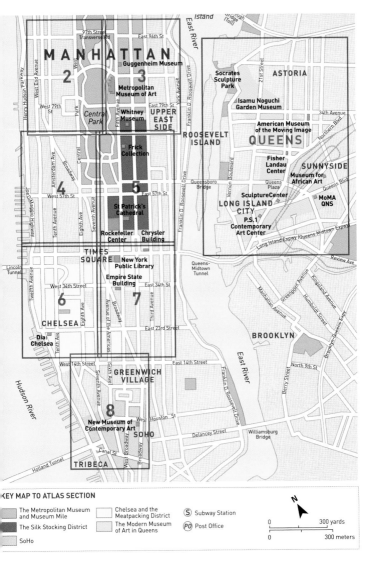

KEY MAP TO ATLAS SECTION

- The Metropolitan Museum and Museum Mile
- The Silk Stocking District
- SoHo
- Chelsea and the Meatpacking District
- The Modern Museum of Art in Queens
- Ⓢ Subway Station
- Ⓟ Post Office

N

0   300 yards

0   300 meters

Broadway

West 104th Street

West 103rd Street

West 102nd Street

West 101st Street

West 100th Street

West 99th Street

West 97th Street

West 96th Street

West 95th Street

West 94th Street

West 92nd Street

West 90th Street

West 89th Street

West 88th Street

West 86th Street

West 85th Street

West 83rd Street

West 81st Street

West 79th Street

West 77th Street

West 75th Street

West End Avenue

Amsterdam Avenue

Columbus Avenue

Manhattan Avenue

Central Park West

West Drive

East Drive

Broadway

UPPER WEST SIDE

Conservatory Garden

Muse the C New

The Pool

CENTRAL PARK

Eas Mead

97th Street Transverse Road

Jacqueline Kennedy Onassis Reservoir

Jewish M

Cooper- National M

National Aca of D

Gugge Mu

86th Street Transverse Road

CENTRAL PARK

The Great Lawn

Metropolitan Museum of Art

79th Street Transverse Road

The Ramble

The Lake

East Drive

Rose Center for Earth & Space

American Museum of Natural History

New York Historical Society

8

West 12th Street
Jane St
West 12th Street
Greenwich Avenue
Bank Street
West 11th Street
Charles Street
Perry Street
Charles Street
West 10th Street
Christopher Street
Seventh Avenue South
Barrow Street
Morton Street
Bedford Street
Leroy Street
St Luke's Pl
Clarkson Street
Charlton Street
King Street
Houston Street
West Houston Street

Fifth Avenue
West 11th Street
East 10th Street

GREENWICH VILLAGE

East 12th Street
Third Avenue
East 11
Saint Ma
East 9th Street
East 8th Street
East 7t
East 6t
East 5
East 4

West 8th Street
East 8th Street
Waverly Place
Washington Sq North
Grey Art Gallery
Waverly Pl
Washington Pl
Washington Sq South
West 3rd Street
Great Jones St
Bond Street
Bleecker Street

Laguardia Place
Avenue of the Americas (Sixth Avenue)

West Houston Street
West Houston Street
New York Earth Room
New Museum of Contemporary Art
Prada Store
Prince Street
SOHO
Dean & DeLuca
NOLITA

Hudson Park

Hudson Street

West Street

PO

Varick Street

West Broadway

Wooster Street
Greene Street
Mercer Street
Broadway
Lafayette Street

Broken Kilometer
Spring Street
Swiss Institute
Broome Street
Kenmare St
Broo
LITT ITA
The Drawing Center
Grand Street
Artists Space
Grand
PO
Holland Tunnel
Canal Street
Watts Street
Hester

Hudson River Park

Hudson River

Greenwich Street
Hudson Street
Varick Street
Church Street
West Broadway
Broadway
Centre Street

Walker Street
Canal
Baxa
CHINATOWN
Franklin Street

TRIBECA
Harrison Street
Duane Street
Worth Street
Reade Street
Chambers Street
Chambers Street
Par

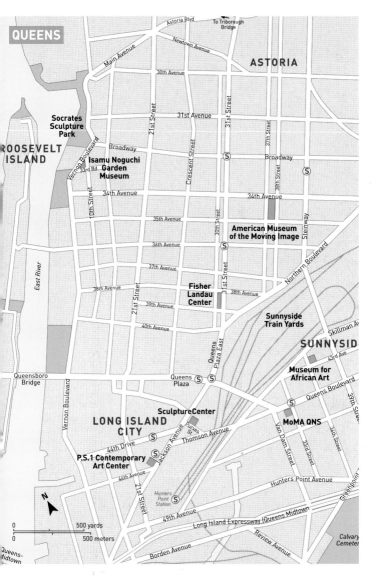

First edition 2004

Published by A&C Black Publishers Ltd
37 Soho Square, London W1D 3QZ

ISBN 0-7136-6791-2

Published in the United States of America by
WW Norton & Company, Inc
500 Fifth Avenue, New York, NY 10110, USA

ISBN 0-393-32594-6

Published simultaneously in Canada
Penguin Books Canada Limited
10 Alcorn Avenue, Toronto, Ontario M4V 3BE

Series devised by Gemma Davies
Series designed by Jocelyn Lucas
Editorial and production: Gemma Davies, Jocelyn Lucas, Lilla Nwenu-Msimang, Miranda Robson, Kim Teo, Judy Tither

Maps and plans by Mapping Company Ltd: pp 10–11, 79, 215–223; floor plan on p 79 reproduced by kind permission of The Frick Collection. Map of New York Subway (inside back cover) © Metropolitan Transport Authority

Printed and bound in Singapore by Tien Wah Press (Pte.) Ltd